Syria and the United States

Syria and the United States

Eisenhower's Cold War in the Middle East

David W. Lesch

Westview Press
BOULDER •SAN FRANCISCO •OXFORD

Copyright © 1992 by Westview Press, Inc.

Published in 1992 in the United States of America by Westview Press, Inc., 5500 Central Avenue, Boulder, Colorado 80301-2877, and in the United Kingdom by Westview Press, 36 Lonsdale Road, Summertown, Oxford OX2 7EW

Library of Congress Cataloging-in-Publication Data
Lesch, David W.
  Syria and the United States : Eisenhower's Cold War in the Middle East / David W. Lesch.
     p.   cm.
  Includes index.
  ISBN 0-8133-8582-2
  1. United States—Foreign relations—Syria.   2. Syria—Foreign relations—United States.   3. United States—Foreign relations—Middle East.   4. Middle East—Foreign relations—United States.
  5. United States—Foreign relations—1953-1961.   6. Eisenhower, Dwight D. (Dwight David), 1890-1969.   I. Title.
E183.8.S95L47   1992
327.7305691'09'045—dc20

                                                            92-25519
                                                            CIP

10   9   8   7   6   5   4   3   2

To my wife, Suzanne

Contents

Preface

The climax of American-Syrian relations in the 1950s occurred in the late summer and early fall of 1957, the so-called "Syrian crisis," or what will be referred to in this book as the American-Syrian crisis. The incident was ignited by the discovery of a covert American effort to overthrow in Syria a regime that the Eisenhower administration (1953–1961) perceived as being aligned with the Soviet Union. The events surrounding the American-Syrian crisis had repercussions in the regional and international arenas and precipitated a diplomatic confrontation between the two superpowers that could have been converted into a military confrontation.

There have been numerous studies that have focused upon what were the main attractions for the United States in the Arab world in the 1950s, i.e., Egypt's Gamal 'Abd al-Nasser, the rise of Nasserism, and the Arab-Israeli dispute. But few scholars have examined the role Syria played during the same period, primarily because it was viewed as a sideshow in the Egyptian-Iraqi struggle for regional supremacy, yet it was one of the key features in this regional cold war. What scholarship that exists in the United States regarding Syria during this period has tended to focus on the American-Syrian crisis and the covert efforts initiated by the Eisenhower administration.

This book is not only a case study of American-Syrian relations in the 1950s but also a multi-dimensional examination of the regional context of this relationship. By analyzing the motivations and actions of the other players in the Middle East who influenced or were influenced by the consequential American-Syrian relationship, a more complete and detailed picture will result, particularly the evolution of events that led the Eisenhower administration to initiate "corrective" measures in Syria. The recent declassification of pertinent American and British government documents from this period was instrumental in shedding new light on this subject.

One point is to be made. There are those who have dismissed the "American plot" in Syria in 1957 as a hoax concocted by the Syrian government in order to improve its position domestically. This faulty conclusion hampers an overall analysis of the important role played by outside powers who influenced, and in many cases determined, the course of events in Syria. This book contends that the United States was actively involved in clandestine operations throughout 1957 in an effort to bring down the Syrian regime, the discovery of which precipitated the American-Syrian crisis. This claim is based on the following: circumstantial evidence gathered from various archival sources; interviews with high-level American intelligence personnel who were associated with or had knowledge of covert operations in Syria; corroborating evidence from transcripts of the trial in Baghdad in August 1958 of former Iraqi military officers, some of whom purported to have had intimate knowledge of American plans in Syria; the Syrian indictment of the American plot in the summer of 1957;[1] and a detailed description of the covert plot given by a Syrian officer who was reportedly recruited by American embassy personnel but was actually in the service of Syrian intelligence.[2]

A special military tribunal was set up by the Syrian government in October 1957 to try those involved in the American "conspiracy." It was composed, quite unexpectedly, of officers who had a record of being pro-American. The United States Embassy in Damascus described the members of the tribunal as having had "untarnished" backgrounds and possessing "relatively high integrity." There are a number of possible explanations for the composition of this tribunal. One reason might be that the political complexion of these individuals had changed (or had been wrongly assessed from the beginning). Maybe they were under pressure to hand out guilty verdicts, which would have been convincing proof of the fairness of the trial. It also could have meant that the Syrian government had such an iron-clad case that they were certain that any tribunal, regardless of its ideological composition, would return a verdict of guilty.[3]

This body of evidence does not preclude the fact that the Syrian government took advantage of the American conspiracy to secure its position domestically—it certainly did. But armed with this knowledge, we are better able to assess the actions of the Syrians and the very real and legitimate concerns they had for their political survival in the face of what seemed to be incessant intervention by outside powers. The details of covert activities in Syria are not a central feature of this book—this type of study must wait for the declassification of "smoking gun" American and British government documents (an occurrence not likely to happen in the near future). There are a number of studies that have attempted to trace American and British covert operations in Syria, but on the whole they are rather devoid of any analysis which placed these clandestine activities in their proper context or answered the more important questions revolving around American foreign policy and the regional objectives of the countries in the Middle East that contributed to an environment in which covert efforts were deemed necessary.[4]

There are many individuals and organizations that contributed in varying degrees to the completion of this book. They all helped me convert a rather rough and embryonic idea into a full-fledged manuscript. I would like to thank: the Center for Middle Eastern Studies at Harvard University, Patrick Seale, Sadiq al-'Azm, James Gelvin, Zachary Lockman, Philip S. Khoury, F.G.K. Gallagher, and Sir George Humphrey Middleton. I also would like to thank the personnel at the various archives I visited, with a special note of appreciation to the staff at the Dwight D. Eisenhower Library for their extraordinary efficiency and dedication to their work. The Marion and Jaspar Whiting Foundation awarded a fellowship that enabled me to travel to Syria, Turkey, England, and France; for that, I am most grateful. Three individuals are worthy of particular mention: Louis Cantori, Robert O. Freedman, and Nadav Safran. They not only selflessly assisted me with this manuscript but also helped me shape my academic career and thoughtfully advised me at various critical junctures of my academic life. Any credit or recognition I might receive in the future can be traced back to the foundations they laid.

David W. Lesch
Trinity University
San Antonio

Notes

1. Foreign Broadcast Information Service (hereafter FBIS), October 1, 1957, pp. C1–18.

2. FBIS, August 16, 1957, pp. C6–17.

3. DA Intelligence Report, October 30, 1957, Entry 85, Intell. Doc. File, 2062641, Record Group 319 (hereafter RG319), National Archives and Records Administration, Suitland, Maryland (hereafter NARA).

4. See Jonathan Bloch and Patrick Fitzgerald, *British Intelligence and Covert Action: Africa, Middle East and Europe Since 1945* (London: Brandon Junction, 1983); William Blum, *The CIA: A Forgotten History* (London: Zed Books, 1986); and John Prados, *President's Secret Wars: CIA and Pentagon Covert Operations Since World War II* (New York: William Morrow, 1986). All three of these studies are based, practically verbatim, on Patrick Seale's investigations and the rather dubious validity of the assertions made by Wilbur Crane Eveland in his book, *Ropes of Sand: America's Failure in the Middle East* (1980), which was based on his activities as a CIA operative in Syria; also, see Douglas Little, "Cold War and Covert Action: The United States and Syria, 1945–1958," *Middle East Journal* 44, 1 (Winter 1990), pp. 51–75.

Note on the Text

In this book, the author has employed the direct transliteration from Arabic to English, unless a particular individual's name is more commonly written in another fashion; for example, "Nasser" is used instead of "Nasir" or "Faisal" instead of "Faysal."

Most of the United States government dispatches to and from its various embassies in the Middle East (and elsewhere) and the records and memoranda of conversations between diplomatic personnel all have one common feature: laconism. In an effort to be concise and morphemic, these documents are often without definite articles, prepositions, conjunctions, etc. In the numerous quotes from government documents in the text, I have bracketed missing grammatical lexica or clarification where necessary in order to assist the reader.

Finally, when referring to Syria, the terms "chamber," "Chamber of Deputies," or "parliament" are one and the same — all three are used only for the sake of avoiding repetition.

Abbreviations

ALCSP	Arab League Collective Security Pact
ALM	Arab Liberation Movement
ASRP	Arab Socialist Resurrection Party
BMEO	British Middle East Office
CIA	Central Intelligence Agency
DDEL	Dwight D. Eisenhower Library (Abilene, Kansas)
DMZ	Demilitarized Zone
ESS	Egyptian-Syrian-Saudi defense pact
FBIS	Foreign Broadcast Information Service
FO	Foreign Office
FRUS	*Foreign Relations of the United States*
MACs	Mixed Armistice Committees
MEC	Middle East Command
MEDO	Middle East Defense Organization
NA	National Archives (Washington, D.C.)
NARA	National Archives and Records Administration (Suitland, Maryland)
NSC	National Security Council
NYT	*New York Times*
PRO	Public Record Office (London)
RCC	Revolutionary Command Council
RG	Record Group (RG84 = Record Group 84, RG59 = Record Group 59, etc.)
SSNP	Syrian Social Nationalist Party
UAR	United Arab Republic
UN	United Nations
UNEF	United Nations Emergency Forces
UNTSO	United Nations Truce Supervision Organization
USIA	United States Information Agency

Syria

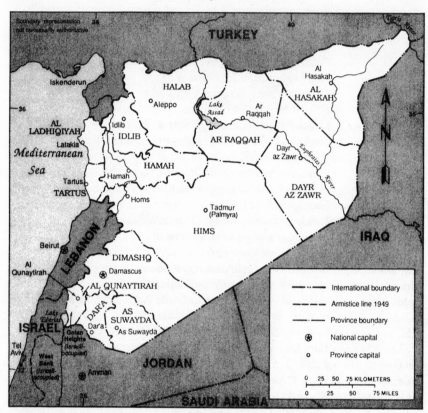

Source: Thomas Collelo, ed., *Syria: A Country Study* (Washington, D.C.: Federal Research Division, Library of Congress, 1988).

1

Introduction

Syria After World War Two

Syria emerged from the Second World War as a newly independent state freed from the shackles of the French mandate imposed upon it following World War One. The last contingent of French troops departed Syria in April 1946. The country was now in the hands of a group of politicians who had gained popularity from their long struggle against Ottoman and French suzerainty; however, they also had very little experience in the everyday operations of running a government and, in some cases, had become disreputable in the view of many Syrians for having cooperated with and been too conciliatory toward the French mandate regime in the interest of obtaining and maintaining their political and economic power positions.[1] But, on the whole, they were identified with the independence movement of the inter-war years and as a result (also by default) this group, the National or Kutla Bloc, maintained power immediately after World War Two under the guise of a parliamentary democracy led by President Shukri al-Quwatli.

The 1947 parliamentary elections gave visible indications of the growing fragmentation of the Syrian polity as well as the increasing public disenchantment with the Kutla Bloc politicians. The election process catalyzed a split within the Kutla Bloc, leading to the formation of the Nationalist Party, which consisted of members of the ruling wing of the bloc such as Quwatli, Jamil Mardam, Faris al-Khuri, Lutfi al-Haffar, and Sabri al-'Asali, all of whom were identified as Damascene politicians. The opposition wing of the bloc, consisting of members who generally had been identified as dissidents since 1939 (primarily over the issue of Alexandretta/Hatay and the obsequious actions of the ruling wing of the Kutla Bloc in allowing the French to "give" the Alexandretta region to Turkey—which subsequently referred to it as Hatay), was based in Aleppo and counted among its members Rushdi al-Kikhia, Nazim al-Qudsi, and Mustafa Barmada. The latter group began to coalesce in 1947 but officially formed a party, Hizb al-Sha'b or Populist (People's) Party, in August of 1948. Both parties were economically and politically conservative and tended to look to the West when military and/or economic assistance was sought, and in the case of the Populist Party, its Aleppan base steered it toward an allegiance toward the pro-West regime in Iraq (and toward a frequently proposed union with it) that only distanced it from the Nationalist Party over an issue that generally divided the Syrian polity, i.e., the direction of Arab unity and the integrity of the Syrian republic. This split within the Kutla Bloc would never be healed completely, and it would allow the more nationalistic and leftist elements of the Syrian polity an opportunity to subsume their *own* differences in their ultimately success-ful challenge for political leadership.[2]

The elections in 1947 also introduced outside observers to the Ba'th or Resurrection Party, an ardently nationalistic group operating under a pan-Arab socialist doctrine. It would systematically improve its power position in Syria to the point of virtually dictating by 1955 the government's neutralist and largely anti-West foreign policy. The Ba'th Party was primarily the product of the ideological meeting-of-the-minds of two men, Michel 'Aflaq and Salah al-Din Bitar. At first "flirting" with communism while studying together in Paris from 1929 to 1934, both ultimately rejected communist doctrine and promoted the "trinity" of "indissolubly fused" ideas: Arab unity, freedom, and socialism.[3] This trinity of ideas, however, meant a "simultaneous assault on 'reaction' at home and 'imperialism' abroad."[4] The Ba'th became the foremost proponent of Arab neutralism a decade before Nasser made the term famous. The communists were also opposed to the reactionaries and imperialists, but they were under suspicion from the Ba'th because their ideology was anything but home-grown and their actions were dictated by another outside power, the Soviet Union. They would, however, arrange a marriage of convenience at various times in the 1950s when the country was confronted by the ominous and more imminent threats posed by the West (specifically Great Britain and the United States) and their "imperialist tools" in the Middle East (primarily Israel, Iraq, and Turkey). They shared the objective of ridding the country of malevolent outside influence and maintaining Syrian independence, but that was the extent of their cooperation, and when this objective was achieved their latent differences typically manifested themselves into an open breach.

The Ba'th might have remained an ideological party of the periphery if it were not for its association with the parliamentary deputy from Hama, Akram al-Hawrani, who ultimately provided the "muscle" for the Ba'th with his close ties with various elements of the Syrian army, which would soon become the final political arbiter in the country. The relationship would prove to be symbiotic, for Hawrani's Arab Socialist Party was in need of an ideological foundation, one which the Ba'th was amply qualified to provide. A foreshadowing of their alliance occurred during the 1947 elections when Hawrani supported the Ba'th (and the Populists) in their successful cam-paign for free and universal suffrage. The formal merger occurred in

November–December 1952 while all three men were in exile in Lebanon, a propitious occurrence that had a lasting effect upon the future of Syria, for the new Arab Socialist Resurrection Party (ASRP or still simply referred to as the Ba'th) was now endowed with the political wherewithal to seriously contend for power in Syria by 1954 and thereafter force upon the regime the increasingly popular foreign policy edicts of vehement anti-Zionism, nationalism, and Arab neutralism. The Ba'th became the voice of the opposition to the West, Israel, and anyone in the government who was seen as collaborating with either one of them.

The seminal event during this period, however, was the 1947–1949 Arab-Israeli war that resulted in the emergence of the state of Israel in 1948. The regime of Shukri al-Quwatli was utterly discredited by its corrupt mishandling of a war that resulted in a humiliating defeat for Syria (the repercussions were similar in Egypt, Jordan, and Lebanon). The discontent among the populace and in the military created an opening for the entrance of the army into Syrian politics with the overthrow of Quwatli by General Husni al-Za'im in March 1949, a position from which they have yet to retreat. The coup signaled an end to Syria's brief encounter with parliamentary democracy and created the foundation for the important alliance between the ASRP and the army.

The politicization of the army only exacerbated the divisions in the already unstable Syrian polity (save for the relative stability of a military dictatorship), and added another player to the political power game to be for or against, bought and sold, or influenced by outside powers. Indeed, the country's parochial and particularistic society offered ample fodder for the intrigues of external forces interested in promoting their own sets of objectives, and they could usually find willing partners in Syria eager to extol these interests for the sake of political aggrandizement.[5]

The United States was primarily interested in Syria in terms of the extent of its relationship with Moscow, fearing that it could become a Soviet base for subversive activity in the region. The Kremlin, in turn, did not want Syria to become ensnared in the Western "containment" defense net, and wanted to extend its influence to a country that was more amenable to Soviet inroads than most in the region in an attempt to secure an indispensable role for itself equal to that of the other great powers in the Middle East. France viewed its former mandated territory as its last area of ingress into the heartland of the region and would, and did, do everything it could to preserve, its largely fictitious position among the great powers in the area. To Great Britain, also on the wane as an imperial power, Syria at first was not that important, as London was reluctant to step on the toes of the French and was primarily concerned with its position in Iraq, Jordan, and Egypt; however, as its relationship with Egypt deteriorated, and as its influence in the area was being systematically replaced by the United States, Britain began to value Syria in terms of reducing Egypt's influence in the region, while at the same time enhancing its own stature in the area by augmenting that of its client-state Iraq. Turkey, already nervously exposed to the Soviet Union on its northern border, saw its southern neighbor as a possible strategic threat to its southern flank and, especially after joining NATO in 1952, began to amplify the communist "buildup" in Syria in an attempt to depict itself as the West's outpost in the region against Soviet/communist expansionism. Iraq was mainly interested in Syria in terms of its vision for Fertile Crescent unity and as a means to isolate Egypt in its drive for Arab leadership. Egypt, responding in kind in this regional cold war, wanted a Syria that looked to it rather than Iraq, as Syria held the key as to whether one or the other would triumph as the leader of the Arab world. Saudi Arabia was concerned about the disposition of Syria lest it fall into the camp of the rival Hashemite House ruling Iraq, enhancing that regime's stature and power at the expense of the House of Sa'ud — thus for a time Egypt and Saudi Arabia cooperated in an attempt to keep Syria and Iraq apart. The generally pro-West regimes of Jordan and Lebanon wanted a Syria that looked to the West but were not willing to take the initiative against their stronger neighbor, and, for the most part, essentially hoped it would be a benign partner in the Arab world. And finally, Israel wanted Syria to remain weak and non-threatening, hoping to create a more secure northern border zone out of the still unsettled border demarcation question that emerged from the 1947–49 war — and like Turkey, the Israelis did their best to portray Syria as a budding Soviet/communist outpost in the Middle East so as to tug at the hearts of the American public and government in an attempt to persuade it to provide Israel with the desired amount of military hardware.

As one can readily see, Syria was at the center of a tug-of-war with many different ropes and on several different planes. All of the international and regional interests that the aforementioned nations held regarding Syria were sometimes superimposed on, sometimes integrated into the domestic political and economic situation in the country — simultaneously pushing together and pulling apart the fabric of its society. During the period under discussion, Syria presents a classic paradigm of the consequences of external intervention, not only for the victim but also for the protagonist. Within this paradigm, the American-Syrian relationship allows us to examine and analyze the full purview of this tug of war.

Eisenhower, the Cold War, and the Middle East

The Eisenhower administration engineered what has frequently been viewed as successful covert campaigns to install pro-American regimes in Iran in 1953 and Guatemala in 1954. The repressive and elitist policies of the individual the United States brought back to power in Iran, Muhammad

Reza Shah Pahlavi, precipitated the 1979 Iranian revolution that severed the American-Iranian tacit alliance and destabilized the Persian Gulf area. The succession of military dictatorships in Guatemala following the 1954 coup has made this Central American nation one of the foremost offenders of human rights in the world and one of the poorest economically. In retrospect, the Eisenhower administration's "success" vis-à-vis Iran and Guatemala should be reevaluated.

This foreign policy was based on containment of the Soviet Union and communist expansion. The Eisenhower administration was preoccupied, if not obsessed, with this foreign policy objective. With the decolonization process having occurred in the former Soviet Union and the democracy movements having broken out in the former Soviet satellite countries in Eastern Europe, the containment policy inaugurated by the Truman administration and continued under Eisenhower is now being labelled in many circles as having been the right policy for the right time. According to this view, American activities in the Third World succeeded in at least making it much more difficult, i.e., expensive, for the Kremlin to attempt to counter American efforts, which ultimately led to the traumatization of the Soviet economy to an extent that forced Moscow into military retrenchment and economic and political reform along the Western model. This analysis, however, tends to ignore the negative consequences for many nations in the Third World, the battleground of the superpower zero-sum competition for client-states — a contest that heated up in the 1950s.

The revisionist scholarship on the Eisenhower administration, beginning for the most part in the early 1970s, has also tended to overlook the administration's policies toward the Third World. Much of this literature was based on newly declassified archival material that revealed President Eisenhower to be the man in charge of American foreign policy during his time in power, contrary to earlier scholarship that portrayed Secretary of State John Foster Dulles as the sole architect of American foreign policy and Eisenhower as his passive "yes-man."[6] This revisionism led many scholars to attribute to Eisenhower a more subtle ingenuity and presidential know-how than had been the case in the past, especially in his apparent use of Dulles as his "front-man" to absorb the criticisms of the press, public, and congress. Almost instantly this reinterpretation of the efficaciousness of Eisenhower the man led to a more positive reevaluation of the Eisenhower administration; as a result, it moved steadily up lists of presidential performance to the "near great" category. Robert Divine writes that "nearly all of Eisenhower's foreign policy achievements were negative in nature. He ended the Korean War, he refused to intervene militarily in Indochina, he refrained from involving the United States in the Suez crisis, he avoided war with China over Quemoy and Matsu, he resisted the temptation to force a showdown over Berlin, he stopped exploding nuclear weapons in the atmosphere." Divine goes on to state that following the lessons learned from Vietnam, "a President who avoids hasty military action and refrains from extensive involvement in the internal affairs of other nations deserves praise rather than scorn."[7] Stephen Ambrose, Eisenhower's preeminent biographer, reflecting the new positive interpretation of his presidency, stated that he "gave the nation eight years of peace and prosperity. No other President in the twentieth century could make that claim."[8] But as Stephen Rabe correctly asserts, the debate over the Eisenhower foreign policy "has focused on the means of presidential leadership, not the ends; it has concentrated on strategy, not results."[9]

There has been some recent scholarship on the Eisenhower administration that has shown that indeed the president was very active in the decision-making process related to foreign policy issues, but was not the totally benign, peace-loving leader he has been made out to be.[10] Blanche Wiesen Cook, who has done extensive work on the Eisenhower administration and contributed greatly to the revisionist interpretation of his presidency, stated that while "Eisenhower's commitment to peace was real, it was limited to nuclear detente and the prevention of large-scale international warfare," yet in the process of trying to contain communism and promote American interests abroad, the alternatives to war "involved a range of political warfare activities that included covert operations and counterinsurgency" that involved the elements of "repression and reaction."[11] Slowly, scholars are beginning to identify the "interventionist" Eisenhower in his administration's policies toward various regions of the globe. One of the objectives of this book is to attempt to uncover this particular trait during the Eisenhower years as seen in American policy toward Syria—a "re-revisionism" so to speak.

The Eisenhower administration came to power in 1953 with the intention of implementing its New Look foreign policy in an attempt to correct what it viewed were the deficiencies inherent in the approach of the Truman administration as defined in the 1950 policy paper commonly referred to as NSC-68 (National Security Council Resolution No. 68). Indeed, in some important ways, the New Look differed from NSC-68, in others, however, it was basically a carbon copy. Containing the Soviet Union from expanding its influence beyond that which already existed was the paramount foreign policy objective in both administrations; however, the means by which this was to be accomplished changed when Eisenhower became president. This change had an important impact upon the Middle East, affecting the political dynamics that had already produced tensions in the area at the regional and domestic levels.

National Security Council Resolution No. 68 was loosely based on George F. Kennan's theory of containment of the Soviet Union and postulated that the United States should meet any communist advances, wherever they occurred, with a direct reciprocal response. One of the authors of NSC-68 defined it in terms of "an immediate and large-scale buildup in our military and general strength and that of our allies with the intention of righting the power balance and in the hope that through means other than all-out war we could induce a change in the nature of the Soviet system."[12] Following the "loss" of China in 1949 and the beginning of the Korean War in 1950, the Republican Party launched a vocal attack on the Truman administration for "allowing" the former to occur as a result of its acceptance of the status quo division of the bipolar world, and in the latter case, for its strategic conception that gave the communists the initiative in fomenting trouble anywhere it so chose, requiring a costly American military posture in order to symmetrically respond to these advances in a timely fashion.

The budget conscious and economically conservative republican platform in 1952 preached a foreign policy that would more effectively meet at less cost what they viewed as the global communist threat. Before assuming his post as secretary of state, Dulles stated that "already the free world has been so shrunk that no further substantial parts of it can be lost without danger to the whole that remains."[13] Eisenhower would write the following to Winston Churchill in 1955:

> We have come to the point where every additional backward step must be deemed a defeat for the Western world. In fact, it is a triple defeat. First, we lose a potential ally. Next, we give to an implacable enemy another recruit. Beyond this, every such retreat creates in the minds of neutrals the fear that we do not mean what we say when we pledge our support to people who want to remain free.[14]

The most important aspect of the cold war to the Eisenhower administration, especially as articulated through Dulles, was winning the zero-sum game against the Soviets in the new battleground called the Third World. The secretary of state was convinced the Kremlin was attempting to encircle the United States until the latter was "strangled into submission."[15] Communism was viewed in Washington as a monolithic and devious force that would "enslave" the vulnerable nations of the Third World — unless it was checked by the free nations of the West. Behind every problem encountered by the Eisenhower administration in the international arena was seen the guiding hand of Soviet communism, "designed to accelerate Communist conquest of every country where the Soviet government could make its influence felt."[16]

Dulles remarked in 1954 at the Caracas Conference, convened to discuss the "communist drive" in Guatemala, that the "Soviet Communists have constantly taught and practiced the art of deception, of making concessions merely in order to lure others into a false sense of security, which makes them the easier victims of ultimate aggression."[17] And as John Lewis Gaddis aptly noted, "this perception of tactical virtuosity on the Russians' part made administration officials extremely wary of the surprisingly conciliatory gestures that began to emerge from the Kremlin upon Stalin's death."[18] This would become particularly evident in the Middle East, where the Kremlin's persistent peaceful diplomatic overtures during the course of 1956–1957, promulgated in an effort to be taken seriously as a major player in the region, were for the most part rebuffed by Washington.

With this type of mentality prevailing in Washington, it was little wonder that when successive Syrian governments during the Truman and Eisenhower years refused to embrace the United States as its patron, and more importantly, from the perspective of the White House, when Syria began to flirt with the Soviet bloc and apparently allow communism to gain a foothold in the country, relations with it were conducted on the plane of the cold war battleground between East and West. This was done to the exclusion of other elements of the equation, both regional and domestic, that also defined the American-Syrian relationship and the role that each played in the Middle East.

To meet the simultaneous desire for global defense against communist expansion and a more economically efficient foreign policy, Eisenhower and Dulles formulated the New Look. It was based on the proposition that the American people should not and would not suffer the debilitating effects of a lower standard of living just to maintain the high military profile ordained under NSC-68. To circumvent this problem, Dulles proposed, and Eisenhower accepted, the idea of asymmetrical strategic deterrence, or as it is more popularly termed, "massive retaliation."[19] This portended a reliance on the threat of using nuclear weapons to retaliate directly against the perpetrator of communist aggression in order to deter such aggression a priori rather than be placed in a defensive position by being forced to react via the much more costly means of conventional forces sent half-way across the globe (as in Korea) to meet communist advances *after* they had been initiated. In this fashion, conventional force levels could be reduced at the same time since the focus was on maintaining, at much cheaper cost, an adequate nuclear deterrent that would enable the administration to counter the Keynesian economic policies of previous administrations by balancing the federal budget and allowing the people of the United States to maintain the high standard of living to which they had become accustomed.[20]

The focus on nuclear weapons, however, tended to obscure other facets of the Eisenhower-Dulles foreign policy that were also important components of the New Look, such as alliances, psychological warfare, and covert operations, all of which were intended to meet the so-called communist threat. The construction of alliances to confront Sino-Soviet "aggression" was largely a continuation of the policy under Truman, except that under Eisenhower the emphasis was again on the deterrent power of such alliances rather than their use in actively combatting Sino-Soviet advances (which, however, did not preclude the latter function if necessary). To implement this strategy, the Eisenhower administration concentrated on forming associations, either through multilateral pacts (such as SEATO and the Baghdad Pact/CENTO), bilateral agreements (as with Pakistan and Iraq), or unilateral enunciations of intent through congressional resolutions (such as the Formosa Resolution and what became known as the Eisenhower Doctrine), that would encircle the Soviet Union and the People's Republic of China. In his 1954 article in *Foreign Affairs,* Dulles even listed alliances as more important to the security of the "free nations" than the nuclear deterrent.

In addition to this deterrent effect, alliances fell in line with the concern with economy of resources in the Eisenhower foreign policy by developing "within the various areas and regions of the free world indigenous forces for the maintenance of order, the safeguarding of frontiers, and the provision of the bulk of ground capability."[21] This also tended to distance the United States (it was hoped) from action that could brand it as imperialist, a label which Eisenhower was sensitive to avoid. This last point, as we shall see, was particularly evident in the administration's relationship with Turkey vis-à-vis the 1957 American-Syrian crisis.

Other aspects of the New Look strategy beyond nuclear weapons and alliances focused on the increased emphasis on covert operations and psychological warfare. They were intended to prevent nations deemed susceptible to communist advances from actually turning communist and toward the Soviet Union. They were also employed in an effort, more imagined than real, to "liberate" those nations that had fallen under the yoke of communism, primarily the countries of Eastern Europe, rather than be satisfied, as Truman was accused of being, that they were forever "lost." Fundamentally, however, their use originated out of the necessity to fill the gaps in the overall strategic approach of the New Look.

Eisenhower responded early on to Dulles' asymmetrical strategic deterrence in the following manner:

> There is only one point that bothered me. . . . It is this: What should we do if Soviet political aggression, as in Czechoslovakia, successively chips away exposed positions of the free world? So far as our resulting economic situation is concerned, such an eventuality would be just as bad for us as if the area had been captured by force. To my mind, this is the case where the theory of "retaliation" falls down.[22]

In other words, how was the United States to counter indirect aggression or subversion engineered through non-military means. The administration never adequately addressed this flaw in its strategic perception, made all the more apparent with the enunciation of the Eisenhower Doctrine in 1957 and the subsequent problems in Syria.[23] The doctrine essentially offered American military and economic aid to those nations in the Middle East that requested it in order to fend off the advances of other states who were, in the official opinion of the administration, dominated by "international communism." The Eisenhower administration, however, at the height of the cold war and its manifestations in political rhetoric, was absolutely focused on the Soviet Union, and despite knowing full well (as indicated in numerous statements and analyses) that such things as Arab nationalism, the Arab-Israeli conflict, the regional tug-of-war between Egypt, Iraq, Saudi Arabia, and Syria, etc., were at the root of the instabilities in the Middle East, it chose to address the area at the international level. Even at this level, the doctrine's intent did not conform with the reality of the situation. It was intended to counter the Soviet Union's non-military activities in the region by means that were actually designed to counter expected military advances; this clearly betrayed the administration's distrust of the Kremlin and the dominant view held in Washington (sincerely held and for public consumption) that the Soviets were ruthless and totally devoid of "moral scruples" — in other words, the possibility that the Soviet Union may not have been at all interested in military expansion in the region did not come into play.[24] The Eisenhower Doctrine, then, was attempting to deter something that was itself deterred by other factors, such as the fear of initiating a nuclear war.[25] And since the only official Middle East policy of the United States at the time did not directly address the regional and domestic problems at the heart of the instabilities in the area, especially those that ran counter to American interests, the task of dealing with such concerns was left to means of a covert nature, such as that which was applied in Syria throughout much of 1957 — this, of course, only succeeded in exacerbating tensions in the region and between the superpowers. As George and Smoke wrote: "Because the doctrine specifically mentioned only armed aggression and said nothing at all about subversion, it is clear that U.S. leaders envisioned a relationship between the two that would allow the U.S. implicitly to bridge the gap between them and deter the latter by explicitly deterring the former."[26] The American-Syrian crisis exposed the administration's inability to lawfully bridge this gap, and as we shall see, Eisenhower and Dulles wrestled with this problem throughout the incident, especially as the focus of the crisis shifted to the United Nations, a forum where the exposure of such discrepancies are readily and eagerly revealed.

Contributing to the Eisenhower administration's misinterpretation of events occurring in the Middle East was its failure to grasp the distinct relationship between nationalism and communism in the revolutionary movements that broke out in the Third World as a result of the decline in

European colonialism following World War Two, and the international and regional interests of the United States in the area. The nationalists in the Middle East had been and were struggling to emerge completely from under the yoke of dominant influence exerted by the West, a battle that not only pitted them against the West but also against those indigenous elements who had vague or real associations with the West. Washington was convinced that these national liberation movements were susceptible to communist "penetration" directed from Moscow, and would inevitably lead to their total subordination to the Soviet Union. It was not a totally illusory assessment since the hard-core nationalists themselves in Syria were suspicious of communist "infiltration" within their own movement and were fearful that it would just lead the country into a colonial relationship with the Soviets – this was one of the main reasons behind their push for union with Egypt (finally consummated in 1958). But from the American standpoint, the nationalist-communist combination in Syria, brought together by the common goal of promoting Syrian independence in the face of real and embellished threats from the West and its allies in the region, was just that much more lethal. As William Stivers points out, the strategic desire, from the American point of view, to create and/or maintain a pro-West stability in the area was endangered principally by the Soviet Union and "unfriendly indigenous nationalisms," but the "interlinking" of these two threats was even more "disquieting."[27] To prevent the Soviets from taking advantage of "disorder" in the region, American administrations, including Eisenhower's, chose for the most part to "support the status quo" and oppose the forces of nationalism (i.e., change) in the Middle East.[28]

It was not a case of the Eisenhower administration not being able to distinguish between the nationalists or the communists – numerous State Department reports and statements by Eisenhower and Dulles indicate it could – but all that was really important was the perception in Washington that no matter what vehicle was carrying the burden of Soviet interests, the reality of the situation was that the Kremlin was indeed increasing its influence in the Middle East, with all the supposedly calamitous repercussions that this portended for the United States. This viewpoint not only precluded a cogent and sagacious analysis of the nationalist movement in Syria itself, but more importantly, it denied to the Syrians, both the pro-American and anti-American elements, the root causes of their very real domestic and regional concerns in favor of superimposing the East-West conflict upon them. As Eisenhower noted in 1953:

Nationalism is on the march and world Communism is taking advantage of that spirit of nationalism to cause dissension in the free world. Moscow leads many misguided people to believe that they can count on Communist help to achieve and sustain nationalistic ambitions. Actually what is going on is that the Communists are hoping to take advantage of the confusion resulting from destruction of existing relationships and in the difficulties and uncertainties of disrupted trade, security and understandings, to further the aims of world revolution and the Kremlin's domination of all people.[29]

Dulles would state in April 1957 that "international communism is on the prowl to capture those nations whose leaders feel that newly acquired sovereign rights have to be displayed by flouting other independent nations. That kind of sovereignty is suicidal sovereignty."[30] The secretary of state also remarked at the Caracas Conference that communism is "not a theory, not a doctrine, but an aggressive, tough, political force, backed by great resources and serving the most ruthless empire of modern times."[31] But the Kremlin, for the most part, was not looking to foment revolution, but to enhance Soviet influence, exactly what the United States was attempting to do.[32] And contrary to the heavy-handed tactics imposed by Stalin vis-à-vis Eastern Europe, the new Soviet leadership was conscious of its own limitations and sensitive to the concerns of Washington and the lengths it was prepared to go (apparent after travelling half-way across the globe to Korea) to protect its interests. The Eisenhower administration, however, would continue to view the Kremlin leadership in Stalinist, and even Hitlerian, terms.

The Soviet Union often adopted measures specifically designed not to provide a convenient pretext for American intervention. Indeed, as Barnet states, the "post-Stalin leaders began to make a major play for the support of Arab governments by becoming a partisan of Arab nationalism and discouraging independent revolutionary activity of local communists."[33] This is one of the reasons why the Kremlin could befriend Egypt's Gamal 'Abd al-Nasser at the same time the latter was persecuting the communists within his own country. Ironically, Moscow's attempt to circumvent American opprobrium by supporting nationalist movements only increased the concern felt in Washington since the great fear was that these popular movements would turn to the Soviet bloc for support.

The United States would not have the success of "winning over" the nationalist elements in the Middle East that the Soviet Union enjoyed since it was hamstrung by its commitment to Israel and the construction of a pro-West regional defense system to ward off Soviet "expansionism" as defined in military terms. It was much more economical to employ covert means to ensure the preeminence of pro-American forces (i.e., the status quo or status quo ante), as was successfully applied in Iran in 1953 and in Guatemala in 1954.[34] American efforts to cement the loyalty of countries in the Third World often focused upon the role of a single individual leader to the exclusion of the domestic and regional repercussions of his/her policies (and when this individual fell from power, the

United States was inevitably caught in the wave of animosity emanating from the respective populations against their former regimes). An NSC staff study in 1952 concluded, "the problem of leadership is crucial. We should make full use of our military and economic programs to support, or develop, *leaders* whose maintenance in, or advent to, power gives such promise."[35] (emphasis mine).

It was also easier for the administration to construct alliances and dictate congressional resolutions in an effort to keep the Soviets out of the Middle East, relying more and more on military solutions. As Ernest May writes, "before mid-1950 containment seemed to involve primarily an effort to create economic, social, and political conditions assumed to be inhospitable to communism, whereas from mid-1950 onward, the policy seemed primarily one of preserving military frontiers behind which conditions unsuited to subversion could gradually evolve."[36] But such things as the Baghdad Pact, the Eisenhower Doctrine, the Suez war, the perceived threat from Israel, and the interminable covert efforts to maintain in power or put in power pro-West elements, presented to most people in the Middle East a threat much more real and dangerous than anything emanating from communism or the Soviet bloc.

Notes

1. For an excellent detailed discussion of Syria under the French Mandate, see Philip S. Khoury, *Syria and the French Mandate: The Politics of Arab Nationalism, 1920–1945* (Princeton: Princeton University Press, 1987); also, see Stephen H. Longrigg, *Syria and Lebanon under French Mandate* (New York: Oxford University Press, 1958); for a discussion of Syria during the later stages of the Ottoman Empire, see Philip S. Khoury, *Urban Notables and Arab Nationalism: The Politics of Damascus 1860–1920* (New York: Cambridge University Press, 1983).

2. For more on the political constitution of Syria during this period, see Patrick Seale, *The Struggle for Syria: A Study of Post-War Arab Politics 1945–1958* (New Haven: Yale University Press, 1986), pp. 24–33; and, Gordon H. Torrey, *Syrian Politics and the Military 1945–1958* (Columbus, OH: Ohio State University Press, 1964), pp. 73–103.

3. Seale, pp. 148–158; for a discussion of the position of the Ba'th in relation to communism, see Salah al-Din Bitar and Michel 'Aflaq, *al-Ba'th wa al-hizb al-shuyu'i* (Damascus, 1944); and Hanna Batatu, *The Old Social Classes and the Revolutionary Movements of Iraq* (Princeton: Princeton University Press, 1978), pp. 722–748.

4. Seale, p. 157.

5. For more on Syria's political divisions, see Pierre Rondot, "Tendances particularistes et tendances unitaires en Syrie," *Orient*, 2, 1958.

6. For a discussion on this issue, see Richard H. Immerman, "Eisenhower and Dulles: Who Made the Decisions?" *Political Psychology,* I, 1979, pp. 3–20.

7. Robert A. Divine, *Eisenhower and the Cold War* (New York: Oxford University Press, 1981), p. 154.

8. Stephen E. Ambrose, *Eisenhower: The President* (New York: Simon and Schuster, 1984), p. 627.

9. Stephen G. Rabe, *Eisenhower and Latin America: The Foreign Policy of Anticommunism* (Chapel Hill: The University of North Carolina Press, 1988), p. 175.

10. See recent works on the Guatemalan coup in 1954: Richard H. Immerman, *The CIA in Guatemala* (Austin: University of Texas Press, 1982); Stephen G. Rabe, *Eisenhower and Latin America* (Chapel Hill: The University of North Carolina Press, 1988); and Stephen Schlesinger and Stephen Kinzer, *Bitter Fruit* (Garden City, NY: Anchor Books, 1983).

11. Quoted from Rabe, p. 5; Cook's most influential works on the Eisenhower Administration are: *The Declassified Eisenhower: A Divided Legacy* (Garden City, NY: Doubleday, 1981); and *Dwight David Eisenhower: Antimilitarist in the White House* (St. Charles, MO: Forum Press, 1974).

12. Stephen E. Ambrose, *Rise to Globalism: American Foreign Policy, 1938–1970* (Baltimore: Penguin Books), as quoted in Thomas G. Paterson (ed.)., *The Origins of the Cold War* (Lexington, MA: D.C. Heath, 1974), p. 181.

13. Dulles speech to the French National Political Science Institute in Paris, May 4, 1952, *Vital Speeches,* XXVIII (June 1, 1952), p. 495.

14. Eisenhower to Churchill, March 29, 1955, Ann Whitman File, DDE Diary Series, Box 6, Dwight D. Eisenhower Library, Abilene, Kansas (hereafter DDEL). An NSC paper (NSC 5501), approved by Eisenhower on January 7, 1955, stated the following: "As the lines between the Communist bloc and the Western coalition have come to be more clearly drawn over the last few years, a situation has arisen in which any further Communist territorial gain would have an unfavorable impact within the free world that might be out of all proportion to the strategic or economic significance of the territory lost." (White House Office: Office of the Special Assistant for National Security Affairs, Box 1, DDEL).

15. Speech by Dulles to the American Society of International Law, April 27, 1950, Department of State *Bulletin,* XXII (May 8, 1950), p. 717.

16. Eisenhower to Frank Altschul, October 25, 1957, Ann Whitman File, DDE Diary Series, Box 16, DDEL. Interestingly, this comment was made during the waning moments of the American-Syrian crisis.

17. Department of State *Bulletin,* XXX (March 15, 1954), p. 379.

18. John Lewis Gaddis, *Strategies of Containment: A Critical Appraisal of Postwar American National Security Policy* (New York: Oxford University Press, 1982), p. 140–141.

19. See article by John Foster Dulles, "Policy for Security and Peace," *Foreign Affairs*, XXXII (April 1954), pp. 357–359. The New Look was officially formulated from the deliberations and policy recommendations of "Operation Solarium," which was designed to consider and suggest options for the administration in its construction of a defined foreign policy.

20. For more on the strategic perception of the Eisenhower Administration, see John Lewis Gaddis, *Strategies of Containment: A Critical Appraisal of Postwar American National Security Policy* (New York: Oxford University Press, 1982), pp. 127–197; Robert A. Divine, *Since 1945: Politics and Diplomacy in Recent American History* (New York: John Wiley & Sons, 1979), pp. 55–69; H.W. Brands, "The Age of Vulnerability: Eisenhower and the National Insecurity State," *The American Historical Review*, vol.94, no.4 (October 1989), pp. 963–989; Douglas Kinnard, *President Eisenhower and Strategy Management: A Study in Defense Politics* (Lexington: The University of Kentucky Press, 1977), pp. 1–36; Elmo Richardson, *The Presidency of Dwight D. Eisenhower* (Lawrence: the Regents Press of Kansas, 1979), pp. 64–68; Samuel P. Huntington, *The Common Defense: Strategic Programs in National Politics* (New York: Columbia University Press, 1961), pp. 64–87; Robert A. Divine, *Eisenhower and the Cold War* (New York: Oxford University Press, 1981), pp. 34–39; Dwight D. Eisenhower, *Mandate for Change 1953–1956* (Garden City, NY: Doubleday & Company, 1963), pp. 445–458.

21. Eisenhower quoted in General Goodpaster memorandum, March 29, 1957, Ann Whitman File, DDE Diary Series, Box 13, DDEL.

22. Eisenhower to Dulles, April 15, 1952, Eisenhower Papers, 1916–1952, Box 33, DDEL.

23. For an excellent critique of the Eisenhower Doctrine, see Alexander L. George and Richard Smoke, *Deterrence in American Foreign Policy: Theory and Practice* (New York: Columbia University Press, 1974), pp. 309–358.

24. Ibid., p. 319.

25. Ibid., p. 322.

26. Ibid., p. 321.

27. William Stivers, *America's Confrontation with Revolutionary Change in the Middle East, 1943–1983* (London: MacMillan, 1986), p. 4.

28. Ibid., p. 5.

29. January 6, 1953, Ann Whitman File, DDE Diary Series, Box 5, DDEL.

30. Department of State *Bulletin*, April 22, 1957, XXXVI (May 6, 1957), p. 719.

31. Richard H. Immerman, *The CIA in Guatemala: The Foreign Policy of Intervention* (Austin: University of Texas Press, 1982), p. 10.

32. Richard J. Barnet, *Intervention and Revolution: The United States in the Third World* (New York: World Publishing, 1968), p. 135.

33. Ibid., p. 137.

34. Eisenhower commented at a press conference on January 19, 1955, discussing the first two years of his presidency, that ridding Guatemala of the communist "threat" was one of his proudest accomplishments. (Immerman, p. 5).

35. NSC Staff Study, "The Position of the United States with Respect to the Area Comprising the Arab States, Iran, and Israel," January 18, 1952, NSC 129/annex, RG273, National Archives, Washington, DC (hereafter NA).

36. In Joseph S. Nye, Jr. (ed.), *The Making of America's Soviet Policy* (New Haven: Yale University Press, 1984), p. 221.

2

American Policy Under Truman

The Truman administration (1945–1953) viewed Syria in terms of its strategic location in the heart of the Middle East "athwart oil pipelines and air routes; its possible role in a crisis as an area of ingress from the Eastern Mediterranean; and the vigorous activity of its government and people in the politics and cultural affairs of the Arab world."[1] Syria became important to the United States in terms of its relevance to other regional issues and problems that were of interest to the Truman administration.

As far as the Middle East as a whole was concerned, the administration's most developed objectives were delineated in National Security Council resolution 129/1, signed by President Truman on April 24, 1952, and superseding those outlined in NSC 47/2 of October 20, 1949, NSC 65/3 (Tripartite Declaration) of May 19, 1950, and NSC 47/5 of March 17, 1951. The objectives of NSC 129/1 (entitled, "United States Objectives and Policies with Respect to the Arab States and Israel) were the following: a) to overcome or prevent instability that threatened the West's interests in the region; b) to prevent the extension of Soviet influence and to enhance the West's influence; c) to insure that the resources of the area (i.e., oil) are available to the United States and its allies for use in strengthening the free world; d) to strengthen the will and ability of these countries to resist possible future aggression by the Soviet Union; and e) to establish within the community of nations a new relationship with the states of the area that recognizes their desire to achieve status and respect for their sovereign equality. In order to achieve these goals, the administration held as a minimum objective the stability of the various regimes in the region and an Arab-Israeli peace agreement as the maximum objective.[2]

The Truman administration feared that instability in the area would only create openings for the Soviet Union, enabling the latter to establish a foothold in the Middle East by means of an association with the growing leftist movements who had been identifying themselves with an anti-Zionist and anti-West platform.[3] This approach fell in line with the administration's containment policy as articulated in NSC-68. From Washington's point of view, of course, this "stability" in the Middle East was defined in terms of a regime aligning itself with the West and not with the Soviet bloc. It also meant a willingness on the part of the Arab regimes to come to terms with the new state of Israel, which would prevent the festering Arab-Israeli dispute to become a disruptive factor that could impede safe and easy access to oil and create opportunities for the Kremlin to exploit to its own advantage. Under this definition, however, the most "stable" regime was not necessarily the one that looked to the West or was willing and able to negotiate a settlement to the problems resulting from the 1947–1949 Arab-Israeli war, such as border demarcation and the status of the Arab refugees. This dilemma became apparent when the United States intervened in Syria in early 1949 to place an individual in power who American officials admitted was a "Banana Republic dictator type" who "did not have the competence of a French corporal" but did have a "strong anti-Soviet attitude" and showed he was willing to talk peace with Israel.[4]

In assisting General Husni al-Za'im overthrow the discredited Shukri al-Quwatli regime in March 1949, the United States felt it was riding a wave of popular discontent in Syria toward establishing a regime that would bring stability to a country rife with factionalism. It would also bring to power a leader with whom Washington could work to improve the chances of achieving peace with Israel and fitting Syria nicely into the West's schemes of preventing an increase of Soviet/communist influence in the region.[5] Indeed, Za'im was all and more of what the United States thought he could be. He concluded an armistice agreement with Israel, showed tangible signs of favoring peace negotiations with the Israelis, approved the TAPLINE (Trans-Arabian Oil Pipeline) concession which transported ARAMCO (Arab-American Oil Company) oil from Saudi Arabia to the Mediterranean, improved relations with NATO member Turkey, cracked down on communists and leftists in Syria, and displayed a willingness to accept American military assistance. When Za'im was himself overthrown less than five months after he assumed power (primarily because of his domestic excesses and the vitriolic issue of possible union with Iraq), American policy toward Syria under Truman, resting as it was on an individual leader, was essentially ruined before it ever had a chance to get started.

The overthrow of Za'im would come to characterize the Syrian political scene, one that consisted of chronic instability at the top, with revolving governments and the ever-present threat of actual or rumored coups. Unsure of the political vectors of the mercurial Syrian leadership, the United States reverted to a relatively low-level approach in its attempt to ensure a stable Syria which looked to the West and not to the East. Beginning in 1950, this took the form of encouraging technical and economic assistance to Syria under the Point Four Program and possible military aid under the Mutual Security Program (as established by the Mutual Security Act of 1951).[6]

The Point Four Program (the fourth major point of Truman's inaugural address in 1949) and the Mutual Security Program were initiated to provide technical and military assistance to the less developed countries in an effort to prop them up economically and militarily in order to eliminate any inroads for Soviet/communist influence. The program ran into numerous obstacles in Syria. One major obstacle was the relationship between the United States and Israel and America's commitment to somehow broker an Arab-Israeli peace. Most Syrians viewed the United States as primarily responsible for the creation of Israel; therefore, any regime had to be wary of the domestic repercussions of negotiating with Washington. The irony, of course, is that the Soviet Union, because of its military aid—via Czechoslovakia—and its diplomatic support at the United Nations, was much more responsible for Israel's birth than was the United States. But it is perceptions that matter, and at a minimum, the United States had to give enough tangible assistance as to provide the Syrian regime the wherewithal to withstand expected domestic and regional criticism from the anti-Zionists and anti-imperialists. Even so, the Syrians called on the Americans to pressure Israel to abide by the 1947 United Nations resolution on the division of Palestine as the quid pro quo for an agreement. The United States, on the other hand, had its own set of conditions for giving any significant aid to Syria, primarily the latter's cooperation regarding regional defense plans and concessions of its own on the Arab-Israeli issue. Each felt they had leverage on the other, but neither was willing to budge.

The United States again thought it potentially had someone in Syria with whom it could work when Colonel Adib al-Shishakli engineered the third coup d'etat within a year in December 1949 (the coup based mainly on the issue of union with Iraq, i.e., Shishakli was against it whereas his predecessor was close to consummating it). Shishakli chose to rule behind the throne (manipulating seven different civilian cabinets in the next twenty-three months[7]) until late 1951, when he came out into the open and established a military dictatorship. The Syrians, however, were not seriously interested in Point Four assistance. Khalid al-'Azm, wealthy landowner, opportunistic leader of the left-leaning Independent bloc, and two-time prime minister under Shishakli, stated that nothing counted regarding political influence in Syria except the willingness to supply arms.[8] Syrians generally felt that they would be the next victim of Israeli expansionism. And Israel was doing nothing to dispel this notion with its frequent armed sorties along the Syrian border. The Israelis claimed they had the right to till the soil of the disputed area; Syria rejected this claim. Like most Arabs, Syrians, looking introspectively, believed the 1947–1949 debacle was caused by corruption, ill-preparedness, and an underestimation of the enemy; if given the arms and proper leadership, they could redress the issue in their favor, or at least negotiate from a position of strength. The Israeli threat was by far the most popularly espoused issue in Syria, and only unconditional military assistance could satisfy the public.

The Point Four program was, in addition, very unpopular, and nations targeted as recipients felt threatened by it. The British ambassador to Syria described a conversation he had had with his American counterpart, Cavendish Cannon, "he told me how horrified he had been to find the Lebanon teeming with Point IV officials all busy 'programming' instead of getting down to the execution of projects. As a result, Point IV was already beginning to acquire a very bad reputation in the Lebanon, and it was not to be wondered at that the Syrian government should fight shy of these hordes of foreign officials."[9]   The Syrian regime was more interested in tangible benefits than receiving technical and survey teams that made recommendations for the implementation of long-term projects.[10]

The Syrian economy, while in better shape than that in most of the other Arab states, definitely could have used the Point Four assistance. American officials were genuinely perplexed that the Syrians did not immediately accept their offers. Syrian equivocation on Point Four became so distressing that Cannon referred to his staff in Damascus as "prophets of frustration."[11] American officials, however, did not understand the depth of feeling in Syria against Israel or the Syrian fear of falling under the domination of another "imperialist country" (after having so recently rid themselves of the French). This fear, as it turned out, was quite legitimate, as evidenced by the following conclusion made at the United States Chiefs of Mission Conference held in Istanbul in 1954: " . . . our most useful tool in maintaining our position of influence [in the Middle East] is technical assistance, both in the form of our military training mission and our Point Four experts."[12]

Complicating matters even further with respect to Point Four aid was the attempt by the United States to link the issue to the resettlement of Palestinian refugees, of whom there were over one million from the 1947–49 war. Syria was designated as the Arab nation most capable, in geographic and economic terms, to house the large portion of these refugees. With this in mind, Washington and the World Bank negotiated with Syria during most of 1952 to channel aid and loans through the United Nations Relief and Works Agency (UNRWA) to help the Syrian regime cope with the anticipated influx of Palestinians.[13]

Shishakli balked on this account since the regime would be seen as doing more for the refugees than for the Syrian people.[14] In any event, an acceptance of the refugees would legitimize Israel's right to the land it conquered in the 1947–49 war beyond the UN partition zones without compensation for those Palestinians that left or were forced out — and many Syrians resented the linkage. Ma'ruf al-Dawalibi, a leader of the Populist Party and minister of national economy at the time, stated in Cairo that "should the American pressure on the Arab countries, which is intended eventually to Judaize them, continue, I hope that a referendum will be held in the Arab world so that all and sundry will know that the Arabs would prefer a 1000 times to be a Soviet republic rather than a palatable Jewish morsel."[15] It is interesting to note that the American army attache in Damascus analyzed Dawalibi's statement to be part of a Soviet "black propaganda" drive aimed at driving out American influence rather than what it probably really was, i.e., an embellished expression of the perceived unequal threats posed by Israel and the Soviet Union and/or a political maneuver to gain domestic support in the ongoing power struggles in the Syrian polity.[16]

Before any agreement regarding Israel could occur, Shishakli demanded sufficient economic aid for the Syrian people to offset that directed at the refugees. He also insisted on American enforcement of the 1947 UN partition as a "gesture" of goodwill.[17] This, of course, from an economic and political standpoint, was out of the question as far as the United States was concerned. The Point Four program in Syria never overcame these obstacles and did not advance beyond the planning stage. As the British Foreign Office concluded, the Point Four program failed because the United States did not realize that it was "not possible with money and persuasion alone to bring a region in a short time to a stage of development at which American technical and administrative assistance is both palatable and capable of absorption by the national and social systems to which it is applied."[18] The overall program was, indeed, generally hampered by the fact that the "long-run, indigenous developmental considerations were generally subordinated in United States aid policy to more immediate measures designed to insure the recipient against actual or anticipated Soviet influences."[19]

Arms for Sale

The issue of military aid to Syria also presented the Truman administration with a variety of problems, although the prospects for an agreement being reached in this sphere were much better since this was the type of assistance in which the Syrians were primarily interested. But the ability of the United States to provide Syria with enough military aid to satiate its needs were also hamstrung by a number of factors.

One was the French. France had only recently been forced to relinquish its' mandate over Syria and therefore still maintained a significant amount of cultural and economic influence in the country, as well as strong ties with many Syrian politicians and army officers who basically owed their positions to the French. Reluctant to accept their waning status as a great power, France was not about to acquiesce to the inevitable and calmly hand Syria over to the next highest bidder. They would do everything they possibly could, at times at the expense of American interests in blocking Soviet inroads into Syria, to keep their position in the country viable. Most importantly, they wanted to guard against and frustrate the attempts by their erstwhile allies, the British and Americans, to increase their own influence in Syria.[20] They did not have the wherewithal of the British, and certainly not that of the United States, to compete on equal terms in the international jockeying for materially winning friends in Syria. The French government maneuvered effectively within the Syrian political landscape, taking advantage of the contacts it had built up during the mandate years. As a result, the French were widely accused in Washington and London of playing into the hands of the Kremlin.

Another obstacle to American attempts to secure a military aid agreement with Syria was the actions of the British. At the time, London was caught in the dilemma of wanting Washington to involve itself in the Middle East since it no longer had the wherewithal to go it alone, but it did not want the United States to involve itself to the point where it began to replace British influence in the region. British officials knew their country could not compete with the economic and military might of the United States for friends in the Middle East; therefore, even though London and Washington had what largely amounted to coinciding interests vis-à-vis Syria (i.e., bring it into the West camp and out of Soviet reach), Britain was not all that forthcoming in helping the Americans curtail or thwart French obstructionism or make it any easier for Washington to enter into significant arms deals with Arab nations.[21]

The British were especially sensitive to their position in Iraq and were concerned over how they would look in Iraqi eyes if Syria all of a sudden was to receive huge amounts of arms from the United States. The recovering British economy was not up to the task of meeting any additional Iraqi requests. This issue would cause some low-level friction between the United States and Britain when Iraq began to seek military aid from the Americans. Most British officials during this period, however, understood the inevitable and considered it a fait accompli that the United States would eventually surpass them in the Middle East, and it was much more desirable to concede defeat and work in concert with the Americans to "contain" the Soviets than to openly challenge them. Nevertheless, differences between the three Western powers could not be hidden completely, and the Syrians certainly tried their best to play one off against the other in their attempts to obtain the best deal on military hardware that they could get. Soviet propaganda also tended to exploit the disaccord, portraying the West as selfishly hungry imperialists out to take advantage of weaker nations.

Another hindrance to Washington's attempts to sell arms to the Syrians was the Tripartite Declaration of 1950, in which the governments of France, the United Kingdom, and the United States basically agreed to limit arms sales and transfers in the Middle East so as to prevent an arms race between Israel and the Arab states.[22] If any significant arms deal was struck with

Syria, immediately Israel, and even other Arab states (such as Iraq, Jordan, and Lebanon), would demand more military aid to maintain the balance of power in the region.[23]

The Israeli government, along with its numerous supporters in Congress, lobbied extremely hard against American arms transfers to the Arab states, especially those residing on its border. An administration that was for the most part sympathetic to Israel's needs and, indeed, played a significant role in its creation, was hesitant to provide military aid to any Arab country that was not willing to peacefully come to terms with the Israelis. And since 1952 was an election year, the Truman administration did not want to offend the American Jewish community for fear of losing their votes and campaign support.

Finally, the Syrians themselves made it very difficult to successfully negotiate an aid agreement. Their equivocation on the issue, no matter what the political color of the regime in power, reflected the deep distrust of the West in Syria and the extreme distaste for making agreements with a country that had been supporting Israel. Even if a Syrian leader showed great interest in obtaining arms from the United States, and certainly Shishakli was one of them, he had to tiptoe around the issue for fear of arousing intense opposition in the Chamber of Deputies (the Syrian parliament), in the streets, and throughout the Arab world. The United States was forced by its commitment to Israel to ask for certain guarantees from Arab countries that military aid would only be used for defensive purposes (i.e., not used against the Israelis); however, no Syrian leader, who naturally publicly proclaimed himself a sworn enemy of Israel, could agree to these terms. Even so, any American arms package along the generous lines of that given to Turkey (which was the type of deal Shishakli desired), was a moot point, since the United States was constrained under the terms of the Tripartite Declaration, British and French opposition, and, most of all, apprehension that these arms, regardless of Syrian guarantees, would indeed be used against Israel — the volatile and unpredictable nature of the Syrian polity did not render confidence in its ability to honor any guarantees.[24] The Syrians would not act on this issue and go out on the proverbial limb in the Arab world until other Arab states in the region, namely Egypt, had done so.

These obstacles prevented the United States from gaining a foothold in Syria through the vehicle of military aid. All of these deterrents would continue to rear their heads and hamper the efforts of the Eisenhower administration in its attempt to arrange an arms deal with Syria. Despite this, however, embassy personnel in Damascus would continue to press the administration to deal with the Syrians. When Shishakli dissolved parliament and established his military dictatorship (although he himself only retained the title of chief of staff, choosing to rule through his acolyte Colonel Fawzi Selu), the United States thought this to be an opportune moment to push for an arms agreement. Indeed, Shishakli took firm control of the reins of power partly in reaction to Ma'ruf al-Dawalibi's rise to the post of prime minister (lasting only a day before Shishakli removed him). The United States regarded Dawalibi as pro-Soviet, a view primarily derived from his exhortations against the regional defense plans of the West, such as the Middle East Command or Middle East Defense Organization, that were designed, following the precepts of NSC-68, to "contain" the USSR.[25]

There is some indication that the United States might have encouraged Shishakli's coup, although it is not yet known what role, if any, it played; whether or not it had a role in the coup, the Truman administration was pleased with the results.[26] Shishakli was not a disappointment, as he showed a willingness to consider a peace treaty with Israel, resettle the refugees under certain conditions, negotiate a mutual defense agreement with Turkey, reach an agreement with the United States on military aid, and join the Middle East Command.[27]

Negotiations with Shishakli, however, became protracted. All of the obstacles described above came into full play throughout the year 1952. Each side was unwilling to take the initiative, or as one official commented, "Syria won't cooperate with us until we offer a small sprat and we won't offer a small sprat unless Syria is more cooperative."[28] In any event, American offers of military aid at this time were clearly politically motivated in an attempt to reorient the Shishakli regime in a more pro-West direction, as opposed to providing it with military hardware for a specifically designed role within MEDO. Shishakli seemed to understand this and consequently called Washington's bluff by holding out for a much better offer, and in doing so, he exposed the constraints upon the Truman and Eisenhower administrations' ability to provide assistance.

Notes

1. Policy Statement: Syria, June 26, 1950, 611.83/6-2650, RG59, NA.
2. Ibid.
3. There were (and still are) so many factors involved in Syria that demarcate political boundaries—economic, social, familial, religious—that have very little to do with ideology or Western definitions of left-wing or leftists and right-wing or conservatives. Fundamentally speaking, in Syria during the period under discussion, the leftists were those who favored a regime that reflected their views of Arab nationalism, neutralism, anti-imperialism, anti-Zionism, and, to a lesser extent, anti-feudalism and anti-old guard cum corrupt politicians, and in doing so tended to support Nasserism and a closer relationship with the Soviet bloc. The right-wing or conservative elements, having held power for a decade since the end of World War Two, represented those groups who wanted a maintenance of the status quo when

in power and a return to power when the leftists became predominant (certainly the case by late 1956). Having had vested interests in relations with the West, and recognizing the growing leftwing attachment to the Soviet bloc, a symbiotic relationship developed between these groups and the Western powers (namely, the United States and Great Britain) and as a result were generally identified as being pro-West.

4. Quoted in Douglas Little, "Cold War and Covert Action: The United States and Syria, 1945–1958," *The Middle East Journal,* vol. 44, no. 1 (Winter 1990), pp. 55–56.

5. For further information on American covert actions in Syria during the Truman years see Little, pp. 51–60; also see Miles Copeland, *The Game of Nations* (New York: Simon and Schuster, 1969).

6. For details on Point Four assistance to Syria, see State Department Memorandum, "Point IV," September 18, 1950, State Department Post Files, Cairo Embassy, 1950, RG84, NARA; On Eisenhower's foreign economic aid policy in general, see Burton I. Kaufman, *Trade and Aid: Eisenhower's Foreign Economic Policy 1953–1961* (Baltimore: The Johns Hopkins University Press, 1982).

7. For composition of the various cabinets, see Gordon H. Torrey, *Syrian Politics and the Military 1945–1958* (Columbus, OH: Ohio State University Press, 1964), pp. 405–415; also, see R. Bayly Winder, "Syrian Deputies and Cabinet Ministers, 1919–1959," *Middle East Journal,* vol. XVII (1963), pp. 35–54.

8. British Embassy-Damascus, April 7, 1952, FO 371/98921, Public Record Office, London (hereafter PRO).

9. British Embassy-Damascus, April 28, 1952, FO 371/98921, PRO. A British report on the United States Chiefs of Mission Conference held in Damascus in December 1954 described the "meeting as unanimously hostile to Point Four on account of excessive number and poor quality of staff and over ambitious nature of some of the programme." (British Embassy-Damascus, December 20, 1954, FO 371/110775, PRO).

10. As Shishakli stated in an interview on March 18, 1953, with American journalists: Point Four "does not serve our purpose since its objective is to undertake studies of projects and not to implement these projects." American Embassy-Damascus to Department of State, March 25, 1953, State Department Post Files, Cairo Embassy, 1953, RG84, NARA.

11. Letter from Cavendish Cannon, U.S. Ambassador to Syria, to Edwin A. Locke, Coordinator of U.S. Economic and Technical Assistance in the Near East, March 17, 1952, State Department Post Files, Cairo Embassy, 1952, RG84, NARA.

12. "Summary Record of the Conference of U.S. Chiefs of Mission in the NEA Area Held at Istanbul May 11–14, 1954," State Department Post Files, Cairo Embassy, 1954, RG84, NARA.

13. For pertinent UN resolutions regarding this subject, see Resolution No. 302 (IV) of December 8, 1949, "Establishing the U.N. Relief and Works Agency for Palestine Refugees (UNRWA)," and Resolution No. 513 (VI) of January 26, 1952, "Endorsing a three-year UNRWA programme for relief and reintegration." George J. Tomeh (ed.), *United Nations Resolutions on Palestine and the Arab-Israeli Conflict, Volume I: 1947–1974* (Washington: Institute for Palestine Studies, 1975), pp. 18 and 24 respectively.

14. Shishakli did agree, however, to settle the 80,000 Palestinian refugees already in Syria in exchange for $ .3 million from UNRWA. British Foreign Office, "Syria: Annual Review for 1952," January 8, 1953, FO 371/104965.

15. *al-Misri,* April 12, 1950.

16. For Army Attache's comment, see Milattache Damascus Syria From SA From Keeley to Comgenusareur, Dept of Army, April 28, 1950, 783.00/4-2850, RG59, NA.

17. Funkhouser to Kopper, May 26, 1952, 783.00/5-2652, RG59, NA; American Legation, Damascus to Department of State, June 30, 1952, 783.5 MSP/6-3052, RG59, NA; Memorandum of Conversation, Department of State, November 15, 1952, 611.83/11-1552, RG59, NA.

18. British Middle East Office (BMEO), July 7, 1953, FO 371/104258, PRO. An example of this incongruency, according to the British, was the transatlantic thinking of applying the Tennessee Valley Authority plan (on which the Johnston Plan for redistribution of the Jordan River waters was based — discussed below) to the Middle East. (Ibid.)

19. Harold G. Vatter, *The U.S. Economy in the 1950's: An Economic History* (Chicago: The University of Chicago Press, 1963), p. 17.

20. For comments on French actions, see British Embassy-Damascus, no date, 1952, FO 371/98925, PRO; British Embassy-Washington, March 1, 1952, FO 371/98925, PRO; British Foreign Office, "France and the Middle East," April 29, 1952, FO 371/98242, PRO; American Embassy, Ankara to Secretary of State, February 6, 1952, 783.13/2-652, RG59, NA; British Embassy-Washington, April 12, 1952, FO 371/98921, PRO; British Foreign Office, April 9, 1952, FO 371/98921, PRO.

21. The British were also hindered from taking decisive action against the French by the Non-substitution Agreement between the two countries in 1945. The agreement, inter alia, stated that "each Government affirms its intention of doing nothing to supplant the interests or responsibilities of the other in the Middle East, having full regard to the political status of the countries in question," of which Syria was one. British Foreign Office, December 13, 1945, FO 371/110770.

22. For text of Tripartite Declaration, see Ralph H. Magnus (ed.), *Documents on the Middle East* (Washington: American Enterprise Institute, 1969), p. 163.

23. It is interesting that in testimony before the Senate Foreign Relations and Armed Services Committee on January 15, 1957, Secretary of State Dulles said that the British and French had stated that the declaration was no longer binding on them, but that it was still an expression of United States policy. (U.S. Congress, Senate, Committee on Foreign Relations and Committee on Armed Services, *The President's Proposal on the Middle East. Hearings* on S.J. res. 19 and H.J. res. 117, 85th Congress, 1st session, 1957).

24. Typical of Syrian comment at the time is the following extract from the Damascus paper *Barada* of January 31, 1952: "It is difficult to understand how the Western powers and America in particular have supplied our Turkish neighbor with all types of arms and made her an important military power but at the same time prevented the Arabs from obtaining necessary arms for their forces."

25. The British-inspired Middle East Command (MEC) was ostensibly a defense organization proposed in the summer of 1951 to resist (Soviet) "aggression" in the Middle East. The initial participants envisaged included the United States, Great Britain, France, Australia, New Zealand, South Africa, Turkey, and Egypt. The plan was basically an attempt by the British to protect their specific interests in the Middle East under the cover of regional security. It was also the main reason why they wanted an American commitment to the Middle East, for lacking this, the organization would be militarily hollow. The consummation of the project revolved around the participation of Egypt, which would lead the way for other Arab states to join (including Syria), but the lack of an agreement between Britain and Egypt over the former's orderly departure from Egyptian territory (an agreement which was finally reached in 1954) precluded Egypt from taking part in the plan. The United States was also not going to participate until an Anglo-Egyptian accord was reached for fear of upsetting the Egyptians, with whom it was trying to gain increasing influence at the expense of the British. The United States envisioned after an agreement, Egypt would then be seen as more amenable to an Arab-Israeli peace settlement, thus making American accession to a Middle East regional defense system that included Arab states more palatable to Israel and its supporters in the United States.

By 1952, the MEC was being called the Middle East Defense Organization (more passive nomenclature!), which was basically the same animal, although it was intended to be a regional defense group rather than including countries from half-way across the globe. It was still an Anglo-American creation and Egypt was still the linchpin for attracting other Arab states (Egypt was also strategically necessary because of its location astride the Suez Canal). For the "Proposals Presented to Egypt by the Governments of the United States, United Kingdom, France and Turkey, October 13, 1951" and the "Rejection by Egypt of the Joint Proposals: Statement of Regret by the Secretary of State, October 17, 1951," see Magnus, *Documents on the*

Middle East, pp. 75 and 77 respectively. For more on this subject, see John C. Campbell, *Defense of the Middle East: Problems of American Policy* (New York: Harper and Brothers, 1960), pp. 39–48.

26. Little, p. 60.

27. The British Embassy in Damascus made the following assessment of Shishakli: "He would like Syria to be a member of a Middle East Defence Organization, not only because he would expect thereby to obtain arms in greater quantity and on more favorable terms but also because he knows, and he has publicly admitted, that neutrality is impossible. It is, however, difficult for him to speak his mind on this subject until his internal position is impregnable. It seems that only a decisive step by Egypt into the Western camp would remove this inhibition." (British Embassy-Damascus, "Syria: Annual Review for 1952," January 8, 1953, FO 371/104965).

28. British Embassy-Damascus, March 21, 1952, FO 371/98921.

3

Eisenhower's Turn

When the Eisenhower administration came to power in January 1953 there existed much optimism in the Arab world that American policies might change in its favor. This was based largely on Eisenhower's and Secretary of State Dulles' known disposition to direct foreign policy in the Middle East on a more even-handed basis between Israel and the Arabs.[1] The new administration also recognized the increasing strategic importance of the Middle East's oil reserves, its oil transport routes, and its position on the southeast flank of NATO bordering the south-central regions of the Soviet Union. It was thought that this, combined with concern over the waning ability of the British to protect Western interests in the Middle East and the volatility of the Arab-Israeli dispute, might provide an opening for the Soviets to increase their influence in the area. As Dulles stated in June, "it is high time that the United States Government paid more attention to the Near East and South Asia. . . . "[2]

As early as January 27, 1953, Dulles warned against communist encirclement of the West. He believed that the communists in the Middle East were trying to "inspire the Arabs with a fanatical hatred" of the United States.[3] As evidence of Soviet interest in the Middle East, Dulles stated that "Stalin when he was negotiating with Hitler in 1940 said that that area must be looked upon as the center of Soviet aspirations."[4] The State Department, indeed, had been tracking with consternation the rise of left-wing and communist influence in Syria. Certainly statements such as the one made by Ahmad al-Hajj Yunes, a member of the Syrian parliament, as early as 1951, when he proposed an alliance with the Soviets, only heightened the sense of vulnerability to Soviet inroads in the area.[5] The Syrian ambassador to the United States, Farid Zayn al-Din, in a speech at a conference in January 1953 of the American Friends of the Middle East, remarked that Soviet propaganda was extremely persuasive and that the Soviet Union's attitude on Palestine, Morocco, Tunisia, and other issues of colonialism had been "at least ten times more effective in swaying opinion" than all the work by American information services over the years.[6] American embassy personnel felt that the most effective way to keep the Soviets out of the region was to meet the immediate worries of the Arabs rather than press for an Arab-Israeli peace agreement or be constrained by what they believed were embellished concerns over Israel's security. They knew that for military and political reasons, Syria's real fear of Israel had to be addressed with a military aid package, and if not, it would eventually look elsewhere for protection.[7]

The initial optimism in the Arab world for the Eisenhower administration was met with reciprocal dismay on the part of Israel and its supporters in the United States. The Israelis were reportedly very worried about the new administration, viewing it as less "open-handed" than the Truman administration had been in assisting Israel financially. It was perceived by Tel Aviv as being more susceptible to be "tempted to try to win Arab military cooperation with deliveries of arms."[8] Israel was also apprehensive over the possibility that the United States would impose a peace settlement upon it and force it to give up territory in exchange for an agreement. The Israeli government, aware of the red-scare mentality of Dulles (and indeed most of the United States at the time), began a campaign through the American press that attempted to link communism with anti-Zionism, especially by focusing on anti-Semitic activities in the Soviet Union.[9]

The United States Embassy in Tel Aviv reported that the Israelis felt that their backs were against the wall as a result of the following chain of events: 1) anti-Semitism in the Soviet bloc countries (focusing on the Prague trials); 2) the "intensification" of Arab collective action against Israel; 3) Arab "obstructionism" that increased Israeli economic difficulties, notably by putting pressure on West Germany and other Western governments to delay the German World War Two reparation payments to Israel; 4) British supplying the Arabs with jet planes, possibly presaging a change in Western arms policy in defiance of the Tripartite Declaration; and 5) disappointment with the anti-Israeli policy of Egypt's President Muhammad Naguib and Syria's strongman Adib al-Shishakli, two men the Israelis (and the Americans) had hoped would be more favorably disposed toward peace negotiations.[10]

As far as Syria was concerned, however, the Israelis had less to worry about than they had anticipated. Eisenhower and Dulles, although more willing to encourage arms agreements with Arab countries, immediately encountered a Syrian regime that was considerably less anxious to come to an agreement with the United States. The main reason for the change in outlook of the Shishakli regime was the attempted coup by leftist forces in Syria only a month before Eisenhower came to power. The coup was allegedly incited by Akram al-Hawrani and the two Ba'thist leaders Salah al-Din Bitar and Michel 'Aflaq. All three were forced to take refuge in Lebanon, where they decided to combine their two movements into the Arab Socialist Resurrection Party (the Ba'th).

While smothering the coup attempt, Shishakli was forced to dismiss some twenty-four military officers, including old friends and supporters. And despite his attempts during the course of 1952 to create a political party that would back his policies (the Arab Liberation Movement or ALM), by the beginning of 1953 Shishakli was still without any significant organized political support. Under these conditions, it would have been impossible for him to make concessions to the West or consummate a deal with the United States for arms, unless, of course, it was an offer of such magnitude that he could not refuse it. However, Syria's internal instability and the rise in popularity of anti-Zionist and anti-imperialist slogans with which the left-wing became identified, forced Shishakli to placate the opposition's concerns in his own country by playing hard to get with the United States. He was obviously shaken by the December coup attempt and realized now that he would have to cater to both sides of the political fence in order to maintain power. It is interesting to note that the ALM charter of March 1953 was decidedly non-controversial. Of the thirty-seven articles in the charter, thirteen dealt with social issues, eight with political concerns, fourteen on economic matters, one on military policy, and only one minor reference to foreign policy.[11] Shishakli definitely did not want to rekindle the opposition's criticism by delving into East-West issues.

Shishakli immediately went on the offensive to counter charges from the leftists that he was a "stooge" of the West. He began to publicly emphasize that the West must satisfy the nationalist aspirations of the Arabs and insisted that Arab collaboration be on a basis of equality.[12] He also did an about-face on the oil pipeline negotiations with the Iraq Petroleum Company (IPC), demanding at least forty-nine percent of the savings that resulted from the transport of oil across Syria.[13] "Squeezing" the oil companies was always a popular move by Arab governments as an indication to their publics that they were not cowering in the face of economic imperialism. In February 1953, in an interview with an American journalist, Shishakli, in an "unusually frank" manner, stated that American aid offers were insufficient and that it would be impossible for Syria to join any Middle East defense plan until it was "confident of the security of its frontiers [i.e., Israel], its national entity and its vital interests"[14] (insert mine). In other words, the burden was on the United States.

So the issue of a military or economic agreement between the United States and Syria when Eisenhower came to power was stillborn. The American ambassador in Syria, James S. Moose, wrote the State Department in January that it might "wish to consider leaving negotiations for a bilateral aid program in abeyance until the United States has a more comprehensive type of program to offer or until the Syrian authorities show more active interest in the kind of program now authorized."[15] Either of these two possibilities were unlikely to occur until the administration got settled in and formulated an approach to the Middle East. One of the reasons Shishakli was obdurate throughout much of 1952 in relation to an arms deal with the United States might have been because he was expecting the Eisenhower administration to make a more enticing offer. The president felt, however, that the entire Middle East policy of the United States needed a reevaluation; therefore, no new initiatives would be undertaken until this rather cumbersome process was completed. To facilitate this, Eisenhower sent his secretary of state on a tour of Middle Eastern and South Asian capitals.

John Foster Dulles in the Middle East

Dulles' trip lasted from May 11 to May 29, 1953. He met with Adib al-Shishakli in Damascus on May 15. The Syrian leader expressed to Dulles his great hope that the new administration would adopt a foreign policy not "poisoned" by Zionist propaganda. He emphasized that he was not one of those Arabs who claimed that Israel does not exist nor was he committed to pushing it into the sea, but he reiterated the fact that Israel must adhere to the UN resolutions relating to the refugee problem, border demarcation, and the internationalization of Jerusalem before he could lead his country into some sort of association with the West. Shishakli also restated his country's need for military defense, appealing to American sensitivities by appearing to want these arms to enable Syria to defend itself internally against the spread of communism. He claimed that Syria must spend half of its budget on defense and pointed out that the United States had the capability through economic and military assistance to keep Syria independent.[16]

The secretary of state's response was to give Shishakli the "strongest and most categorical assurance" that the United States was opposed to any expansion of the existing frontiers of Israel. He also wanted the Syrian people to know that the United States did not favor Israel at the expense of Syria. While wanting to give "greater confidence to Syria that Israel will not attack it," Dulles did emphasize that "one element related to U.S. military assistance is that the United States must be confident that Syria would not attack Israel." Dulles told Shishakli that he realized that Israel was Syria's number one concern, but the primary concern of the United States was the "balance of power between the Soviet and non-Soviet world." He admitted that MEDO was probably not the best way to go about arranging a regional security system (especially after learning of Egypt's extreme distaste for it on his first stop on the trip in Cairo), and even asked Shishakli for his advice on the matter, but the Syrian leader just reiterated the standard Arab policy that before he could participate in any regional defense plan there must be security in the Middle East, i.e., the overall problem of Israel must be resolved and, to a lesser extent, a settlement reached on the Suez Canal Zone between the British and the Egyptians.[17]

The preceding exchange made it apparent that the obstacles to an American-Syrian agreement were still essentially intact. Despite this, Dulles was impressed with Shishakli and came away with an appreciation of the vital strategic role Syria could potentially play in the Middle East.[18] He concluded that Syria offered "some promise" since it had greater economic potential at less cost and was the only Arab country that could absorb large numbers of refugees, which, in his view, would be a good start for the "liquidation of the problem which poisons all Arab relations" with the United States.[19] Dulles was impressed with Shishakli's weltanschauung, which he felt was more accurate (i.e., in line with American interests) than that of the Egyptian leadership, and found solace in the fact that Syria seemed "less engrossed" with the Suez problem and more aware of the Soviet threat because of its proximity to the USSR.[20] Egypt, however, was still the prize in the Middle East as far as American foreign policy interests were concerned, and Dulles admitted that Syria could not act as an adequate substitute.[21]

The overall conclusions that Dulles made during his sojourn in the Middle East were, inter alia, the following: 1) that American policy vis-à-vis the colonial interests of France and Great Britain has become "unnecessarily ambiguous" and that the United States should pursue its "traditional dedication to political liberty," for it is in the West's interests to have an "orderly development of self-government" in Middle East nations; 2) the United States should "seek to allay the deep resentment against it that has resulted from the creation of Israel" and it must be "made clear" that the Eisenhower administration "stands fully behind" the Tripartite Declaration; 3) the Arabs are "more fearful of Zionism than of communism, and they fear lest the United States become the backer of expansionist Zionism"; 4) that the "parties concerned have the primary responsibility of bringing peace to the area," but the United States "will not hesitate by every appropriate means to use its influence to promote step-by-step reduction of tension in the area and the conclusion of ultimate peace"; 5) that MEDO is a "future rather than an immediate policy" since "many of the Arab countries are so engrossed with their quarrels with Israel or with Great Britain or France that they pay little heed to the menace of Soviet communism," but "where the Soviet Union is near" (i.e., the northern tier countries), there is an appropriate appreciation and awareness of the danger; 6) that the "political stability required for internal progress and building of defensive strength of [the] area is lacking" and that the "position of the Western powers has deteriorated to the point where they are not at present serving as factors of stability"; 7) that it is of the "utmost importance that U.S. assistance to the area be somewhat increased and the Point IV concept sharpened in its application" with the primary utilization of funds directed toward water development which would help alleviate the refugee problem and a "small amount of military equipment" provided to "certain selected States."[22] Dulles' findings were essentially crystallized into policy in NSC resolution 155/1, approved by the president on July 11, 1953.

Dulles' trip to the Middle East enabled him to assess more accurately the American position in the region and the sentiments of the various leaders and populations in the area concerning the more salient issues affecting them. He recognized that MEDO was an unreal possibility and that the extent of the hostility the Arabs engendered toward Israel had deleterious effects on American-Arab relations. The question still remained, however, if the United States could meet Arab demands to the point where it was seen as not abandoning Israel, while at the same time enabling the local Arab governments to rationalize an agreement to their respective populations and opposition groups. This was particularly relevant to the situation in Syria. The short and long-term answer was no; the Eisenhower administration was not able to juggle the interests and demands of the countries concerned and integrate them neatly into American plans.

Dulles continued to push the Point Four program and started the negotiations for water development (known as the Johnston Plan) in the region in an attempt bring the Arabs and Israelis together through common economic interest.[23] The Point Four program in Syria was at a standstill, and even though the Shishakli regime showed some interest in the Johnston Plan, it was never in a position to accede to something that involved cooperation with Israel unless the Syrians felt they were militarily secure through the acquisition of arms and with a settlement of the border dispute with the Israelis. Dulles was only willing to give a "small amount" of military aid to "selected states" in the region while emphasizing economic aid, which was essentially the same line the Syrians had been listening to since the Truman administration came to power.[24] The budget conscious Eisenhower administration knew that large amounts of military aid would immediately win over the hearts of the Arabs, but the obstacles to this still basically remained in the wake of Dulles' trip; therefore, Syria would remain aloof of Western defense plans and economic integration projects designed to secure the region from Soviet encroachment and create an atmosphere that would be conducive to an Arab-Israeli peace settlement.

Eisenhower and Dulles favored multilateral defense and peace plans in the Middle East that were initiated from within the region and not imposed from the outside, preferring to work with individual states who were disposed to cooperate with the West. The countries in the region had the "primary responsibility" to bring peace to the area. Yet, the United States would employ "every appropriate means" to assist in the attainment of this outcome. It wanted to influence events in the area in pursuit of Western objectives and American strategic interests (which were not always compatible), while at the same time careful not to be tainted by the label of imperialism which colored the British and French. It also did not want to be caught in the middle of the Arab-Israeli dispute (to the detriment of American relations with Israel and such strategically important countries as Saudi Arabia and Egypt). It was indeed an impossible juggling act. And while the Eisenhower administration would come to view professed neutrality in the region vis-à-vis the cold war as being anti-West, Syria and others in the area regarded the professed impartial policy of the United States in the Arab-Israeli dispute as being anti-Arab. The only real leverage the Arabs had vis-à-vis Israel was the threat that they would align themselves with the Soviet bloc in order to obtain what they felt was the necessary protection from "Zionist aggression." This, in their view, would hopefully convince the West, primarily the United States, to pressure Israel to make concessions that would pave the way for arms and economic agreements with the Arab countries in such a way as to make them palatable to the indigenous populations. But Washington would not take this threat seriously.

Constraints on Shishakli

Shishakli's meeting with Dulles had the expected effect in Syria of opening up the regime to further criticism from opposition groups labelling him an instrument of the West. This, of course, only made it more difficult for him to negotiate an agreement with the United States unless he was given "substantial inducements" to justify such steps to his countrymen.[25] To demonstrate his detachment from Western "schemes," Shishakli concluded a Treaty of Friendship with Iran on May 24, 1953. Iran, at the time, was ruled by the nationalist Mossadegh regime (in its last months of office before being overthrown by forces loyal to the Shah in a coup that was covertly engineered by the United States), and as a political gesture, Shishakli proclaimed his solidarity with Iran against the imperialist designs of the West.

Internally, Shishakli was attempting to consolidate his position. After "cleaning house" following the December 1952 aborted coup attempt, Shishakli felt that it was a propitious time to demonstrate the support in the country for his regime. A referendum was held during the summer (1953) and a constitution was adopted by a large majority (primarily because the opposition parties boycotted the referendum and the fact that Shishakli supporters "stuffed" the ballot boxes). On July 10, 1953, Shishakli was elected president of the republic. On October 9, general elections were held for the Syrian parliament, in which some sixty of the eighty-two seats went to the Arab Liberation Movement. The election was described, however, as being held in an "atmosphere of almost complete apathy," with the rigging of votes to obtain the positive results for the ALM.[26] These steps taken, Shishakli felt secure enough in his position to allow a certain amount of freedom of the press and initiate democratic reform. He even allowed

Hawrani, Bitar, and ʿAflaq to return to the country on October 16 from their exile in Lebanon.

The relative political freedom was effectively exploited by the opposition parties, especially the Baʿth Party and the communists. Anti-Shishakli criticism surfaced in certain sections of the press, in pamphlets distributed throughout the country, and at organized meetings. The Baʿthists were able to place themselves in the position of representing the general opposition to Shishakli among the masses regardless of ideology. This meant that they were able to channel the opposition to Shishakli's dictatorial domestic behavior into additional support for their neutralist, anti-imperialist, and anti-Zionist foreign policy program. This only made it tougher on the Shishakli regime to come to some arrangement with the United States regarding economic or military aid or negotiate in good faith the border dispute with Israel. The Israelis, however, only added to Shishakli's problems by undertaking action that played into the hands of the Syrian opposition.

Israel had basically been acting in the Israeli-Syrian demilitarized zone (DMZ-negotiated as part of the armistice agreement following the 1947–49 Arab-Israeli war) as if it was Israeli territory instead of territory where "sovereignty is in abeyance pending a final peace settlement."[27] The main cause for concern for the Syrian government was the Israeli attempt to unilaterally divert the waters of the Jordan River, in defiance of United Nations' calls to cease this activity (and in defiance of the proposed Johnston Plan), through the construction of the Banat Yaʿqub canal, which would "leave dry an important system of eight canals in Syrian territory" and allow the Israelis to use the Jordan River as an "adjustable" military barrier by means of opening and closing the canal spillways.[28] The Syrians officially brought the matter to the UN Security Council on October 12, 1953, blaming Israel for refusing to comply with the order of General Vagn Bennike, the chief of staff of the UN Truce Supervision Organization (UNTSO), to cease and desist construction on the Banat Yaʿqub. Up to this point, by most accounts, the Syrians had been rather favorably disposed to an agreement with Israel concerning the division of the DMZ. The negotiations took place through the Mixed Armistice Committees (MACs) formed after the 1947–49 war. United Nations representatives in Israel believed that a Syrian-Israeli agreement "could have been had" had it not been for Israel's reticence.[29] Israel asserted that it had been adamant Arab refusal to negotiate that had created the impasse, but the American representative in Jerusalem countered this argument by noting that the Syrians for "over a year" had been willing to discuss the division of the DMZ.[30]

All hopes of resolving the Israeli-Syrian border problems were dashed on October 14–15, 1953, when Israeli troops (dressed as "irregulars") attacked the Jordanian village of Qibya, killing some fifty-three men, women, and children. The official Israeli view sanctioned the attack as retaliation for numerous fedayeen (literally translated as "self-sacrificers" but more akin to freedom fighters or guerrillas) attacks from the Jordanian occupied West Bank. The Syrian army was put on alert and two-thirds of its strength (about 24,000 men) was sent to the Israeli front. The outcry in the Arab world against Israel was sufficiently intense. The United States, Britain, and France led the condemnation of Israel in the UN Security Council and agreed to express their "strong censure."[31] The Israelis blamed the incident on the "constant provocative infiltration" emanating from Jordan, but Dulles pointed out that Jordan had been doing its best to restrain such attacks and that the Israeli approach of "belittling" Jordan's efforts was "out-of-line."[32] Summarily, Dulles announced on October 20 that all economic aid to Israel had been suspended, basing this action on Israel's refusal to comply with General Bennike's orders vis-à-vis construction in the DMZ.

But whatever points the United States gained in Arab eyes from its action in the UN and it suspension of Israeli economic aid were effectively negated by Dulles' decision on October 28 to resume an economic aid grant to Israel of $26 million that had apparently been previously allocated.[33] Reportedly, intense pressure on the State Department by Israel's supporters in Congress was enough to force Dulles to reverse his decision.[34] The American embassy in Damascus, however, lamented that the "manner and magnitude" of the resumption of aid to Israel had lessened Syrian confidence in the United States and in the professed impartiality of the Eisenhower administration, recalling the conditions that existed under Truman.[35] Not only was the United States hamstrung by its commitment to Israel but also the State Department feared that too much condemnation of Israel would cause problems for the governments of Syrian and Jordan, who had been in the process of negotiating indirectly with the Israelis and were receiving intense criticism all along from their respective opposition groups for doing so. Any condemnation could backfire against the regimes of Shishakli and King Hussein, possibly resulting in their fall from power and their replacement by more leftist and anti-West regimes. This also could have been a rationalization for acquiescing to Israeli demands.

The Qibya massacre took place alongside Eric Johnston's visit to the area to discuss his water development plan. Naturally, the incident effectively made his task impossible for the moment. When he talked to Shishakli on October 30, the latter just replied that he would study the plan, but demanded that Israel must first comply with UN resolutions.[36] That the Syrian president did not outright reject the plan or refuse to meet with Johnston in the wake of Qibya shows just how close the prospects for a resolution of the various Syrian-Israeli problems might have been prior to the incident, the disruption of which may well have been one of the reasons for the Israeli action in the first place.

Shishakli's room for maneuver was thus severely limited, and any military aid agreement with the United States was out of the question for the time being. Washington had made one last pitch to Shishakli for a military aid agreement, programming in September two-thirds of the $30 million allocated for the Middle East by Congress toward Syria and Iraq (each to get $10 million).[37] The State Department admitted that the main object for this allotment was to produce "political dividends."[38] The conditions for this aid to Syria contained the following points: 1) an engagement that Syria would not employ these arms offensively against Israel; and 2) an engagement that Syria would consider entering upon staff talks to defend the Middle East against a possible Soviet attack.[39] To ensure that these two conditions were followed, Dulles proposed to dispatch survey missions to study the exact character of equipment and training to be furnished and establish joint military planning between the United States and the recipient countries to increase American control on the use of the weapons and enhance American influence in each of the recipient countries.[40] The Defense Department concluded that no fiscal year 1954 funds for military aid to Syria would be allotted unless a "strong case" could be made that such action would be important for the attainment of American political objectives, and that the "appropriate conditions" for such aid included a cooperative attitude on the part of Syria regarding refugee resettlement and the Unified Plan for water development (Johnston Plan) as well as a readiness to sign a military agreement with the United States and accept military survey teams.[41]

Everything about this plan was contrary to Syria's interests. We have already discussed Syria's demand for unconditional aid and their legitimate distaste for survey missions and technical teams "overrunning" the country. The amount allocated for Syria under the proposal was less than they had wanted or expected. This was partially due to the fact that the majority of foreign aid distributed by the Eisenhower administration toward the Middle East at this time was directed toward Iran and Egypt, two nations which were viewed upon by the State Department as essential to American interests in the Middle East. This left very little to be allocated toward any other countries in the region.

This relative parsimony fell in line with the economically based strategic outlook of the Eisenhower administration. Eisenhower was intent on balancing the national budget, which obviously restricted the amount of foreign aid that could be legislated. This was one of the campaign slogans that got him elected to the presidency and Congress was intent on following through on it. The sums that were allocated were given to the countries that were of the most strategic importance to the United States. As one British official commented, the Eisenhower administration "is keenly interested" in the Middle East but "is prohibited by the exigencies of its strategic planning and by its budgetary problems" from adopting a more "forward policy."[42]

Shishakli had gained enough of a false sense of security from his political manipulation during the summer of 1953 to the point of encouraging American officials to continue to pursue economic and military aid agreements with his country. His "secure" position was made all the more chimerical by Israeli intransigence and its disruptive behavior during the autumn months. The growing opposition to Shishakli manifested itself in December 1953, when there occurred violent student demonstrations against the regime in Damascus and Aleppo. The Syrian University was closed down in January 1954 for fear of further disturbances. The opposition press attacked the regime for its dealings with the Zionists and the "creators of the Zionist state," the United States and Britain. Shishakli's shell was cracking and soon would be completely broken, along with American hopes to include Syria in the Western defense net.

Notes

1. A February 25, 1953, State Department report entitled, "United States Policies and Programs in the Middle East and South Asia," made the following point: "While we continue to give Israel some financial assistance, we should demonstrate to the Arab world that we do not intend to sponsor Israel exclusively nor to give her discriminatory preference. At an appropriate date we should reaffirm the Tripartite Declaration of May 1950. We should make it clear that it is our will that national borders should be respected." (Policy paper for NSC 155/1, February 25, 1953, RG273, NA.) Eisenhower commented on one occasion that the aid which Israel received from the United States had caused Arab enmity and "has delayed the possibility of a settlement by enabling Israel to avoid facing the issue that, unless she trades with the Arab countries, she cannot be a viable state." Memorandum for the Acting Secretary of State from Eisenhower, April 23, 1953, Ann Whitman File, Dulles-Herter Series, Box 7, DDEL.

2. Speech by Dulles entitled, "Six Major Policy Issues," made on June 1, 1953, in Ralph H. Magnus (ed.), *Documents on the Middle East* (Washington: American Enterprise Institute, 1969), p. 78.

3. *New York Times* (hereafter *NYT*), January 28, 1953.

4. Ibid.

5. American Embassy, Damascus, May 16, 1951, State Department Post Files, Cairo Embassy, 1951, RG84, NARA.

6. *New York Herald Tribune,* January 31, 1957.

7. Donald Bergus, acting executive secretary for the regional coordinating committee for the Near East, wrote to John D. Jernegan, deputy assistant secretary of state for Near East affairs, that the difference in aid criteria as applied between Israel and the Arab states "serves to point up the wide gap which has developed between the views of the field and those of the [State]

Department." (Letter from Bergus to Jernegan, August 4, 1953, State Department Post Files, Cairo Embassy, 1953, RG84, NARA.)

8. *NYT,* January 19, 1953.

9. See several articles on this topic in *NYT,* January 20, 1953 — one headline read. Also, see article by former congressman Jacob Javits, "Should the U.S. Sell Arms to Israel?" *Foreign Policy Bulletin,* vol. 35 (February 15, 1956), p. 84.

10. American Embassy-Tel Aviv, January 23, 1953, State Department Post Files, Cairo Embassy, 1953, RG84, NARA.

11. British Embassy-Damascus, March 31, 1953, FO 371/104966, PRO.

12. British Embassy-Damascus, Political Summary No. 1 for the Month of January, 1953, FO 371/104966, PRO.

13. Ibid.

14. American Embassy,Damascus to Department of State, February 24, 1953, 783.00/2-2453, RG59, NA.

15. American Embassy-Damascus to Department of State, early January 1953, 611.83, RG59, NA.

16. Memorandum of Conversation, May 16, 1953, in Moose to Deputy Assistant Secretary of State for Near Eastern, South Asian and African Affairs John D. Jernagan, May 21, 1953, 611.83/5-2153, RG59, NA.

17. Ibid.

18. *Time* magazine, May 25, 1953, p. 29.

19. John Foster Dulles to Eisenhower from Baghdad, May 18, 1953, Ann Whitman File, Dulles-Herter Series, Box 1, DDEL.

20. Ibid.

21. Ibid. For a summary of Dulles' views toward each specific country he visited see, "Important Points of Trip," no date, John Foster Dulles Papers, Box 73, The John Foster Dulles Collection, Seeley G. Mudd Library, Princeton University, Princeton, New Jersey.

22. For points 1–5 see speech by Dulles, "Six Major Policy Issues," on June 1, 1953, in Magnus, pp. 78–81; for points 6 and 7, see "Conclusions on Trip," no date, John Foster Dulles Papers, Box 73, The John Foster Dulles Collection, Seeley G. Mudd Library, Princeton.

United States aid to Israel between 1945 and 1953 amounted to approximately $250 million while that to all the Arab and African states during the same period of time amounted to about $108 million. (Harry Byrode, "The Development of United States Policy in the Near East, South Asia and Africa during 1953," Department of State *Bulletin,* XXX, March 8, 1954, p. 367.)

23. The Johnston Plan was based on the Tennessee Valley Authority and named after Eric Johnston, who was Eisenhower's presidential emissary sent to discuss with countries in the Middle East a project to irrigate the Jordan Valley through the redistribution of the Jordan River waters (which would

then lead to further refugee resettlement). For more on this, see Faiz S. Abu-Jaber, "Eisenhower, Israel and the Jordan Valley Authority Scheme," *Middle East Forum*, vol. XLI, no. 2 (1969), pp. 51–63.

24. Donald Bergus, acting executive secretary for the regional coordinating committee for the Near East, wrote to John D. Jernegan, deputy assistant secretary of state for Near East affairs, that there is "great fear" in the field that the United States "may be changing a few of the spices" but serving up "the same old hash" of the last three to four years. (August 4, 1953, State Dept. Post Files, Cairo Embassy, 1953, RG84, NARA.)

25. American Embassy, Damascus to Department of State, June 9, 1953, 783.00/6-953, RG59, NA.

26. British Embassy-Damascus, February 12, 1954, FO 371/111137.

27. Memorandum of Conversation, Department of State, September 29, 1953, State Dept. Post Files, Cairo Embassy, 1953, RG84, NARA.

28. Ibid.

29. American Consulate-Jerusalem, October 29, 1953, State Dept. Post Files, Cairo Embassy, RG84, NARA.

30. A speech by the Israeli ambassador in Washington (printed in October 28, 1953, *Jerusalem Post*) did not help matters much when he stated that Israel should have complete control of the Jordan River flowing between Huleh and Kinneret and that the Arabs should be satisfied with their "undisputed possession of the vast, abundant Rivers Tigris, Euphrates, Nile and Litani." Also see *NYT*, October 19, 1953, for an article by James Reston on Israel's uncooperative approach toward regional development.

31. *NYT*, November 21, 1953.

32. Department of State, Memorandum of Conversation Between Israeli and U.S. Officials, October 19, 1953, State Dept. Post Files, Cairo Embassy, 1953, RG84, NARA.

33. For text of statement, see Department of State For the Press, no. 604, "Aid to Israel," October 28, 1953, John Foster Dulles Papers, Box 71, The John Foster Dulles Collection, Princeton.

34. British Embassy-Washington, November 6, 1953, FO 371/104258, PRO.

35. American Embassy, Damascus to Department of State, November 9, 1953, 611.83/11-953, RG59, NA.

36. British Embassy-Damascus, Political Summary No. 10 for the Month of October, 1953, FO 371/104966, PRO.

37. Secretary of Defense, Charles E. Wilson to John Foster Dulles, September 8, 1953, 611.83/9-853, RG59, NA.

38. British Embassy-Washington, September 9, 1953, FO 371/104240, PRO.

39. British Embassy-Damascus, September 16, 1953, FO 371/104974, PRO.

40. Secretary of Defense Charles E. Wilson to John Foster Dulles, September 8, 1953, 611.83/9-853, RG59, NA.

41. American Embassy, Damascus, December 18, 1953, 783.5 MSP/12-1853, RG59, NA.

42. British Embassy-Washington, November 6, 1953, FO 371/104258, PRO.

4

The Swinging of
the Pendulum in Syria

By early 1954 the line of demarcation in the Middle East between those regimes and groups that were associated with the West and those that were anti-West and/or linked to the East was becoming more distinct. The more this became apparent in Washington, the more opportunities were seen available to Moscow to portray itself as the champion of the anti-West groups. The Eisenhower administration, frustrated with its attempts to resolve the Arab-Israeli issue and its related inability to implement its regional defense plans, decided to address the prospect of increased Soviet influence in the Middle East by adopting Dulles' northern tier approach, which was designed to divorce (or delink) the regional defense issue from the intricacies of inter-Arab and Arab-Israeli politics. The administration continued to pursue resolutions to some of the outstanding problems in the Arab world, namely an acceptable Anglo-Egyptian accord and an Arab-Israeli peace settlement, but it could no longer wait for these events to occur before addressing what it thought was an imminent threat from the Soviets in the area. The strategic desire for Egypt to be included in a defense pact still existed, but it would have to wait until after it had come to terms with Britain and Israel.

The strategic focus of the northern tier was based on the Eisenhower administration's emphasis on the concept of "massive retaliation," which involved "the availability of advantageously located bases from which to launch an attack on the centers of Soviet power, as well as an increased dependence on local forces to deal with local aggression on the Communist periphery and to protect these bases."[1] The project, as it was originally drawn up, did not envision Iraq becoming a member of the defense pact, as the United States "was never really comfortable about . . . an Arab country being included in it."[2] Iraq, which would later become the linchpin (and only Arab member) of the Baghdad Pact, was led into the arrangement by the British, who were anxious to use the pact as a substitute for the Anglo-

Iraqi treaty due to expire in 1957, and as a way to maintain some measure of influence in the area. The Soviets, however, would find a way to circumvent the Eisenhower administration's containment policy.

The Fall of the Shishakli Regime

Shishakli gave indications in early 1954 that he was willing to come to some sort of an arrangement with the United States regarding military and/or economic aid. Embassy personnel in Damascus could not figure out if Shishakli's renewed interest was "real or simulated" and postulated that it either reflected his strengthened position, thereby enabling him to risk an agreement with the West, or a sign of his weakness and now was in need of help from the West.[3] Both the British and the Americans believed Shishakli had a sufficient grip on the country and would remain in power for some time; however, both did acknowledge a growing undercurrent of dissatisfaction that could erupt at any moment and potentially topple the regime. But with the loyal support of most elements of the army, Shishakli was viewed as being more than capable of handling any attempted putsches directed against him.[4] It is likely, then, considering Shishakli's megalomania, that the Syrian president felt that his political manipulations of the previous year had sufficiently empowered him to pursue a more reconciliatory course with the West. He even brought up the possibility of improved relations with the Turks to a group of British ministers and commented on the desirability for a Syrian-Turkish defense pact.[5]

What may have been even more paramount in the mind of the Syrian president than the extent of his control over the country, however, was his concern that Syria might be left out of and isolated from America's northern tier concept. It had been known for some time (especially after Vice President Nixon's visit to Karachi in December 1953) that the United States and Pakistan were negotiating a military aid agreement in line with Dulles' northern tier strategy and preference for dealing on an individual basis with the countries in the area. It was also known that Pakistan was negotiating a security pact with Turkey. Rumors were swirling in diplomatic circles in the region that Iraq was also earmarked for a role in the budding regional defense network. As anticipated, Eisenhower announced on February 25, 1954, an agreement with Pakistan for American military assistance (signed in May); on April 2, 1954, Turkey and Pakistan signed a security pact; and on April 21, the United States and Iraq exchanged notes on a military aid agreement.

Observing all of this activity, Shishakli was concerned that his country would be left out of the regional defense system that was taking shape; Syria would not then be in a position to acquire arms on preferential terms. He was also worried that the prestige of Iraq and Turkey would be enhanced at

Syria's expense, and on a more practical level, he was very concerned that these two countries would now have the military and political wherewithal to advance their various territorial ambitions vis-à-vis Syria.

Shishakli's suspicion of Iraqi intentions rose to a new level when Iraqi Premier Fadil al-Jamali proposed the formation of an Arab Federation at the Arab League Council meeting in January 1954, reviving the idea of Fertile Crescent unity that portended the union of Iraq with Syria. Shishakli could not openly oppose the popular idea of Arab unity, but the Syrian press took the lead in rejecting the Jamali plan, essentially saying that while Syria favored the general idea of unity, this particular scheme was inspired by "foreigners," and that before Arab unity could become a reality all foreign influence in the Arab world must be eliminated. In this light, Shishakli's renewed interest in American arms and improved relations with Turkey could be viewed as his attempt to "jump on the bandwagon" before it was too late, even though his attack against the Jamali plan led him to condemn outside influence (which only shows how contradictory policies can be followed at the same time when dealing with events at different levels).[7] The Syrian government's official hostility during December 1953 and January 1954 to the American proposal to supply arms to Pakistan was the flip side of its desire not to see Iraq and Turkey associated with the West's defense plan (as well as ingratiating the anti-imperialist sentiment of the public). Shishakli either wanted to scuttle the evolving regional defense initiatives (however his ability to do so was limited) or place Syria in a position where it was assured equal consideration in any defense scheme. That he pursued both policies simultaneously reflected the rather untenable position he was in regarding the administration of Syrian foreign policy.

Faced with this predicament, Shishakli used the Soviet threat to appease his domestic opposition and as leverage against the United States in an attempt to hasten a military aid package. He did so by exploiting the Soviet veto in the United Nations Security Council in January 1954. The veto nixed what the Syrians viewed as a rather watered down American-British-French resolution condemning Israel for its activities in the DMZ during the previous fall. The Syrian press hailed the Soviet veto as a victory for the Arabs — no longer did the West have an exclusive say on matters concerning the Middle East.

With the veto, the Soviet Union had entered the diplomatic fray in the region — to the heightened consternation of the West, which, despite its valiant attempt, discovered it could not wholly divorce the Arab-Israeli issue from its plans for regional defense. Indeed, the festering dispute finally offered the Soviets the entrance into the region the Eisenhower administration had feared since coming to power. It also gave an indication of how the Arab-Israeli issue would allow the Soviets to strategically leapfrog the northern tier, something they would continue to do in coming years.

By trying to delink the Arab world and its various quagmires from the strategic goal of a regional defense system, Dulles actually succeeded in opening the door for the Soviet Union in the Arab heartland – in those countries that felt in desperate need of arms to protect themselves from Israel. As long as there was the prospect of Arab (specifically Egyptian and Syrian) participation in a pro-West defense scheme, the United States was viewed as a guarantor of security against Israel (leverage which the Arabs unsuccessfully tried to use to secure Israeli concessions and from which the Eisenhower administration tried to escape with the northern tier). Once the United States was seen as focusing instead on the non-Arab nations along the Soviet border, Moscow was then viewed as a legitimate alternative. Impatience in the West, Israeli intransigence, and Arab equivocation helped secure this outcome.

Before Washington could take advantage of Shishakli's new-found interest in coming to terms, however, the Syrian president was overthrown by a group of left-wing officers, led by Colonel 'Adnan al-Malki, in a bloodless coup on February 25, 1954. This section of the army had become dissatisfied with Shishakli's arbitrary dismissals and transfers, as well as the totalitarian manner in which he was running the military and civilian bureaucracies. Adding fuel to the fire of their discontent, some of the officers had family ties with the civilian politicians who were ordered arrested by Shishakli at the end of January in his attempt to crackdown on the opposition. After some initial confusion following the coup, agreement was reached among the leaders of the political parties to revert to the constitution of 1950, dissolve the Shishakli parliament, and install the octogenarian statesman, Hashim al-Atasi, as president, a position from which he had been removed by Shishakli in December of 1951. A right-wing coalition government of Nationalists and Populists was formed on March 1 led by Prime Minister Sabri al-'Asali, and the holding of parliamentary elections was promised as soon as the situation stabilized and the register of voters revised.

Inter-Arab Politics

That the Jamali plan occurred contemporaneously with the Iraqi government's rising interest in obtaining American arms and in associating itself with the Turkish-Pakistani pact was by no means a coincidence. Iraq could not be seen as abandoning the aspirations of Arab nationalism by exclusively associating itself with the West. Primarily for domestic public consumption, the government rationalized its acquisition of arms from the United States and its eventual inclusion in the Baghdad Pact as enhancing its ability to successfully confront Israel.[8] Employing this rationale in the inter-Arab arena, the Iraqis additionally put forth the Jamali plan to mitigate the expected strong opposition from Egypt and Saudi Arabia by appearing to take the lead in implementing the much talked about but little acted upon plans for Arab unity.

Nasser was concerned that Iraq's actions would enable it to challenge Egypt for leadership in the Arab world. The Saudis, for their part, were adamant in their opposition to any project or scheme that enhanced the status of the rival Hashimites ruling Iraq and Jordan. Egypt and Saudi Arabia had been on good terms with Shishakli because of his hostility toward Iraq, and both countries deeply regretted his overthrow. The fact that Iraq had a hand in Shishakli's fall from power only made the Saudis and Egyptians that much more suspicious that the Jamali plan would be forcibly implemented.[9] In order to allay Egyptian anxiety, the Iraqis offered to defer adherence to the Turkish-Pakistani pact until an Anglo-Egyptian agreement was reached on the Canal Zone[10] (the Canal Zone dispute was resolved several months later in October 1954 and Iraq did not accede to the Turkish-Pakistani pact, thus forming the Baghdad Pact, until February 1955). In this fashion, Arab solidarity (and bargaining power) would not be broken until an issue of immediate importance to Egypt was resolved, and thus the raison d'etre of their criticism against the Iraqis would be removed for the time being.

The pro-West Iraqi leader, Nuri al-Sa'id, who resumed the premiership during the summer of 1954, envisioned Iraq as the link between the Arab states, the northern tier countries, and the West, thus enhancing his country's status in all three spheres and making it indispensable as a military bulwark against the Soviet Union and Israel. If successful, Iraq would have automatically reduce Egypt's status to that of a junior partner in the contest for Arab leadership. This is why Syria became the key to Iraq's success, for if Egypt and/or the Saudis were able to wean Syria into their own camp, Iraq would be isolated in the Arab world. On the other hand, if Iraq was able to win over Syria (through union or alliance), Jordan and Lebanon would most likely follow, resulting in Egypt's isolation.

Confronted with this expostulation, Egypt had to cleverly maneuver around the Jamali plan. Egyptian leadership in the Arab world was predicated on Arab acceptance of the idea of non-alignment; in other words, the Arabs should rely on themselves for their own defense through the Arab League Collective Security Pact (ALCSP), which, of course, was dominated by Cairo.[11] Amidst all the talk of American-inspired pacts at the end of 1953, Egypt, on January 4, 1954, stepped up its anti-West propaganda campaign by increasing its "Voice of the Arabs" broadcast air-time from half an hour a day to one and three quarters hour per day; on July 4, Cairo extended the on-air time to four hours a day.[12] At first, Egypt felt secure that Syria would not follow Iraq's lead since Shishakli had consistently rejected plans for union with Iraq and generally looked to Egypt and Saudi Arabia in the inter-Arab arena. It was even reported that Egypt constructed an agreement with Shishakli that it would see to it that the Jamali plan was "politely shelved" in return for Syrian support in the Canal Zone negotiations with the British.[13]

Egyptian hopes were dealt a severe blow in the form of Shishakli's overthrow and the subsequent return to power in Syria of many elements who had gone on record as favoring union with Iraq (namely the Populists). There was also a measure of instability in Egypt itself as the struggle between Colonel Gamal 'Abd al-Nasser and President Muhammad Naguib within the ruling Free Officers junta came out into the open, resulting in the latter's resignation on February 24, 1954, and the former's assumption of the posts of prime minister and chairman of the Revolutionary Command Council.[14] The domestic situation in Saudi Arabia was also not completely sanguine at the time as the death of King 'Abd al-Aziz ibn Sa'ud in 1953 left a vast political void that his unproven son and successor, King Sa'ud, attempted to fill. The fact that Egypt and Saudi Arabia were experiencing domestic political problems only made the Iraqis feel more comfortable in taking the diplomatic initiative.

Also troubling the Egyptians and Saudis were indications that the new 'Asali government in Syria was prepared to come to terms with the Iraqis, something they had feared would happen in the wake of Shishakli's fall. In an interview with *New York Times* correspondent Kenneth Love, 'Asali declared his "open endorsement" for the Turkish-Pakistani pact, and, while attacking American policy vis-à-vis Israel in pro forma fashion, he commented that Defense Minister Ma'ruf al-Dawalibi, who had been labelled by the State Department as pro-Soviet, was not inherently anti-American and that he only tried to play off the United States against the Soviet Union to benefit the Arabs.[15] Dawalibi himself stated that Syria wished to collaborate with the West and hoped that the United States would use its economic leverage to restrain Israel as a measure of goodwill toward his country.[16] 'Asali's foreign minister, Faydi al-Atasi, who was considered to be pro-West, also expressed cautious approval of the Turkish-Pakistani pact.[17] On May 8, 1954, General Arthur Trudeau, United States deputy chief of staff, visited Damascus amid rumors that he had come to negotiate a military aid agreement—the Syrian government denied that such was the case.[18] 'Asali also held a secret meeting at the Lebanese mountain resort of Brummanah on June 8, 1954, with Jamali and Mikhail Ilyan, an Aleppan pro-Iraqi Nationalist Party leader, reportedly discussing plans to bring about Fertile Crescent union through the instrument of an Iraqi invasion of Syria—this occurred only three days prior to the fall of the 'Asali government.[19]

Egypt was not particularly in the best of shape to prevent Syria from uniting with Iraq if it so chose; however, Cairo was not content to just let things take their natural course and apparently mustered its assets in Syria in opposition to the 'Asali regime (including those who, while not friendly with Cairo, had a concurrent interest in keeping the Iraqis at bay). There were "well-substantiated" reports that there was a coup attempt by a group of junior officers around the end of March 1954.[20] Indeed, there were student protests on March 29 in Damascus that the United States Embassy described as communist-inspired, indicating "a concerted Soviet campaign to discourage Arab adherence to the proposed Turkish-Pakistani pact."[21] Although a change in regime would have been in the Kremlin's interest, and one would suspect that the Soviet representation in Syria did in fact contribute in some form to the disturbances, the conclusion that it was a Soviet plot gives an indication of how American officials misinterpreted the motivations behind the coup attempt – it had much more to do with the internal dynamics in the Syrian officer corps and its relationship with the civilian cabinet, as well as the question of union with Iraq.

The dissident group was comprised primarily of former Shishakli supporters who were prepared to hand over civilian control of the new regime to Akram al-Hawrani, one of the leaders of the leftist Ba'th party and someone who had intimate connections among the ranks of the army, especially its junior classes. The junior officers apparently were afraid of losing the prestige and influence that would be a concomitant outcome if it withdrew from politics, something that Dawalibi had been actively pressing for and "rigidly" enforcing.[22] In addition, the junior officers felt that if union with Iraq occurred, it would be at least twice as difficult to be promoted, especially considering the better equipped and trained Iraqi army. One of the leaders of the group was (then) Captain 'Abd al-Hamid Sarraj of G-1, who would soon become a prominent figure in Syrian politics and who would become known for his close ties to and affinity for Nasser. The coup was apparently nipped in the bud by Syrian authorities and the dissident officers were dispersed to less threatening areas of Syria or "diplomatic" exile abroad (Sarraj was appointed as assistant military attache in Paris). It is certainly not hard to imagine the Egyptians and/or Saudis playing a role in instigating the coup attempt in order to place a more amenable (i.e., anti-Iraqi) regime in power.

Rumors of coups continually haunted the 'Asali regime during its short tenure in power. It publicly tried to steer a neutral course between Iraq and Egypt in its official task as a caretaker government that would prepare the way for parliamentary elections. Many of the politicians in power purposely tried to avoid discussion of the possibility of union with Iraq for fear of playing into the hands of the leftists in the upcoming elections.[23] Despite this, however, the 'Asali government probably offered the last realistic chance for uniting Syria with Iraq, though it only had itself to blame for not bringing it off. The 'Asali coalition was weak and divided, and in reality, subservient to the pro-Ba'thist army faction led by Colonel 'Adnan al-Malki, who led the coup against Shishakli. The Populist Party was split on the subject of union with Iraq and could never attract the domestic support needed to bring the issue to a head. Many Syrian politicians, of all shades, were reluctant to meet the finality that a union with Iraq would bring, i.e., the perpetual instability in the Syrian polity would come to an end and thus terminate the lucrative payoffs originating from outside powers. The dynamics of Syrian politics compelled various parties, factions, and individuals to align themselves with external interests, but once this was accomplished, rarely did they carry through with their a priori commitments (and this was particularly true in the case of Iraq).[24]

In the end, the 'Asali regime self-destructed, not being able to placate the army or remain totally neutral in the inter-Arab and international arenas. It was replaced on June 19, 1954, by a non-partisan government led by Sa'id al-Ghazzi amid serious rumors of another coup attempt instigated by pro-Iraqi forces who wanted to install a government that could successfully bring about the sought-for union. The Ghazzi government secured its position by immediately proclaiming its absolute neutrality on domestic, regional, and international issues, relegating its function solely to that of conducting "free and fair" parliamentary elections in September.[25]

Reversing Course

United States policy toward Syria during the period following Shishakli's fall can be described as being fairly passive. This is not surprising since the Eisenhower administration was focusing on the northern tier strategy. Washington regretted Shishakli's departure since it had at least a working relationship with him, even though he had stalled on the issues of military and economic aid. More importantly from the American point of view, Shishakli had injected some measure of stability to a country that had known little of it in its brief life as an independent state. With the uncertain political situation in the wake of Shishakli's fall, the Eisenhower administration was not about to press Syria on the issues of aid or Israel. On the Syrian side of the equation, President Hashim al-Atasi informed Ambassador Moose that his government could make no commitments on such matters as the Johnston Plan or military/economic aid.[26] If anything, the Eisenhower administration was determined not to prejudice the chances of the pro-West Nationalist-Populist elements in the September elections by pressing for a Syrian-Iraqi union or propagandizing heavily on Iraqi adherence to the Turkish-Pakistani pact.[27]

The administration was also intent on building up the perception in the Arab world that it was an impartial player in the Arab-Israeli dispute. Toward this end, the Tripartite Declaration was reaffirmed on May 1, 1954. In addition, the United States Information Agency (USIA) began broadcasting in Arabic to the Middle East speeches by administration officials that indicated the intent to implement an objective foreign policy.[28]

While appearing passive on the outside, on the inside the administration became even more concerned about the increase in Soviet influence in the Middle East. Despite the intent of the northern tier strategy, the Soviets had effectively exploited the Arab-Israeli dispute to their advantage, gaining a tremendous propaganda victory over the West by supporting the Arabs' position vis-à-vis Israel in the United Nations. The Soviets again employed their veto in the UN Security Council in April 1954 to shoot down an American-sponsored resolution calling on Egypt to lift restrictions on traffic through the Suez Canal bound for Israel. The Progress Report on NSC 155/1 of July 30 listed as the number one problem in the Middle East the "increased USSR activity in the area, and particularly Soviet support of the Arab position versus Israel"; and secondly, the "growing Arab-Israel tensions" which, of course, provided more openings for the Kremlin.[29] At a conference of the American chiefs of mission in the Middle East held in Istanbul from May 11–14, 1954, the members concluded that they were "convinced that it is one of the objectives of the Soviet Union to bring the Middle East behind the Iron Curtain and that the Soviet Union is constantly maneuvering with the purpose of facilitating the attainment of this objective."[30] Officials, however, concluded that despite the increase in Soviet activities, the United States had been "keeping pace, *except* in Jordan and Syria."[31] (emphasis mine). American personnel in Damascus noticed a "marked increase" in the Syrian press of pro-Soviet statements due to the Kremlin's vetoes in the UN, as well as a general feeling in Syria that the United States was only "uttering fair words" while the Soviet Union was supporting the Arabs through concrete measures.[32] In addition, the Soviets increased their subsidies to various Syrian newspapers and generally were seen as having intensified their propaganda activities throughout the country.[33] The Eisenhower administration was also worried about the rising influence of the ASRP within the Syrian army, and was concerned that the disunity and divisions among the conservative parties would, following the elections, result in a "disciplined leftist minority" that may "wield disproportionate influence over parliamentary affairs" and lead the country into a closer relationship with the Soviet Union.[34] Actual events would soon prove this prediction correct.

One of the major problems with American foreign policy toward the Middle East at this juncture was that while the Eisenhower administration recognized the need for a more active posture to combat what it viewed as Soviet advances in the region, the policy actually set down in writing in various NSC resolutions was intended for more limited involvement. United States policy in the region, namely the implementation of the northern tier strategy, seemed "to go beyond the cautious limits explicitly sanctioned by those [NSC] documents."[35] The incongruency was admitted to by officials in the administration and a warning was sounded that the "concerted United

States effort to inspire a defense arrangement . . . implies a forward defense strategy in the Middle East. . . . "[36] In addition: "The countries directly involved must assume that this is in fact United States policy—a policy which would seem to carry with it a willingness on the part of the United States to supply leadership, assistance and support. In the formal policy documents, however, there is as yet no explicit statement that such is in fact our intent."[37] The northern tier envisaged an association of indigenous forces under an indigenous command, with the implication that the commitments and responsibilities of the United States would be less than that envisioned under the British-led MEDO. But what was becoming apparent was the fact that the United States was "alone . . . taking the initiative in fostering a security arrangement of Middle East states which could never have evolved in the absence of strong encouragement from us."[38] In other words, contrary to the intention of the northern tier concept, the United States was entering the dangerous territory of inter-Arab and Arab-Israeli politics by appearing to take a more forward defense policy toward the region, thus creating the perception of American omnipresence as well as accelerating the arms race.

America's approach to the Middle East also created some problems with the British. As long as the administration pursued the northern tier regional security strategy, "it was possible for the United States to move decisively without the complication of prior consultations with the British, who betrayed certain symptoms of schizophrenia on the subject. . . ."[39] Great Britain was only informed of the Turkish-Pakistani arrangement after the fact.[40] But London was not about to relent passively to American dominance in the region, and it consequently pushed for Iraq's inclusion into the burgeoning defense system. Britain's acquiescence to the American-Iraqi military assistance agreement not only reflected its realization of the inevitable greater wherewithal of the United States to provide arms but also the correct prediction that this would enhance Iraq's chances to fulfill Nuri al-Sa'id's dream of being the link between the West and the Arab states, enabling London to circumvent the dissolution of its relationship with Iraq through the termination of the Anglo-Iraqi treaty and maintain a position of influence in the region through its client-state.

Contrary to the intent of the northern tier concept, many in the State Department began to see the possible value of including Iraq, "for the adherence of Iraq will crack the structure of the Arab League clear through its foundations, and bring to an end the unyielding negativism and obstructionism of that organization. . . . Iraq, for example, is probably the key to the political success of the venture, and here the British are firmly entrenched. We need to make a success of our program of military assistance there in order to induce the Iraqis to take the further step into the security arrangements, and we need British cooperation to assure this success."[41] Administration officials saw this as an opportunity to resolve some of the problems with the British resulting from America's go-it-alone approach, because "by appearing to threaten the remaining British position in the Middle East we have rubbed nerves already raw from the frictions which have accompanied the postwar retreats from positions of empire."[42] The administration also became wildly optimistic:

> For after Iraq takes the plunge, it seems likely that with some encouragement from the United States, Lebanon and Syria would shortly follow. The pressure on Egypt to come to terms on the Suez would mount steadily. Recalcitrance would seem a less attractive policy to the Saudis. In short, the prospects would seem good for moving a major part of the Near East into overt alignment with the free world, thereby delivering a telling blow to Asian-African neutralism, and effecting a really significant shift in the global balance of power. In such a context, even the Arab-Israel problem might not prove so utterly intractable as it has been these several years.[43]

So the Eisenhower administration, by favoring Iraq's accession to the Turkish-Pakistani pact, was essentially relinking its defense initiative with the intricacies of inter-Arab politics, and inexorably with it, the problems of the Arab-Israeli dispute. Without a coherent policy, and without staying within the limitations of the policy that had been delineated, although ambiguously, in previous NSC resolutions, the above contradictions were able to rear their ugly heads and force the administration along paths which it was not prepared to walk.[44] It is true that the administration was not totally responsible for the creation of the Baghdad Pact, for Britain was an active sponsor and Nuri al-Sa'id of Iraq and Prime Minister Menderes of Turkey eagerly welcomed it. But the United States set the process in motion and created the expectation among the states in the Middle East (and with Britain) that it was pursuing a forward defense policy that it would support with its own active participation. The Turkish-Iraqi pact was signed in Baghdad on February 24, 1955, thus creating the Baghdad Pact. On April 4, 1955, Great Britain adhered to the pact. The United States did not, hoping to recapture the aloofness from inter-Arab and Arab-Israeli politics that it tried to achieve through the northern tier scheme, but the damage had already been done — the contradiction in American policy succeeded in antagonizing the adherents to the pact as well as its foes; the pact itself catalyzed the division of the Arab world, with Syria moving farther and farther away from the West.

The Rise of the Ba'th Party: The September 1954 Elections[45]

If the Eisenhower administration was worried about the leftist presence in Syria prior to the September parliamentary elections, afterward the situation would be described as positively grave. Out of 142 seats, the Ba'th Party gained an unprecedented twenty-two seats, increasing in strength from five percent in the old parliament to fifteen percent in the new. At the same time, the Populist Party lost fifty percent of its parliamentary share, effectively closing political discussion on the Iraqi question in Syria and forcing its supporters in and outside of the country to look to other (i.e., more interventionist) methods to bring about union with Iraq. And for the first time in the Arab world, a Communist Party member, Khalid Baqdash, became an elected official of government, polling the third highest vote total in Damascus. Running on an anti-West campaign, Baqdash's election proved not so much the strength of the communists in Syria as the popularity of his anti-imperialist and anti-Zionist platform, something which he shared with the Ba'thists. In addition, Khalid al-'Azm led a bloc of some thirty independents into parliament, and though this group was conservative by "temperament and background," they had cooperated with the leftists and campaigned on an anti-West platform. The French were widely believed to have financially backed 'Azm and his bloc, hoping that the more anti-West (thus anti-Turkish-Pakistani pact) elements in the government, the better it would be for the maintenance of their own position in Syria. They were not unhappy about the relative victory of the leftists, despite the fact that it moved Syria a little closer to the Soviet bloc.

The disappointing showing by the conservative elements, particularly the Populists and the Nationalists, was due primarily to the antagonism between the two parties and widespread divisions within each, as well as the fact that they were identified, rightly or wrongly, with the West and, therefore, with Israel. The existence of rumors in Syria of American interference in the elections in support of right-wing candidates did not help the cause of the conservatives; the important point being that whether or not these rumors were true, they were believed by the populace.[46]

Since no one party won a majority in parliament, the stage was set for the formation of a coalition government. After several failed attempts by various party leaders, on November 3, 1954, the seventy-seven year old Faris al-Khuri succeeded in forming a government consisting mainly of Populists and Nationalists. Although this seemed to be a reversal of the leftists' advance in the election, it was really more the result of the fragmentation of the Syrian political scene, as the left-wing parties themselves were not immune to some of the divisions which plagued the conservatives (indeed, the election result spurred the Populists and Nationalists to at least nominally cooperate with each other for the time being). But the issues that the leftists had espoused were still more powerful than the tenuous makeup of parliament and the dynamics of domestic politics in Syria. The Ba'th and 'Azm's newly formed Democratic Bloc refused to take part in the new government, yet despite the known pro-West disposition of Khuri and the formation of a right-wing coalition, the prime minister felt compelled to immediately and publicly proclaim his ministry's opposition to any "pledge, pact or agreement" with a foreign power and its intention to improve relations with the Arab states and pay particular attention to the Palestine problem. The Ba'th's preoccupation with foreign policy and the pressure that it placed on Khuri was evident in the fact that it concentrated its efforts within the chamber to get its nominees elected to the foreign relations committee.[47]

The United States was obviously concerned by the turn of events in Syria. In addition to the election results, there was a noticeable increase in the size of the Soviet legation, as well as an impressive display of Soviet and East bloc hardware and goods at the August International Trade Fair held in Damascus (America and Britain did not have official pavilions). Baqdash's election to parliament seemed to produce and legitimate expanding sales of communist literature throughout Syria and the free distribution of communist papers to the trade unions, where they had already established themselves.[48]

There was, however, some cause for optimism in Washington. There was a right-wing coalition in power led by a pro-West prime minister who appointed a pro-West foreign minister, Faydi al-Atasi. There were also a number of statements by Ba'thists and pro-Ba'thists discounting the allegation that they were in alliance with the communists.[49] In addition, there occurred toward the end of the year a sharp deterioration in relations with Egypt, largely stemming from Nasser's harsh treatment of the Muslim Brethren after the latter tried to assassinate the Egyptian leader in October 1954.[50] Syrians were also generally disillusioned by what they perceived to be Nasser's capitulation in coming to terms with the British over the Canal Zone.

There were other positive signs. Relations between Turkey and Syria had been improving ever since Shishakli's fall and by the end of the year there was a flurry of diplomatic activity flowing between Ankara and Damascus.[51] At about this time, Nasser began to seek an improved relationship with the Turks, at one point stating that "no matter what has happened between us and Turkey in the past or the present, we belong to each other."[52] What seemed to be a move by Nasser to improve relations with the West, however, was actually a counter-action to the tightening relationship between Iraq and Turkey, which, of course, would culminate in the Turkish-Iraqi pact announced in January and signed in February 1955.[53] Once this became apparent, Egyptian-Turkish relations soon returned to their normal, inimical form.[54]

Syrian-Turkish relations also soon returned to their tense state, with many of the outstanding problems between the two countries proving to be intractable (namely the Alexandretta/Hatay territorial dispute); this became even more pronounced after the announcement of the Turkish-Iraqi pact. As a result, these few glimmers of hope for the West quickly faded away and the transparency of the Khuri regime enabled Washington to see through the pro-West facade and observe the growing leftist trend in Syria and its influence upon the regime's foreign policy. By the end of the year, the administration was complaining that "the current trend of Syrian attitudes in the United Nations is moving ever more closely to the Communist line."[55] Commenting on Syria, Allen Dulles, director of the CIA and brother of the secretary of state, said that "the situation in that country is the worst of all the countries in that area."[56]

Notes

1. "The Problem of Regional Security," Department of State, May 8, 1954, State Dept. Post Files, Cairo Embassy, 1954, RG84, NARA.

2. Loy Henderson, deputy under secretary of state for administration, The John Foster Dulles Oral History Project, The John Foster Dulles Collection, Seeley G. Mudd Library, Princeton.

3. W.D. Brewer to The Ambassador and Mr. Clark, "President Shishakli's Position at the Beginning of 1954," January 11, 1954, State Dept. Post Files, Cairo Embassy, 1954, RG84, NARA.

4. Assessing Shishakli's position at the beginning of 1954, the State Department concluded that "there is no evidence of intrigue or disloyalty to the present Government within the Army." The report, however, did recognize that a coup could originate from elsewhere. (Ibid.). The British review of Syrian events in 1953 made the following comment on Shishakli's position at the end of the year: "As in the past, there were dark clouds on the horizon, although there was no reason to suppose that the President could not deal adequately with the situation when the storm eventually broke." (British Embassy-Damascus, February 12, 1954, FO 371/111137, PRO.)

5. For comments on ministers' visit, see British Embassy-Damascus, January 18, 1954, FO 371/111153, PRO; also see British-Foreign Office, January 15, 1954, FO 371/111153, PRO.

6. For Eisenhower's February 25 statement, see *Documents on American Foreign Relations, 1954* (New York: Harper, 1955), pp. 373–374; for text of American-Pakistani agreement, see Department of State, "Mutual Defense Agreement between the United States of America and Pakistan," *Treaties and Other International Acts Series,* no. 2976 (Washington: G.P.O., 1955); for text of Turco-Pakistani agreement, see *Documents on American Foreign Relations, 1954,* pp. 376–378.

Saudi Arabia declined an offer to conclude a military assistance agreement with the United States on January 15, 1954, and cancelled the Point Four agreement. An economic aid agreement was signed with Israel on November 25, 1953, with Jordan on May 13, 1954, and with Lebanon on June 19, 1954.

7. British Embassy-Damascus, January 19, 1954, FO 371/110787, PRO.

8. This is why the Iraqis were particularly upset when Dulles made a statement assuring the Israelis that the United States had only agreed to give

a token amount of military aid to Iraq. (British Embassy-Baghdad, March 17, 1954, FO 371/110787, PRO.)

9. The Egyptian ambassador in Damascus reportedly informed Ambassador Moose that the Saudi embassy there had paid the equivalent of 30,000 British pounds to pro-Shishakli elements to resist the coup. (British Embassy-Damascus, March 1, 1954, FO 371/110787, PRO.)

10. British Embassy-Cairo, March 29, 1954, FO 371/110787, PRO.

11. The ALCSP (initially known as the Treaty of Joint Defense and Economic Cooperation) was proposed by Egypt at an Arab League meeting in October of 1949 and primarily aimed at countering any Syrian-Iraqi bilateral agreement that would presage union between the two countries (to which Cairo was adamantly opposed). The Arab League Council approved the defense pact in April 1950, after Shishakli had come to power in Syria and had successfully quelled, for the time being, any proposals for union with Iraq. The ALCSP itself "pledged collective support for any member faced with aggression; it provided for consultation in the event of an external threat and for coordination and consolidation of armed forces; it set up a permanent military commission to draw up plans for collective defence, as well as a ministerial Joint Defence Council to supervise their execution." (Seale, p. 90.) For more on the beginnings of the ALCSP, see Fayez A. Sayegh, *Arab Unity: Hope and Fulfillment* (New York, 1956), pp. 142–151.

12. Seale, p. 196.

13. British Embassy-Damascus, February 23, 1954, FO 371/110785, PRO.

14. In a series of political maneuvers that enabled Nasser to eventually assume full power in Egypt, the popular Naguib was reinstated as president the next day while Nasser retained the premiership. On March 8, Naguib was reinstated as prime minister and chairman of the RCC, with Nasser resuming his old post as deputy prime minister. On April 17, 1954, Nasser became prime minister while Naguib remained president. Despite what seemed to be a victory for Naguib, Nasser systematically brought his supporters into the government to the point where, amidst problems with the Muslim Brethren, Naguib was finally dismissed from the presidency in November. Nasser formally assumed the title and office of president in June of 1956. For more on this, see P.J. Vatikiotis, *The History of Egypt* (Baltimore: The Johns Hopkins University Press, 1985), pp. 381–385.

15. *NYT,* March 5, 1954.

16. American Embassy-Damascus, March 15, 1954, State Department Post Files, Cairo Embassy, 1954, RG84, NARA.

17. British Embassy-Damascus, Political Summary No. 3 for the Month of March, 1954, FO 371/110787, PRO.

18. Seale, p. 171.

19. Seale, pp. 169–170.

20. This and subsequent information on the coup from: American Embassy, Damascus to Department of State, April 2, 1954, 783.00/4-254, RG59, NA.

21. U.S. Army Attache-Damascus to Department of the Army, April 3, 1954, 783.00 (W)/4-254, RG59, NA.

22. Seale, p. 171.

23. British Embassy-Damascus, March 23, 1954, FO 371/110787, PRO.

24. Seale, p. 167. In addition to these obstacles, Seale points out that Iraq was not wholeheartedly in favor of it. In fact, probably the most important political figure in Iraq, Nuri al-Sa'id, was rather lukewarm on the idea. While he definitely wanted a Syria that looked to Iraq rather than Egypt, he preferred not to add to Iraq's own economic and political problems by incorporating a country that was inherently unstable. (Ibid.)

25. The elections were originally scheduled for August 20, but were postponed to September 24 because of the announced intention of the Populist and National parties to boycott the elections, claiming that the army was interfering in the process at their expense.

26. American Embassy, Damascus to Department of State, March 26, 1954, 611.834/3-2654, RG59, NA; also see British Embassy-Damascus, June 30, 1954, FO 371/110785, PRO.

27. USIA initiated in February a "cautious, low-keyed effort to encourage Iraq to accept military aid from the U.S. and to persuade the other Arab states and Israel to regard such a development favorably. Because it was desired to have this event appear as a spontaneous request on Iraq's part, little material directly attributable to USIA was used while as much favorable indigenous comment was stimulated as possible." (Progress Report on NSC 155/1, Operations Coordinating Board, July 30, 1954, White House Office, National Security Council Staff: Papers, 1948–1961: OCB Central Files, Box 77, DDEL.)

28. For example, two speeches by assistant secretary of state for Near Eastern, South Asian and African affairs, Henry A. Byroade, in Dayton on April 9 and in Philadelphia on May 1, were broadcast to the Middle East. For texts of Byroade's speeches, see Department of State *Bulletin* of April 26 and May 10, 1954; also see Department of State publication 5469, Henry A. Byroade, "The Middle East," Near and Middle Eastern Series 16, Released May 1954, Division of Publications, or see John Foster Dulles Papers, Box 84, The John Foster Dulles Collection, Seeley G. Mudd Library, Princeton.

29. Operations Coordinating Board, "Progress Report on NSC 155/1" July 30, 1954.

30. Summary Record of the Conference of U.S. Chiefs of Mission in the NEA Area Held at Istanbul May 11–14, 1954, State Dept. Post Files, Cairo Embassy, 1954, RG84, NARA.

31. Ibid.

32. American Embassy, Damascus, May 28, 1954, 783.00/5-2354, RG59, NA.

33. Ibid.; also see, British Embassy-Damascus, July 15, 1954, FO 371/11144, PRO; U.S.-Department of the Army, August 7, 1954, 783.00 (W)/8-654, RG59, NA.

34. American Embassy, Damascus to Department of State, July 26, 1954, 783.00/7-2654, RG59, NA.

35. "The Problem of Regional Security," Department of State, May 8, 1954.

36. Ibid.

37. Ibid.

38. Ibid.

39. Ibid.

40. Ibid.; the report mentions that "as for the other Western sponsor of the original MEDO, France has been left on the sidelines, at least for the time being."

41. Ibid.

42. Ibid.

43. Ibid.

44. "The ambiguity of United States policy with respect to Middle East security . . . is itself a fundamental problem which, moreover, complicates our handling of all other problems in this area. Until we decide what our strategic goals are, and how far we are willing to go in seeking them, we are in a poor position to deal with the Middle East states which are present or potential members of the security arrangement, with the British whose cooperation is essential, or indeed with the United States Congress. In view of the formidable complexities of the problem, it is not difficult to understand why a clear-cut and unambiguous policy line has been so long in emerging. We have reached the stage, now, however, where some degree of clarification appears essential." ("The Problem of Regional Security," Department of State, May 8, 1954.) Indeed, it appears they were past that stage.

45. On the rise of the Ba'th Party, see the following: Itamar Rabinovich, *Syria Under the Ba'th 1963–1966: The Army-Party Symbiosis* (Tel Aviv: The Shiloah Center, 1972); Hanna Batatu, *Old Social Classes,* pp. 722–748; Nabil M. Kaylani, "The Rise of the Syrian Ba'th, 1940–1958: Political Success, Party Failure," *International Journal of Middle East Studies,* vol. 3 (1972), pp. 3–23; Salaheddin Bitar, "The rise and decline of the Baath," and "The Baath party," *Middle East International,* no. 3 (June 1971) and no. 4 (July 1971); Sami al-Jundi, *al-Ba'th* (Beirut: Dar al-Nahar, 1969); Bashir al-Dawuq, *Nidal Hizb al-Baath al-Arabi al-Ishtiraki abr Mutamarat al-Qawmiya, 1947–1963* (Beirut: Dar al-Talia, 1971); Gordon H. Torrey, "The Ba'th—Ideology

and Practice," *Middle East Journal,* vol. 23 (1969), pp. 445–470; Seale, pp. 148–159; and John F. Devlin, *The Ba'th Party: A History from Its Origins to 1966* (Stanford: Hoover Institution Press, 1976).

46. Seale, p. 184–185; also, see American Embassy, Damascus to Department of State, October 20, 1954, 783.00/10-2054, RG59, NA.

47. British Embassy-Damascus, November 15, 1954, FO 371/111141, PRO.

48. British Embassy-Damascus, February 4, 1955, FO 371/115742, PRO.

49. Ba'thist leader Akram al-Hawrani, elected to parliament in the election, told *al-Jarida* (Beirut) on October 8 that while the socialists and communists might join together to fight imperialism, that was the extent of their cooperation. He pointed out that the "communists openly call for joining the red banner and siding with the Eastern bloc, but the socialists call for neutrality between the two camps." Chief of Staff Shawkat Shuqayr assured the American embassy that one communist deputy out of 142 could hardly be considered dangerous, adding that the ASRP is fighting communism rather than working with them. (Dunlop to Strong, Office of the Army Attache, American Embassy-Damascus, October 18, 1954, State Dept. Post Files, Cairo Embassy, 1954, RG84, NARA.)

50. There were "large and well organized" demonstrations throughout Syria on December 6 and 8 protesting the death sentences accorded those members of the Muslim Brethren found guilty of trying to assassinate Nasser. (U.S. Army Attache, Damascus to Department of the Army, December 10, 1954, 783.00 (W)/12-1054, RG59, NA.) Under suppression in Egypt, the Muslim Brethren had moved their headquarters to Damascus, and their paper, *al-Manar,* had consistently been severely critical of the Nasserist regime, which naturally brought recriminations and pressure from Cairo on the Syrian government to restrain the its activities.

51. British Embassy-Damascus, December 2, 1954, FO 371/111150, PRO.

52. Reported by Ankara Radio (BBC, no. 524, December 7, 1954), from Seale, p. 209; the American Embassy-Ankara reported that Nasser had instructed his ambassador in Ankara to inform Prime Minister Menderes that Egypt was interested in a "friendship pact" with his country (American Embassy-Ankara, December 30, 1954, State Dept. Post Files, Cairo Embassy, 1954, RG84, NARA).

53. Seale, p. 209.

54. For more on Turkish-Egyptian relations, see Baruch Gilead, "Turkish-Egyptian Relations 1952–1957," *Middle Eastern Affairs,* vol. X (November 1959), pp. 356–366.

55. Letter from Henry Cabot Lodge, representative of the United States to the United Nations, to Dulles, December 31, 1954, 611.83/12-3154, RG59, NA.

56. Phone call from John Foster Dulles to CIA Director Allen Dulles, December 27, 1954, John Foster Dulles Papers, Telephone Calls Series, DDEL.

5

Syria's Choice

Due largely to the pressures placed on it as a result of the evolution of the Baghdad Pact, Syria was coming closer to the day of reckoning, when it would have to make a decisive choice on the direction of its foreign policy. The ambiguity over the question of the extent of its relationship with the West had been a reflection of the divisiveness of Syrian politics and the identification of certain groups, parties, and individuals with different external actors. The political trend in Syria by the end of 1954, however, was markedly leftist in orientation, manifested in a committed neutralist and growing anti-West foreign policy. It was symbolic of the changing situation in Syria that the West's remaining hopes would lie with the aging Faris al-Khuri and his outdated, effectively powerless regime.

It was thought by some in diplomatic circles in the West that the pressure that would come to bear on Syria as a result of the evolution of the Baghdad Pact would force a decisive showdown that would result in the ultimate victory of the pro-West elements in the country. Certainly with the Khuri regime in power, they felt that these elements were as well-placed as they were ever going to be. Evidence of the foreign policy tussles between leftist and conservative forces in Syria was apparent late in 1954. Pro and anti-West papers multiplied their editorials on the question of conditional collaboration with the West or complete neutrality. The foreign affairs committee in parliament met repeatedly in December 1954 to discuss the direction of Syria's foreign policy. Iraqi and Turkish emissaries were frequently visiting Damascus in an effort to persuade the regime to resist leftist demands.[1]

Egyptian leadership on the issue was not forthcoming. A very ambiguous statement upon the conclusion of an Arab League foreign ministers meeting in Cairo in December, denouncing any alliance outside the Arab League Collective Security Pact, yet allowing cooperation with the West under certain conditions, reflected Egypt's own contradictory policy in its relationship with the West, i.e., it took the lead in preaching "uncompromising Arab independence under her leadership" yet eagerly obtained arms and economic aid from the West.[2]

There was parallel ambiguity in Syria, evidenced by Foreign Minister Faydi al-Atasi's statement on December 29 that "as to soliciting means for strength and fortitude . . . none of these means for self-maintenance and self-defense accepted by any Arab states (i.e., Iraq) should restrict its freedom or impair its sovereignty."[3] (insert mine). The United States Embassy in Damascus considered that this statement, while being a "masterpiece of ambiguity," was a sign that the regime was interested in assistance from the West.[4] It was definitely a sign that the battle over foreign policy in Syria had yet to be resolved.

In an interview published in the December 9 Cairo weekly *al-Mussawar,* Khuri stated, "let us accept American arms and defend ourselves against Israel. . . . Accept American weapons and attack Israel when we can. I assure you I can explain our position before the UN and the International Court of Justice. What is important is having the means to attack." While obviously an attempt to placate those opposed to American aid by appealing to anti-Israeli sentiments, Khuri certainly did not endear himself to Congress or Israel's other supporters in the United States who could easily point to such statements as evidence that the Arabs intended to use American arms against Israel. This is a perfect example of the "catch-22" situation in which many Arab leaders found themselves, and the difficulty the United States had in trying to back its assets in the Arab world while supporting Israel at the same time – indeed, it turned out to be a liability for the pro-West Arabs.

Nasser called a meeting of the Arab League premiers in Cairo in January 22–29 and February 3–6, 1955, held ostensibly to censure Iraq for its January 13 announcement of its intention to conclude a military alliance with Turkey. Faris al-Khuri attended the meeting along with Faydi al-Atasi. Knowing what the substance of the meeting would be, Nuri al-Sa'id produced a diplomatic illness as his excuse for not attending, sending former premier Fadil al-Jamali in his place.

Neither Khuri nor Atasi expressed an opinion on the proposed Turkish-Iraqi pact in conversations with Ambassador Moose on January 18, despite the efforts of Turkish Prime Minister Menderes to persuade the Syrian leaders upon his visit to Damascus the day after the issuing of the joint communique with Iraq.[5] Khuri's position entering the conference seemed to be considerably weakened by political machinations on the home front. The chamber's foreign affairs committee, stacked in favor of the left, issued on the eve of Khuri's departure for Cairo a resolution reaffirming the prime minister's neutralist foreign policy stance enumerated the previous November upon his accession to power.[6] The debate within the Chamber of Deputies was, for the most part, won by the leftists. Cairo had also timed a major propaganda onslaught against the Turkish-Iraqi pact to coincide with the parliamentary debate. Khuri, however, defended the ambiguous policy that emerged from the previous December's Arab League foreign ministers meeting, thereby preventing Nasser and the Saudis from issuing a joint communique strongly condemning Iraq's action and calling for the preclusion of any pacts with non-ALCSP members.[7] Jordan and Lebanon, to Nasser's surprise, followed Khuri's lead. The Syrian representatives stated their intention to avoid commitments outside the Arab League, but they did not want to directly condemn Iraq for fear of splitting apart the ephemeral concept of Arab unity (a move, they feared, that would also have domestic repercussions), forcing Iraq to take matters into their own hands, and permanently excluding any cooperation with the West.[8]

Khuri's apparent defiance of the resolution adopted by the chamber's foreign affairs committee proved, however, to be one of the main catalysts toward his undoing. The showdown over foreign policy was seen by the leftists as an opportunity to accelerate their rise to power. It was later revealed by President Hashim al-Atasi that Egypt, Saudi Arabia, and, to a lesser extent, France, had bribed and coerced Syrian politicians to force the regime to take a firm position against the Turkish-Iraqi pact; in doing so, they helped precipitate the cabinet crisis that led to Khuri's fall.[9] Indeed, it was at this decisive moment that the Ba'th moved closer to both Egypt and the Syrian communists for the sake of a common foreign policy goal.

The Baghdad Pact had split the Nationalist Party in two, with Lutfi al-Haffar leading the pro-Iraqi wing and Sabri al-'Asali the anti-Iraqi wing. The Ba'th and 'Azm's Democratic Front enlisted 'Asali's support to form a coalition against the pact. When Haffar and other Nationalists found out about Asali's duplicity, they resigned from the party while others quit the government entirely.[10] This withdrawal from the coalition forced Khuri to hand in his resignation on February 7, 1955. 'Asali was reluctantly called upon by the president to form a government, which he successfully did on the 13th. Khalid al-'Azm, who would come to dominate the new regime, was appointed as foreign minster and acting defense minister. The victory by the leftists was crowned on February 22, when, in his ministerial statement, 'Asali committed his government to a policy of complete neutrality, rejected adherence to the Turkish-Iraqi pact, reaffirmed Syria's "aversion to alliances," labelled Zionism as Syria's number one enemy, and excluded exclusive collaboration with the West.[11] On February 24, the 'Asali government received a vote of confidence from parliament (66–53), ironically on the same day the Turkish-Iraqi pact was signed in Baghdad.

Egypt was quick to rally behind the new regime and make certain Syria's foreign policy stayed in line with its own. On February 26, Egypt's minister for national guidance, Major Salah Salim, arrived in Damascus to begin discussions on an Egyptian proposal for a new Arab defense pact. On March 2, Egyptian and Syrian officials signed a joint communique formally rejecting adherence to the Turkish-Iraqi pact or any other outside alliances and announced the intention to establish a joint Arab defense and economic cooperation pact.[12] After failing to convince Jordan to join the proposed pact,[13] Salim travelled to Riyadh, when at the end of his visit on March 6, 1955, the governments of Syria, Egypt, and Saudi Arabia jointly proclaimed that their armed forces would be placed under a unified command (a Syrian-Egyptian defense pact would not be *signed* until November however).[14] Egypt had met Iraq's challenge, countered it with its political triumph in Syria and apparent success in arranging an alliance of its own as an Arab alternative to the Baghdad Pact.

Beyond Washington's Control

The United States, for its part, could do little to prevent the course of events from occurring in Syria in early 1955.[15] The State Department was certainly even more alarmed than before at the growing leftist influence in the country following Khuri's fall from power.[16] The United States Embassy in Damascus believed that the "continuation of [the] 'Asali Cabinet endangers U.S. interests by giving opportunity to Communist-infiltrated ASRP [to] gain control of essentials of power within [a] few months. Once in full control, ASRP ability to guide Syria into cooperation with Saudis and Egyptians as well as its capacity for embarrassing Iraq, Jordan and Lebanon will be increased; and its grip on Syrian affairs may be difficult to shake off."[17] The embassy went on to state that the pro-West elements in Syria "still have considerable strength but need courage to use their strength at [a] critical moment because they fear [the] army will intervene to install [an] even more radical government."[18] Embassy personnel were, however, at a loss as to what course to recommend to reverse the trend. The State Department believed it was sufficient to instruct the embassy to relate to the Syrian government, "whatever its composition," that the United States "fully supports [the] Turkey-Iraq agreement and Northern Tier defense concept and therefore hopes [the] Syrian Government . . . will not oppose Iraq's efforts [to] develop [a] realistic organization for Middle East defense."[19] It even advised the embassy to "avoid active support [of] pro-Western groups to [the] extent this might encourage belief [of] tangible benefits from USG such as military or sizeable economic aid would soon be forthcoming if pro-Western group came to power."[20] For the time being, the pro-West elements in Syria were forced either to fend for themselves or look elsewhere for support. With or without realizing that its regional defense strategy had fomented many of the problems in Syria, the United States was not yet willing to break its nominal principle of not letting itself get entangled in inter-Arab disputes. It also did not want to take any action in Syria that might inflame the already simmering Arab-Israeli situation.

The situation changed dramatically, however, on February 28, 1955, when Israel launched what it claimed was a retaliatory raid in Egypt's Gaza Strip, killing some forty Egyptian soldiers and wounding many more. The act itself appeared to be primarily motivated by an internal power struggle in Israel in the wake of the Bat Gallim incident the preceding fall and the death sentences carried out in January against Israeli saboteurs associated with what became know as the Lavon Affair[21]; secondarily, its timing also can be attributed to Israel's (specifically, the hawks in the government) attempt to disrupt the Baghdad Pact and the then secret ongoing dialogue between Nasser and Premier Moshe Sharrett of Israel.[22] The Gaza raid was a seminal event in the history of the postwar Middle East. Not only did it force Nasser to actively look for military aid from a more forthcoming source, which of course led to the Soviet Union's de jure entrance into the heartland of the region with the conclusion of its arms deal (through Czechoslovakia) with Egypt in September 1955, but it also framed American policy toward Syria back around the Arab-Israeli problem.

Washington became very tentative in its approach to the changing situation in Syria for fear of causing a level of destabilization in the country that might invite aggressive action from what was then perceived to be a more hawkish and paranoid Israel. An Israeli attack could lead to a regional conflagration that would destroy Dulles' efforts to build up his defense system intended to exclude the Soviets from any meaningful role in the area. This tentativeness was apparent from the State Department's rather hesitant responses outlined above to the embassy's requests for signs of encouragement for the pro-West elements in Syria. It is also clear from State Department policy in reaction to rumors of a possible Iraqi-inspired coup and/or invasion in April to "correct" the situation in Syria.

Iraqi officials had relayed to the American ambassador in Baghdad, Waldemar Gallman, information they had obtained in April 1955 from Syrian President Hashim al-Atasi. Atasi reportedly stated that Sabri al-'Asali and Khalid al-'Azm warned him that unless the Egyptian-Syrian-Saudi (ESS) pact was signed immediately, a coup d'etat would be attempted; in response, Atasi reportedly asked for Iraqi military aid in case such an event occurred.[23] The Iraqis told Gallman that they were prepared to move, cautioning that any military occupation would be temporary and only designed to keep the communists from gaining control of Syria.[24] Dulles responded by giving Gallman the following instructions:

> . . . inform [Iraqi] Foreign Minister immediately U.S. Government would be deeply concerned over Iraqi military intervention [in] Syria even at request [of] Syrian President. We have repeatedly made clear our objections [to] prospective Egyptian, Saudi Arabian, Syrian Pact to Syrians and Egyptians. . . . U.S. Government feels byproducts [of] military intervention incalculable and very dangerous. Gaza situation extremely tense. Intervention would heighten Israeli apprehensions and might tip balance of decision

within Israel in favor [of] activist program which could launch Israeli military action against one or several Arab states. In addition Iraqi military intervention would result in widespread belief in the United States that U.S. arms aid to Iraq now being perverted and that Iraq could not be depended upon to exercise cool judgement in area defense matters which [was] anticipated when U.S.-Iraqi military aid agreement signed. We fear Iraq's action would be widely construed in Near East and elsewhere as outright aggression; that Turk-Iraqi Pact containing no general pledge against aggression was concluded in Iraqi anticipation of freedom of action. Furthermore Department fears mere invitation [by] Syrian President under whatever presumed authority [of] Syrian Constitution might not be considered sufficient expression [of] Syrian popular will and might be vigorously opposed by much of Syrian Army.[25]

Dulles sent a similar note to the embassy in Damascus to relay to Atasi, imploring him not to invite Iraqi intervention.[26] In the face of a more acute situation in Syria than he had originally thought,[27] however, Dulles reversed his decision regarding American recognition of a regime that came to power through force and/or violence and instructed Moose to inform Atasi that the United States would not necessarily recognize a new government installed by army pressure.[28] The whole event turned out to be somewhat overblown and was either the result of miscommunication, Iraqi deception, or Iraq's attempt to test the waters and find out what Washington's reaction would be to a more forward Iraqi policy in Syria.[29] This was revealed to Moose in separate conversations with Atasi and 'Asali on April 16, 1955.[30] Atasi stated that he did not request Iraqi aid and that a coup was not imminent. He did, however, inform Moose that he had learned from "a source other than the Prime Minister" that four army officers, including army Chief of Staff Shuqayr and Sarraj, who claimed to represent 300 junior officers, had called on 'Asali and "threatened unspecified action" if the ESS pact was not "promptly signed." This was also the group responsible for pressuring Atasi to offer a bid to 'Asali to form a government back in February — and no doubt on both occasions with encouragement from Cairo. 'Asali told Moose that his government had worked to construct the ESS pact in a form that was much less anti-Iraqi in tone than what the Egyptians and the Saudis had wanted. This accounted for the postponement of the Arab premiers meeting scheduled to be held in Cairo on March 20 and the delay in the signing of the pact. The Syrians did not want a joint ESS declaration excluding Iraq from future participation or explicitly attacking the Turkish-Iraqi pact.[31]

The reason for Syria's hesitation was primarily the fear of alienating Iraq (and the West) in the face of a more aggressive Israel, evidenced by the Gaza raid. 'Asali wanted to maintain at least the appearance that Israel would face more than Syria alone if it decided to move to the north, and he was not fully convinced that Egypt would come to Syria's aid in such an event.[32] There was extreme pressure on Syria both from within and without regarding the signing of the ESS pact. The Nationalists threatened to resign if 'Azm went ahead and signed the original version of the pact.[33] This, of course, would have broken the tacit Ba'th-Nationalist-'Azm alliance which brought 'Asali to power and the Ba'thist foreign policy to its paramount position. Under these circumstances, the Ba'th and 'Azm relented and agreed not to sign, the fear being that the government would fall and possibly open the door for a right-wing, pro-Iraqi coalition government or outright Iraqi intervention.[34]

The Turks, hoping to persuade Syria not to sign the pact, were making threatening noises both through "heavy-handed" diplomatic pressure in Damascus and by massing troops along the border.[35] While causing the Syrian regime to think twice about the prospect of being totally surrounded by hostile neighbors, the most significant and lasting effect of Turkish actions was to bring the Soviet Union out into the open in support of Syria (for the first time outside the confines of the United Nations). Soviet Foreign Minister Molotov informed the Syrian minister in Moscow on March 23, 1955, that the Soviet Union is prepared, if necessary, "to help Syria maintain its freedom and independence in the face of Turkish pressure."[36] Arab press and radio coverage headlined what was referred to as Molotov's "guarantee." Cairo Radio proclaimed on March 29, 1955, that "if Turkey believes that force will settle the situation in Syria then Turkey must remember that she too has a neighbor who is stronger than she is. . . . "[37] — a threat, by the way, that would become all too familiar during the 1957 American-Syrian crisis. With one eye on Syria and the other on the Bandung Conference of non-aligned nations that commenced in April 1955, the Soviets continued to make statements threatening to bring the issue to the UN and warned they could not remain indifferent to activities occurring so close to their border.

This whole episode regarding Syria and the ESS pact was a good example of the rather unpredictable linkage of cause and effect in the Middle East and the complexities with which American policy had to deal. On the one hand, Israeli actions had actually worked in the West's favor with regard to Syria's hesitation to sign the ESS pact, yet on the other hand, it contributed to the regime's willingness to accept the Soviet Union as its protector, to say nothing of its effect on Nasser's decision to conclude an arms deal in September with the Soviets — a lead the Syrians would soon follow and whose beginnings can be traced to Israel's Gaza raid and Turkey's ill-timed threats.

Israel conveniently assumed that through military pressure the Arabs would be forced to come to the negotiating table on terms favorable to it and the West, similar to what they had done when the armistice agreements were signed following the 1947–49 Arab-Israeli war.[38] This line of thinking was clearly evident in a *Jerusalem Post* editorial stating that "we hope that the Israeli raid has convinced many Syrians that the military pact with Egypt has increased the danger to Syria instead of guaranteeing Syria's defence."[39]

The long-term effect was exactly the opposite as the Syrians sought cover behind the Soviet and Egyptian shield.

The Eisenhower administration lamented that Israel's reprisals "had the effect of sharply increasing Arab-Israel tension and of strengthening the tendency of many Arabs to believe that Israel is their principal if not their only enemy. It will also increase the difficulties of our task of attempting to make the Arabs aware of the reality of the Communist danger and to convince them that in their own interests they should take action to develop a realistic defense organization in association with Turkey and the West to defend themselves from possible Soviet aggression."[40]

The Assassination of Malki

If American hopes at the time were slowly dissipating regarding the prospects for Syria aligning itself with the West, the chances of this actually happening took a sharp turn downward on April 22, 1955: the most influential officer in the Syrian army and a staunch Ba'thist supporter, Colonel 'Adnan al-Malki, was assassinated. He was gunned down while attending a soccer match in Damascus by an individual identified as a member of the fascist-oriented Syrian Social Nationalist Party (SSNP), also known as the Parti Populaire Syrien (PPS).[41] The SSNP had a history of overt and covert contacts with the West, including the United States, but had been on the decline ever since the overthrow of Shishakli. As the arch-enemies of the SSNP, the pro-Ba'thist elements in the army used the assassination as an excuse to conduct a witch hunt of SSNP members and close SSNP offices throughout Syria in an attempt to reduce the organization's influence, although there was reason to believe that the murder was an act of personal revenge and not an SSNP conspiracy. The military also used the incident to round up pro-Iraqi elements in order to lessen resistance to the signing of the ESS pact.[42] As an indication of the tendentiousness in the wake of the killing, the government investigation into the incident was headed by none other than Major Sarraj, who only a month earlier had been appointed head of intelligence (G-2 or deuxieme bureau) by Shuqayr.

The connections between the SSNP and the United States, both real and embellished, were used by the Ba'th and the communists as a way to browbeat the West. The Syrian press and radio began to accuse the United States of masterminding the "plot" to assassinate Malki. Prime Minister 'Asali, in a speech to parliament on April 26, stated that the murder was part of a plot to overthrow the regime and reorient the nation's foreign policy, claiming that the conspirators had "thrown themselves at the feet of a foreign state seeking its help and support in order to make an unethical coup—as they all did—to seize power."[43] Many newspapers in Syria identified the foreign state as the United States. The army claimed that this incident represented a perfect example of the need for Syria to sign the ESS pact in order to protect itself against future imperialist intrigue. Ambassador Moose issued an official public denial of the accusations, and after a discussion with 'Asali, the prime minister made a statement on April 28 that he had not indicated specifically which foreign state was behind the plot, only that the conspirators offered themselves to a foreign state, and added that this foreign state did not respond in the affirmative to the SSNP demarche.[44] But the damage had been done. The communists had taken advantage of the situation to move Syria closer to the Soviets, while the Ba'thists were able to destroy the SSNP dictum of pan-Syrianism in favor of their pan-Arab, neutralist policy, one which simultaneously tightened Syria's relationship with Egypt.

The United States could do little to stem Syria's drift away from the West, even though the Eisenhower administration felt that "if the present trend continues there is a strong possibility that a Communist-dominated Syria will result, threatening the peace and stability of the area and endangering the achievement of our objectives in the Middle East."[45] The administration's estimation of the extent of communist and ASRP infiltration into the ranks of the Syrian army precluded the possibility of an arms deal for fear that any military aid would only strengthen the leftist elements.[46] Indeed, as time passed Syria itself became less enthusiastic about an arms agreement with the United States, which seemed only natural considering the predominance of its anti-West foreign policy and the recent support shown it by the Soviets and Egyptians.[47] In lieu of a forward policy, American strategy vis-à-vis Syria at this time was to consider "developing courses of action" (left unspecified) that *might* "affect the situation in Syria."[48]

A Final Opportunity

The signing of the ESS pact was further delayed by the specter of the August 1955 presidential election in Syria to choose a successor to Hashim al-Atasi, whose term was due to expire in November. Since none of the candidates or their supporters in parliament were willing to come down on the ESS issue on one side or the other, and thus risk alienating a significant bloc of voters, any formal signing was indefinitely postponed. There also developed differences among the ESS members about the exact nature of their proposed military and economic integration—no one wanted to get shortchanged.[49] Under these uncertain conditions, any thoughts of a American-Syrian rapprochement would have to wait until after the election.

The election was held on August 18, 1955. The only serious candidates were Khalid al-'Azm, who had long hoped to gain the presidency and had been vigilantly positioning himself for this moment for some time, and the rehabilitated former president, Shukri al-Quwatli, who was urged to run more by default than by choice. Because of widespread distrust of the opportunistic and unpredictable 'Azm among important sectors of the Syrian polity, Quwatli was elected president, backed primarily by the conservatives. This was not, however, the time or place for someone of Quwatli's limited abilities. He was also hamstrung by the fact that he still owed much political deference to the Egyptians and the Saudis (who supported his candidature).[50]   Aiding Quwatli's cause was the army chief of staff, Shawkat Shuqayr, who resisted the Ba'th and withheld army support for 'Azm. He did so primarily because he knew the United States was dead set against the election of 'Azm, and if the latter had won, it might have precipitated an American counteraction to remove him from power. Shuqayr was also known to have been interested in obtaining arms from the United States and was increasingly worried about communist influence in the army and the security of his position in the face of the rapid advancement of Ba'thist junior officers; he therefore did not want to alienate the United States entirely and supported the formation of a more conservative government coalition.[51]   In reaction, the Ba'th withdrew from the 'Asali coalition and the government subsequently fell on September 6, 1955. The dependable Sa'id al-Ghazzi then formed a coalition government on September 13 that was decidedly less radical than its predecessor.

For a moment, there seemed to be a glimmer of hope that the Ghazzi right-wing coalition could succeed in bringing some political stability to Syria. Combined with Quwatli's election, an arms deal might finally be concluded with the United States. On September 10, 1955, Moose relayed to the State Department a Syrian arms request (initiated by Shuqayr) that would be paid for on a reimbursable basis, strongly advising that immediate action be taken and warning that a negative response would only strengthen the leftists and force Syria to turn to the Soviets.[52]   The response was negative. The State Department informed Moose that it felt that any arms negotiations with the Syrians would "inevitably result" in "renewed controversy re[garding] Middle East defense arrangements . . . in Israel and among [the] Arab states. . . . "[53]   More importantly, it warned that negotiations might disrupt the "current consideration" being given to Dulles' statement regarding a resolution to the Arab-Israeli conflict given on August 25, 1955, in a speech to the Council on Foreign Affairs in New York.[54]

The speech was actually the culmination of the findings of the Middle East Planning Group (code-named "Alpha") that had been authorized by Dulles in late 1953 to concentrate on ways to resolve the Arab-Israeli impasse. The Alpha Plan pledged American assistance to three principal problems left unresolved at the end of the 1947-49 war: the "tragic plight" of the Palestinian refugees, "the pall of fear that hangs over the Arab and Israel people alike," and "the lack of fixed permanent boundaries between Israel and her neighbors." To address these three issues, Dulles proposed the creation of an international fund to enable Israel to pay compensation to the refugees, American assistance to adjust the armistice lines to acceptable boundaries, and a formal treaty engagement between the United States and the pertinent nations in the area ensuring that neither side can "alter by force" the defined boundaries.[55] Dulles outlined three reasons to Eisenhower on why he felt the program should be expedited:[56] 1) Nasser was more favorably disposed to the project at the time; 2) the Johnston Plan was "losing steam"; and 3) there was "relative tranquility" at the moment but something could happen in terms of a Soviet-Arab rapprochement to the point where the United States had to unequivocally back Israel, therefore losing all pretense of impartiality. He stated that "if Alpha is to be done at all, it should be done while we can speak as the friend of both."[57] Dulles also commented that this "positive effort" by the United States needed to be put forth before the "situation gets involved in 1956 politics," referring, of course, to the presidential election campaign.[58] Again, contrary to the intent of the northern tier concept, the administration's interest in preventing Soviet "penetration" in the area through regional defense methods was now held hostage to the Arab-Israeli dispute.

Both the Arabs and Israel heartily rejected the well-intentioned but ill-conceived plan. Thus the fear of disrupting "consideration" of the plan led to the refusal of a possible opportunity to prevent Syria from turning to Moscow for military aid. The State Department believed that if Syria received American arms it might feel it unnecessary to come to terms with the Israelis, who in turn would not be inclined to enter negotiations from a weakened bargaining position. In addition, the United States could not obviously be seen negotiating an arms deal of any significance in the region at the same time it was calling for peace negotiations and giving assurances that it would safeguard boundary demarcations. American commitments at the regional and international levels were made, inter alia, at the expense of a potential improvement in its bilateral relationship with Syria.

The attitude of the Eisenhower administration with respect to an arms deal with Syria, however, came under some reevaluation after the Soviet-Egyptian arms agreement in September 1955.[59] There were reliable reports that the Soviets were trying to follow upon the heels of their triumph in Egypt by offering a similar deal to the Syrians.[60] Obviously concerned about this prospect, the administration began to show signs that it was willing to deal with Syria. It authorized an "informal discussion" of an arms sales agreement with the Syrian government along the lines of the 1953 American-Lebanese military sales agreement (reimbursable military aid agreement), that fell under the provisions of Section 106 of the Mutual Security Act of 1954, which stated that "any equipment purchased" must only be used for "internal security or legitimate self-defense" and will not be employed in "any act of aggression against any other state."[61] Before authorizing the approach to the Syrian government, however, Dulles sought advice from none other than Nuri al-Sa'id on whether or not the United States would be wasting its time. Of primary consideration to Dulles was "whether a favorable decision [would] likely forestall [a] Soviet arms deal and encourage those Syrian leaders prepared [to] rely on [the] West."[62] Ambassador Gallman described Nuri's response as "quick and to the point," quoting him as saying that "no matter what or how much [the] United States does for present Syrian Government . . . that government cannot be relied on by [the] United States."[63] Gallman went on to paraphrase Nuri as saying that only "with a stable, reliable government in power in Syria prepared to help in the defense of the area would he recommend an arms agreement on the U.S.-Iraqi pattern. . . . "[64] In other words, only after a coup d'etat replaced the current regime with one that looked to the West. Nuri's advice against an arms deal with the present Syrian regime seemed to have little or no effect on Dulles' decision, but it did add to the administration's concern that the Iraqi leader was eager to act precipitously.

The Syrian-Egyptian defense pact signed on October 20, 1955 (discussed below), again soured the prospect for a deal from the American perspective, as it was viewed as proof of a pattern "previously observed in Egypt and Saudi Arabia, of asking for U.S. aid and then refusing [it] as justification for obtaining arms from [the] Soviet bloc."[65] Continuing the rollercoaster ride on whether to deal or not to deal, by December, reacting to a "series of urgent telegrams" from the embassy in Damascus that depicted the situation in Syria as critical, the State Department was convinced to follow through with the offer.[66] On December 8, 1955, it authorized the embassy to "inform the Syrian Government that the United States was prepared to exchange notes with Syria which would constitute an agreement for sales of military equipment along the lines of the U.S.-Lebanese agreement . . . ," and on December 10 Ambassador Moose met with Ghazzi to carry out his instructions.[67]

On January 5, 1956, however, prospects for an agreement again took a downturn: the Syrian government informed Ambassador Moose that it would not sign a reimbursable military aid agreement with the United States because it considered the prices too expensive.[68] Money, however, was not the problem. Syria had concluded an agreement with the Iraq Petroleum Company on November 29, 1955, for "greatly increased" pipeline transit payments that provided the government with the needed foreign exchange to purchase arms.[69] Indeed, this agreement was probably one of the main reasons that spurred the State Department to reissue the arms offer to Syria, fearing that it now had the wherewithal to go to the Soviets if it so chose. Apparently, the main reason for the sudden refusal by the Syrian government was related to a concurrent struggle occurring within the Syrian army directed at Chief of Staff Shuqayr and one within the Chamber of Deputies.[70]

The chief of staff was much more of an opportunist than an ideologue, interested more in maintaining his position than the particular political shade of the regime in power. He and the leftist junior officers had been wary of each other ever since Shuqayr withdrew his support from Khalid al-'Azm in the presidential election the previous August. The refusal of the American offer was quite simply the victory of the junior officers over Shuqayr in an internal army struggle that had been brewing for months, and which had been sharpened since the Egyptian-Soviet arms deal, the Egyptian-Syrian defense pact, and of course the American demarche in December. Shuqayr told American officials in Damascus that both he and President Quwatli had wanted to sign the aid agreement, and felt that Ghazzi would "go along" when the time was "ripe."[71] There was, however, another obstacle to the conclusion of an agreement. The deal, if signed, would have required parliamentary ratification, and with the leftist orientation of the chamber, backed by popular opinion opposed to such conditional aid, there was little chance that it could have been approved. The leftists had won this round and successfully prevented action that would have brought Syria a bit closer to the West. The victory also effectively kept the conservative elements demoralized, divided, and devoid of confidence in the United States. On February 22, 1956, Shuqayr informed the American embassy that the Syrian government had decided to buy arms from Czechoslovakia, reportedly obtaining a $22 million line of credit through an Arab bank for the purchase.[72] On March 8, CIA Director Allen Dulles stated at the 279th meeting of the NSC that "the delivery of Soviet bloc arms to Syria had begun."[73]

Even if the Eisenhower administration was more forthcoming toward Syria during this period, there was certainly no guarantee that the Ghazzi regime (or any of the regimes since Shishakli's fall) could have negotiated an agreement. American hopes had been raised before and subsequently dashed, especially during the Shishakli years. The United States and Syria traded back and forth the role of procrastinator and initiator, each role dependent upon and determined by events that had almost nothing to do with any proposed arms deals. The Ghazzi coalition was typically weak and divided. The Nationalists and the Populists could not agree on an acceptable division of cabinet portfolios. In retaliation, the Nationalists refused to participate in the government, thus missing an opportunity to form a stable right-wing regime based on the majority that had voted Quwatli president in August 1955. The Nationalist departure allowed the leftist Democratic Bloc to fill the vacuum in the cabinet, thus maintaining direct leftist influence upon the prime minister and offsetting the pro-West Populists within the inner circle.

Even a stable right-wing coalition would have been hard pressed to go against the neutralist, pro-Egyptian tide in the country, especially after the latter's wildly popular arms deal with the Soviets. It might have been too much to expect a split cabinet at that time to undertake such a policy departure. But the decision by the State Department to refuse an arms deal with Syria had initially been made as least as early as April 1955, long before Dulles' Alpha speech, and thus the opportunity to strengthen the conservative elements prior to the divided Ghazzi coalition was lost. In addition, with the political alignment in the Ghazzi cabinet, Dulles' Alpha plan did not have much of a chance of being deemed acceptable by the Syrians. Accordingly, when Ghazzi made his policy statement in front of the chamber on September 20, 1955, a speech full of diatribes against Israel and Zionism, he said that it was "not in the interest [of Syria] to join the Turkish-Iraqi pact or any foreign pact" and that he would resume negotiations on the ESS accord.[74] This he did, and riding the momentum of the Soviet-Egyptian arms deal in September, Syria and Egypt finally came to terms and signed the Egyptian-Syrian defense pact in Damascus in October 1955. Saudi Arabia also agreed to a similar bilateral pact with Egypt in October, and although this was not exactly the ESS pact as originally envisaged, the bilateral defense pacts with Egypt served the same purpose; indeed, it was much more of a political statement than an effective military organization.

The speed with which the agreement was concluded was probably due to several factors: 1) because of the Soviet-Egyptian arms deal, Egypt could act as a supplier of Soviet arms to the Syrians without arousing the opposition of Iraq, Turkey, or the conservatives in Syria that would most certainly occur if it dealt with the Soviets directly (there were several reports that the agreement contained a secret clause to this effect); 2) the Syrians saw the Egyptian-Soviet arms deal as increasing the possibility of a preemptive attack by Israel, in which Syria might incur the greatest losses, and therefore felt a bit more secure under the Egyptian umbrella (the obverse of this, however, is that if Israel attacked Egypt, Syria might have been reluctantly drawn into the war because of the defense pact); 3) finally, the agreement simply may have been a face-saving way of dropping the failed original ESS pact proposal. In any event, the defense pact definitely enhanced Egypt's influence in Syria at the expense of the Iraqis, the West, and even the Soviets, of whom Nasser was suspicious of gaining the upper hand at *his* expense in Syria.

Notes

1. British Embassy-Damascus, December 30, 1954, FO 371/115482, PRO.
2. Seale, p. 210–211; also contains text of resolutions passed at the Cairo meeting.
3. American Embassy-Damascus, December 31, 1954, State Department Post Files, Cairo Embassy, 1954, RG84, NARA.
4. Ibid.

5. Editorial Note, no date, *Foreign Relations of the United States, 1955–1957,* vol. XIII, pp. 514–515, (hereafter cited as *FRUS*).

6. Ba'thist leader Salah al-Din Bitar was secretary of the committee, which also included Hawrani and Baqdash.

7. British Middle East Office (BMEO) Weekly Political Summary No. 4 for Week Ending January 26, 1955, FO 371/115461, PRO.

8. For comments by Khuri reflecting his posturing, see *Rose al-Yusuf* (Egyptian weekly), January 31, 1955, as well as the January 31 Damascus dailies *al-Hadara* and *al-Nasr.*

9. Editorial Note, no date, *FRUS*, pp. 514–515.

10. Seale, p. 219.

11. Editorial Note, no date, *FRUS*, pp. 514–515; also, see American Embassy-Damascus, February 24, 1954, State Dept. Post Files, Cairo Embassy, 1955, RG84, NARA; and British Embassy-Damascus, February 26, 1954, FO 371/115945, PRO.

12. Salim reportedly described the ALCSP as nonexistent since the signing of the Turkish-Iraqi pact. Chief of Staff Shuqayr expressed his support for Egypt's proposal by recalling how successfully Syrian and Egypt collaborated against the Crusades. (American Embassy-Damascus, March 1, 1955, State Dept. Post Files, Cairo Embassy, 1955, RG84, NARA.)

13. Jordan refused because of its close ties with Iraq, its treaty with both the Iraqis and the British, and the fact that they were militarily and economically dependent on Britain. Jordanian nationalists, however, tried to work out a deal with Egypt, Syria, and Saudi Arabia by which these countries would agree to replace the annual British subsidy in order to free Jordan of its dependent status.

14. Text of the tripartite communique, signed in Riyadh by Prince Faisal, Salim, and 'Azm, can be found in *al-Ra'i-al-'Am* of March 7, 1955. 'Azm was the main proponent of the agreement on the Syrian side.

15. Dulles stated that "it does not appear in [the] Department's present view that there is anything we can usefully do in Syria to affect [the] situation. . . . " (Telegram From the Department of State to the Embassy in Syria, February 16, 1955, *FRUS*, pp. 516–517).

16. British Embassy-Washington, March 10, 1955, FO 371/115945, PRO.

17. Telegram From the Embassy in Syria to the Department of State, March 8, 1955, *FRUS*, p. 519–520.

18. Ibid.

19. Telegram From the Department of State to the Embassy in Syria, February 16, 1955, *FRUS*, pp. 516–517. For a record of the conversation between Moose, Asali, and Azm, in which the former relayed the State Department position to the latter two, see American Embassy-Damascus, February 26, 1955, State Dept. Post Files, Cairo Embassy, 1955, RG84, NARA.

20. Telegram From the Department of State to the Embassy in Syria, February 16, 1955.

21. In an attempt to precipitate an incident that would scuttle the Anglo-Egyptian accord (which Israel saw as removing the British military buffer between it and Egypt as well as opening the door for closer American-Egyptian cooperation at its expense), the Israeli government sent the Bat Gallim, flying the national colors, through the Suez Canal. The maneuver utterly failed, as the ship was impounded and its crew imprisoned by Egypt, and the Anglo-Egyptian treaty was ratified. The Lavon Affair revolved around the attempt by Israeli Defense Minister Pinhas Lavon and other hawks in the government, without the knowledge of Prime Minister Moshe Sharrett, to, again, abrogate the Anglo-Egyptian accord. Lavon set up an Israeli spy ring in Cairo, composed mainly of Egyptian Jews, to carry out terrorist bombings against American and British installations. He hoped that these acts would be attributed to the Egyptians and "create an atmosphere of distrust and suspicion of Nasser's ability to protect foreigners" and control his country, thereby compelling the British to keep their troops in the area. The saboteurs were apprehended, two of whom were hanged on January 31, 1955. The Israeli public thought at the time that Nasser had created the incident for political gain, that is until the Lavon Affair became public in 1960, causing a major political scandal in Israel. See Nadav Safran, *Israel: The Embattled Ally* (Cambridge, MA: Harvard University Press, 1981), pp. 348–351; Charles D. Smith, *Palestine and the Arab-Israeli Conflict* (New York: St. Martin's Press, 1988), pp. 164–166.

22. On the specifics of the Israeli operation, see Donald Neff, *Warriors at Suez: Eisenhower Takes America into the Middle East in 1956* (Brattleboro, VT: Amana Books, 1988), pp. 29–35.

23. Telegram From the Department of State to the Embassy in Iraq, April 13, 1955, *FRUS*, pp. 520–521.

24. Ibid.; the Iraqis, in the event of military intervention into Syria, asked the United States to use their "restraining influence" on the Turks and the Israelis (Ibid.).

25. Ibid.

26. Telegram From the Department of State to the Embassy in Syria, April 13, 1955, *FRUS*, p. 522–523.

27. At an NSC meeting on April 3, Dulles described the situation in Syria as "ripe for a military coup d'etat." (239th Meeting of the NSC, April 3, 1955, Ann Whitman File, Dulles-Herter Series, Box 6, DDEL).

28. Telegram From the Department of State to the Embassy in Syria, April 13, 1955.

29. Wilbur Crane Eveland, a CIA operative in Syria at the time, suggests that Gallman's lack of Middle East experience compelled him to tow the British line in his cables to Washington, which might have made him suscep-

tible to believe the Iraqi officials' overture. (Eveland, *Ropes of Sand: America's Failure in the Middle East* (New York: W.W. Norton & Co, 1980), p. 150. The Iraqis, in turn, probably hoped Gallman's sympathetic view to their position might help convince Dulles to give the green light.

30. Telegram From the Department of State to the Embassy in Syria, April 13, 1955.

31. Ibid.; and BMEO Weekly Political Summary No. 12 for Week Ending March 23, 1955, FO 371/115482, PRO.

32. Indeed, Egypt's statements in the past about the possibility of ceding the Negev to Jordan did not encourage the Syrians since they saw this as an attempt by Egypt to rid itself of a common frontier with Israel.

33. BMEO Weekly Political Summary No. 13 for Week Ending March 30, 1955, FO 371/115482, PRO.

34. 'Azm and Shuqayr flew to Cairo on March 30 to press Egypt to radically change the drafting of the proposed pact. (BMEO Weekly Political Summary No. 14 for Week Ending April 6, 1955, FO 371/115482, PRO).

35. Prime Minister Menderes reportedly sent a "stern message" to 'Asali on March 7 putting the Syrian government on notice that if it signed the ESS pact, Turkey must conclude that it had adopted a hostile attitude toward it under Egyptian pressure. (BMEO Weekly Political Summary No. 10 for Week Ending March 9, 1955, FO 371/115461, PRO). The Beirut press was reported to have been unanimously critical of Turkish pressure on Syria, describing it as Hitlerian and indirectly aiding and abetting the communist cause. (American Embassy-Beirut, March 25, 1955, State Dept. Post Files, Cairo Embassy, 1955, RG84, NARA).

36. American Embassy-Beirut, March 25, 1955, State Dept. Post Files, Cairo Embassy, 1955, RG84, NARA.

37. Seale, p. 234.

38. Ernest Stock, *Israel on the Road to Sinai, 1949–1956* (Ithaca: Cornell University Press, 1967), p. 144; also see Chester L. Cooper, *The Lion's Last Roar; Suez, 1956* (New York: Harper & Row, 1978), pp. 91–92.

39. Quoted in Seale, p. 254.

40. Progress Report on NSC 5428 (Near East), Operations Coordinating Board, April 7, 1955, White House Office, National Security Staff: Papers, 1948–1961: OCB Central Files, Box 78, DDEL.

41. For a detailed study of the SSNP, its beginnings and its ideology, see Labib Zuwiyya Yamak, *The Syrian Social Nationalist Party: An Ideological Analysis* (Cambridge: Harvard Middle Eastern Monographs, Center for Middle Eastern Studies, Harvard University Press, 1966); also, for a summary of the SSNP position during the Shishakli years, see American Embassy, Damascus, to Department of State, "The SSNP's Attitude Toward Arabism and Status Vis-à-vis Colonel Shishakli," March 16, 1953, 783.13/3-1653, RG59, NA.

42. British Embassy-Damascus, April 26, 1955, FO 371/115945, PRO.

43. Editorial Note, no date, *FRUS*, pp. 523–524.

44. Ibid.; there is no evidence that the United States had anything to do with Malki's assassination.

45. Paper Prepared by the Operations Coordinating Board Working Group on National Security Council Action 1290-d, July 7, 1955, *FRUS*, pp. 530–537.

46. Ibid.

47. Progress Report on NSC 5428 (Near East), April 7, 1955, op. cit.; Telegram From the Embassy in Syria to the Department of State, May 7, 1955, *FRUS*, pp. 525–528.

48. Paper Prepared by the Operations Coordination Board . . . , July 7, 1955.

49. BMEO Weekly Political Summary No. 19 for Week Ending May 12, 1955, FO 371/115482, PRO.

50. To make the point that they were quite capable of causing Quwatli some problems if he decided to crack down on their party, the communists held a "mammoth" rally in Damascus for Baqdash on August 26. At the rally, Baqdash stated that he had supported 'Azm in the election because he represented a "national bourgeois class . . . that wanted Syria to be free from foreign ties." In a not-so-subtle threat, he also commented on the power of the "street" to take matters into their own hands if the leadership falters. (American Embassy-Damascus to Department of State, August 31, 1955, State Dept. Post Files, Cairo Embassy, 1955, RG84, NARA.)

51. For record of July 25 conversation between Shuqayr and Moose, see British Embassy-Ankara, August 18, 1955, FO 371/115946, PRO.

52. Telegram From the Embassy in Syria to the Department of State, September 10, 1955, *FRUS*, pp. 540–542. The desired military equipment consisted mostly of trucks, jeeps, and trailers.

53. Telegram From the Department of State to the Embassy in Syria, September 21, 1955, *FRUS*, pp. 542–543.

54. Ibid.; for text of speech, see Department of State *Bulletin*, vol. 33, September 5, 1955, pp. 379–380.

55. Gulshan Dietl, *The Dulles Era: America Enters West Asia* (New Delhi: Lancer International, 1986), pp. 67–68.

56. Letter from Dulles to Eisenhower on Alpha, August 19, 1955, Microform Reading Room, microfiche 000274 (1985), Library of Congress.

57. Ibid.

58. Ibid.

59. For information on the evolution of the Soviet-Egyptian arms deal, see Uri Ra'anan, *The USSR Arms the Third World: Case Studies in Soviet Foreign Policy* (Cambridge, MA: The M.I.T. Press, 1969), pp. 13–172.

60. Telegram From the Department of State to the Embassy in Syria, October 6, 1955, *FRUS*, pp. 546–547.

61. Ibid. and Memorandum From the Assistant Secretary of State for Near Eastern, South Asian, and African Affairs (Allen) to the Under Secretary of State (Hoover), October 11, 1955, *FRUS,* pp. 550–551.

62. Telegram From the Department of State to the Embassy in Iraq, October 12, 1955, *FRUS,* pp. 551–552.

63. Telegram From the Embassy in Iraq to the Department of State, October 13, 1955, *FRUS,* pp. 552–553.

64. Ibid.

65. Telegram From the Department of State to the Embassy in Syria, October 25, 1955, *FRUS,* pp. 557–558.

66. Memorandum From the Assistant Secretary of State for Near Eastern, South Asian, and African Affairs (Allen) to the Under Secretary of State (Hoover), December 8, 1955, *FRUS,* pp. 558–560.

67. Ibid.

68. Ibid.

69. Ibid.

70. Telegram From the Embassy in Syria to the Department of State, January 8, 1956, *FRUS,* pp. 563–564.

71. Telegram From the Embassy in Syria to the Department of State, January 24, 1956, *FRUS,* p. 566.

72. Telegram From the Embassy in Syria to the Department of State, January 24, 1956, *FRUS,* p. 566.

73. Ibid.

74. British Embassy-Damascus, "Extract from Said Ghazzi's Statement of Policy," September 21, 1955, FO 371/115947, PRO.

6

Policy Fragmentation

There was a good deal of confusion in the Eisenhower administration during the latter months of 1955 over what exactly its policy toward the Middle East should be. It recognized the existence of several complex issues that needed to be addressed. There was the question of whether or not to join the Baghdad Pact. The administration was contemplating how it would respond to the Soviet-Egyptian arms deal and wondering if it could keep Nasser from irretrievably aligning Egypt with the Soviet bloc. Looming as large as ever was the prospect of an Arab-Israeli peace and how the United States could pursue this track without upsetting or being upset by other problems in the region. And finally, there was the Syrian question and what, if anything, the administration could do to prevent Syria from becoming a Soviet satellite.[1]

Dulles commented that events in the Middle East were moving so fast that he found himself "obliged to make decisions" and that he would have preferred "to make these decisions with more guidance than it might be possible to get from the Planning Board and the National Security Council in the time permitted."[2] The secretary of state agreed with a recommendation from Vice-President Richard Nixon that the Middle East policy of the United States needed a thorough reexamination and subsequently called on the NSC Planning Board to undertake an "urgent review" of the policy contained in NSC resolution No. 5428.[3] The Soviets, as Dulles stated, had "opened up a new front in the Middle East," and "even though our arms and our military assistance to the Middle Eastern states could not be sufficient to enable these states to halt a Russian invasion, U.S. arms and assistance could have immense political importance in the area."[4] He felt it was of the "utmost importance for the welfare of the United States that we should get away from a political basis and try to develop a national non-partisan policy" regarding the Middle East; "otherwise we would be apt to lose the whole area and possibly Africa. . . ."[5]

The key to American policy, to the extent that there was one, was Nasser. The "Egypt-firsters" in the administration maintained that he had not been completely lost to the Soviets, and with some financial incentive, could be won back over to the West as leader of the Arab world against communist expansionism, reviving the old MEDO concept. With this in mind, Dulles gave a measured reaction to the Egyptian-Soviet arms deal, stating that "it is difficult to be critical of countries which, feeling themselves endangered, seek the arms which they sincerely believe they need for defense."[6] In a change of policy, "instead of plotting an uncooperative leader's overthrow as the Eisenhower administration had done when challenged in Iran and Guatemala, Dulles sent emissaries to protest Nasser's decision and to persuade him to change his mind."[7] The incentive given Nasser was an offer to finance the construction of his pet project, the Aswan High Dam. The funding of the dam, it was hoped, would also provide the United States with financial leverage vis-à-vis Egypt. Dulles pointed out that "we certainly have the capability of clamping down on Israel because of that country's heavy financial dependence on the United States," but what bothered him was "the absence of any comparable pressures which we could apply to Egypt."[8] Concurrently, the United States would try to resolve the Arab-Israeli dispute by bringing Nasser and the Israelis together; the hope being, as always, that Egypt would support the West's defense plans in the region if the conflict was resolved.

This preoccupation with Egypt and the Arab-Israeli issue hampered American policy vis-à-vis other problems in the region. All the members of the Baghdad Pact (which now included Pakistan, Great Britain, Turkey, Iraq, and, soon, Iran) had been calling on the United States to join; indeed, they thought it was the natural step to take considering the United States had itself begun the process that developed into the pact. Without the weight of American military might, they felt the organization could be no more than a paper tiger against the Soviets. But the Eisenhower administration would not join for fear of alienating Nasser at the very moment it was trying to wean him back toward the West. The Israelis had been adamantly opposed to the pact, and an American decision to join would only complicate the Arab-Israeli peace initiative the administration was contemplating, one that depended on the cooperation of both the Israelis and the Egyptians.[9] Dulles also was not confident that the administration could receive the necessary two-thirds vote from Congress to join the Baghdad Pact unless the United States gave a security guarantee to the Israelis, which, of course, "would quickly knock out Iraq."[10] In addition, Dulles was very concerned about the Soviets' reaction. He did not want to provoke Moscow too much, and was especially worried the Kremlin might make a counter-move into Iran in the event the United States joined.[11] In fact, Iran approached the Eisenhower administration at this time regarding its inclusion in the Baghdad Pact, hoping the United States would join as well. Dulles was disinclined to encourage the Iranians because, as he stated at an October 1955 NSC meeting:[12]

... there was genuine concern on the part of the Soviet government as to the
direction of future relations between Iran and the Western Powers. Anything
which we might now do which seemed to indicate that Iran was to be used as
a military base would produce a strong reaction from the Soviet Union. We
still have great hopes that the new relationship between the U.S.S.R. and
Egypt can be held to a minimum of significance. Such hopes would be
abruptly ended if we should urge Iran to join the Baghdad Pact.

The secretary of state reiterated at the NSC meeting that "if we now
undertook to tie Iran into a firm military alliance with the Western Powers,
if we tried to set up a counter-front in the Middle East, all our hopes of
guiding the Soviet-Egyptian transaction would be destroyed" (emphasis
mine).

The self-defeating two-track policy the administration pursued of wanting
a regional defense system to contain the Soviets and supporting in principle
the supplying of arms to the Arabs but not wanting to involve itself directly
for fear of trip-wiring a Soviet response or disrupting the Egyptian-Israeli
negotiations was wearing thin with the other Baghdad Pact members, and
they became extremely exasperated over the equivocal American position.
The Soviets, however, had already responded with the arms deal with Egypt,
and contrary to the "Munich mentality" of the administration that would
color most other aspects of its foreign policy (including that toward Syria),
the United States, within this narrow context, appeared to be interested in
appeasing Nasser and the Kremlin.[13]

For all of these reasons, the administration officially announced on
November 8, 1955, its decision not to accede to the Baghdad Pact, expressing, however, support for its mission and stating that the decision did not
exclude the possibility of future adherence. Dulles also told the British that
he hoped that they, along with the other pact members, would not pressure
other Arab countries (namely Jordan and Lebanon) to join, fearing again
that this would upset both the Egyptians and the Israelis and would reduce
the chances for an Arab-Israeli settlement. The day after the announcement, as if to confirm its impartiality in the Middle East and its role
as an objective arbitrator, the administration again reaffirmed the Tripartite
Declaration of 1950.[14] Without a concise and coherent Middle East policy,
contradictions abounded in the administration's approach to the area, with
Dulles reluctantly having to make ad hoc decisions based on scant evidence
and faulty assumptions. The United States seemed to be "walking many tight
ropes and soon may fall off with a bang."[15]

This state of affairs was keenly felt in Syria. After conversations with
Dulles in Geneva, a British official recorded the secretary of state as describing the Syrian situation in the following manner:[16]

. . . he had never known his advisers, especially on the intelligence side, so divided as they were now about Syria. Half of them thought Syria was gone for good and to the Soviet camp. The other half thought she could be rescued. He did not know what to think. It was clear that he was moving in the direction of being less averse to, if not wholly favouring, a coup d'etat by the Iraqis. He said he was afraid that some day it might not be a question of Iraq making a coup in Syria, but Syrian Communists making a coup in Iraq.

It was at this time that the British and the Iraqis began to seriously entertain the possibility of a more forward Iraqi policy vis-à-vis Syria; these discussions evolved into the failed "Iraqi coup" attempt (also known by the British-American code-word Operation Straggle) during the Suez crisis in the fall of 1956.[17] Dulles was hesitant to go along with this approach despite attempts by British and Iraqi officials to convince him otherwise (including a demarche to the American embassy in Damascus in October 1956 by the Syrian pro-Iraqi Nationalist leader Mikhail Ilyan, who would become a central figure in Operation Straggle).[18] The Iraqis and the British, of course, wanted the White House's cooperation so that Washington could use its considerable influence to prevent the Israelis and Turks from taking advantage of what could be a very unstable situation in Syria following the coup.[19] The State Department believed that an Iraqi move at this time would again complicate its "rescue operation" of Nasser and its pursuit of an Arab-Israeli settlement.[20] In addition, it felt Israel might take military action against Syria if Iraq were to intervene (which, in effect, would have moved Iraq's border to Israel), with all the negative repercussions that this would entail for the American position in the region. There was also a feeling in the department (not shared by the American embassy in Damascus or by the British) that Nuri al-Sa'id had engineered Iraq's accession to the Baghdad Pact solely for the purpose of furthering his schemes vis-à-vis Syria.[21] Seen in this light, the United States was reluctant to support a policy that would confirm the suspicions and propaganda blasts that labelled the pact as an instrument of Western imperialism.

The United States shared the *goal* of the British-Iraqi plans to replace the Syrian regime with one that was pro-Iraqi and pro-West, but differed on the timing and the means. Even Ambassador Moose, who was known to have had a distaste for foreign intrigue, suggested that "protection of U.S. interests may require that thought be given to other methods" to reverse the deteriorating situation in Syria.[22] Under Secretary of State Hoover, after recommending against an arms deal with Syria following the conclusion of its defense pact with Egypt, commented that the administration was "giving urgent consideration to ways and means of strengthening [the] hand of pro-U.S. and pro-Western groups in Syria. . . ."[23]

Dulles was encouraged by the election of Quwatli in August 1955 and the formation of a loose right-wing coalition government, and he preferred at first to let the Ghazzi regime have an opportunity to establish itself, especially in light of the ongoing talks with the Syrians about an arms deal, which he did not want to prejudice with precipitate action by the Iraqis. After the deal fell through, and in light of the subsequent Syrian agreement with the East bloc for arms, Dulles reevaluated the situation and was persuaded to at least acquiesce in the British-Iraqi plans. He was adamant that any action should appear to have sprung up spontaneously from the Syrians themselves and was very careful to limit American involvement in the event the operation failed (which in fact occurred—fortunately for the administration, it avoided being directly accused of engineering the plot).[24] Both the British and Americans agreed, however, that an overt Iraqi invasion of Syria was out of the question; the discussions revolved more around the feasibility of employing covert means to accomplish their objective.

Many of the "Egypt-firsters" in the State Department, however, led by Under Secretary of State Hoover, felt that as long as the United States still had a chance to prevent Nasser from committing himself to the Soviet Union then it might be ill-advised to proceed with the Iraqi plan, that is, unless it were possible to bring Nasser into the operation.[25] In other words, it might be better to work on Syria through Egypt rather than Iraq. The communists had been suppressed, at times brutally, by Nasser in his own country and it was known to American officials that he was not particularly fond of the idea of Syria being dominated by the communists or the Soviets. President Quwatli, with strong ties to Egypt and Saudi Arabia, had expressed to Western officials in Damascus his determination to eradicate communism and the "extreme left thoughts" of the ASRP, although he admitted he would have to move slowly because of the strength of the leftists in the junior ranks of the army.[26] Various elements in the State Department believed Quwatli could be a useful link with Nasser in order to employ Egypt's services vis-à-vis Syria.

The approach to Syria through Egypt, however, was not really a viable alternative. At the time, Nasser was more concerned about the direction of Syria's foreign policy and had energetically contributed to the buildup of the leftist elements in Syria who had brought the country in line with Egypt's regional objectives. He was not about to abandon them for a policy which would probably have resulted in what he had been trying to avoid all along, i.e., Syria turning to Iraq, which had always been a more natural economic and geographic partner than Egypt. In any event, Quwatli's criticism of the leftist elements in Syria was simply domestic political posturing—under any sort of pressure, he would not cross them. The British felt as well that if the West worked through Nasser to get to Syria he would just continue to pursue his own interests against the Baghdad Pact and other objectives of the West in the Middle East.[27]

London continued in its attempt to convince the administration that using the Iraqis was the proper policy, claiming that this approach could achieve their combined goals in Syria through "seduction rather than rape."[28] The British eventually succeeded in persuading the United States not so much because of the attractiveness of the plan itself as the reality that by the spring of 1956 the Alpha plan had failed and Nasser was being perceived more and more by the White House as an impediment to the administration's attempts to accomplish its objectives in the region.[29] As early as January 30, 1956, in a meeting with British Prime Minister Anthony Eden (who had been eager to remove Nasser), Dulles said that "if it should be decided to move against Nasser, it might be wise to consider Syria as well."[30]

The Soviet Factor

While the British eventually convinced the United States to see it their way regarding Syria, on other issues there was less agreement. True, the administration was increasingly concerned over the success the Soviet Union was experiencing in establishing a base of influence in Egypt and Syria, but there were those who also believed that the Baghdad Pact, which had "been a major factor in goading the USSR into action," had been one of the reasons for this success.[31] The administration began to recognize that the Kremlin's shift in tactics in the post-Stalinist era, a strategy confirmed by the 20th Congress of the Soviet Communist Party in February 1956, had met with considerable success in the Third World, especially the Middle East.[32] The Soviets had effectively increased their influence in the region by stressing the use of economic aid and trade between the Soviet bloc countries and the Middle East primarily through the following measures: 1) arms sales funnelled through the satellite nations; 2) loans at long-term and very low interest rates (generally about half the rates offered by the West); 3) sending military, technical, and industrial advisors; 4) creation of a Soviet "Point Four" program; 5) relieving the commodity surpluses of the Arab states, enabling them to pay for Soviet arms through barter deals; 6) pressing for and concluding economic and friendship treaties; and 7) attaching no overt strings to their offers, as opposed to the American offers that had legislatively mandated restrictions.[33] The administration also postulated that the communists' strategy in the Middle East was to move "step by step, to take over one country at a time," using the "same tactics against the Arab countries that the Soviets used so successfully against Eastern Europe."[34] The Soviet recourse to supporting the opposition to pro-West regimes in the area (and not relying exclusively on the communist parties) had paid some handsome dividends in Syria. Khalid Baqdash put it succinctly in the *Cominform Journal* of November 20, 1953:

The National liberation movement, the democratic movement, and the peace movement in all Arab countries organically merge into a single all-embracing movement . . . We Arabians [sic] have but one path, the path of a broad national front which must unite the workers, peasants, middle strata of the urban population, and large sections of the national bourgeoisie.[35]

To achieve the immediate goal of coordinating an anti-West foreign policy while moving simultaneously closer to the Soviets, the communists in Syria subsumed most of their radical domestic reform proposals in order to cooperate with such elements as the Ba'th, 'Azm's Democratic Bloc, and the left-wing Nationalists. Only then could they hope to gain power in Syria.

While recognizing this success, the White House also admitted that the Soviet Union had worked itself into a position where it could not longer be entirely ignored regarding a settlement to the Arab-Israeli dispute. The British did not share this view, preferring to maintain its policy of trying to keep the Soviets out of the Middle East. The last thing they wanted was another superpower gaining ground in the area at the expense of their dwindling presence in the region. The differences on this and related issues between the United States and Great Britain became quite noticeable in the early part of 1956, offering the Soviets and the Arabs ample fodder to exploit to their own advantage.

With a heightened sense of confidence, the Soviets became more active on the diplomatic front, as if to confirm the role they felt they deserved regarding Middle East affairs. In response to the Anglo-American talks in Washington in late January 1956, the Soviets issued a statement on February 13 warning the West against intervention in the Arab world.[36] This was obviously designed to gain propaganda points with the Arabs by portraying themselves as their protector. The statement noted that the Soviet Union "cannot be indifferent to the situation which is developing in the area . . . because it is directly connected with the security of the Soviet Union, situated in contrast to certain other powers, in the immediate vicinity of this area." It went on to state that actions by the West, like the formation of the Baghdad Pact, "have nothing in common either with the national interest of the countries of that region or the interest of peace in general. These events have shown that such actions are obviously contrary to the interests of peace, as well as the vital interests of the peoples of this region." The Syrian press generally welcomed the statement as helpful to the Arab cause and as further evidence of Soviet friendship.

Another problem with the administration's Middle East policy at this time was that it was pursuing two contradictory tracks simultaneously in relation to the Soviets. On the one hand it realistically approached the Arab-Israeli conflict by recognizing the need to include the Soviets in an attempt to resolve the issue. It also did not want to engage in a competition with the Soviets in supplying arms to their respective clients in the region. Therefore, in April 1956 (after the failure of the Alpha plan became evident) the administration proposed to the UN Security Council that it instruct UN Secretary General Dag Hammarskjold to "work on the improvement of the Palestine armistice." The United States drew up a resolution on this basis and, since it required Soviet concurrence, submitted it to the Soviet delegate for approval before it was introduced in the Security Council.[37] An American writer cleverly observed that, "it was profoundly novel . . . that on the Middle East issue Washington was operating more closely with Moscow than with London."[38]

In response to this overture, the Soviet Union made an announcement on April 18, 1956, pledging itself to cooperate with the West for a Middle East peace.[39] While condemning "military alignments" that served the "aims of colonialism" and regarding "with sympathy and ardent support" the independence of the nations in the Middle East, the statement declared that:

1) The Soviet Union will render the necessary support to the United Nations measures directed towards the search for ways and means of strengthening peace in the area of Palestine and the implementation of the corresponding decisions of the Security Council.

2) The Soviet Union is of the opinion that measures should be taken in the nearest future to ease the tension existing in the Palestine area without outside interference, which is contrary to the will of Near Eastern countries and to the principles of the United Nations.

3) The Soviet Union considers it essential, in the interests of strengthening international peace and security, to direct efforts towards a stable, peaceful settlement of the Palestine question on a mutually acceptable basis, taking due consideration of the just national interests of the interested parties.

Expanding on the third point, the statement called on the parties to the conflict "to refrain from any kind of action which may lead to an exacerbation of the situation on the existing demarcation line set up by truce agreements between the Arab countries and Israel. . . . " Most Syrians were less than pleased with the Soviet announcement and it was received with considerable hostility in the press. They felt it favored a pro-Israeli solution to the Palestine issue and indirectly recognized the legitimacy of the Jewish state. The left-wing *al-Ra'i al-'Am* proclaimed on April 19 that it was clear that Soviet policy only served Soviet interests and that now the Arabs must deal with the situation by themselves. Khalid al-'Azm, in an April 20 interview with his party organ, *al-Nasr,* said that the Soviet Union was not an enemy of Zionism in the past (as it was one of first nations to recognize the new

Israeli state in 1948 and supplied it with critical arms during the war), so the recent statement was not surprising; therefore, the Arabs should not be fooled into thinking that the Kremlin shares the Arab aim of eradicating Israel. 'Azm went on to suggest (rather accurately) that the reason the Kremlin issued the declaration was to position itself on a diplomatic par with the West in the Middle East, and therefore should not be attacked too harshly. The Soviets were learning, however, that the desire to play a major diplomatic role in the Middle East usually brought with it the equivocation that made it vulnerable to criticism from both sides to the conflict.

On the other hand, the second track that Washington pursued was more in line with British policy and contradicted the approach that required the cooperation of the Soviets. This became evident when the administration announced that it was sending a high-profile official, Loy Henderson, who was deputy under secretary of state for administration and an adviser on Middle Eastern affairs, to the Baghdad Pact meeting in Teheran. At the meeting, the United States announced that it was joining the economic and counter-subversive committees of the pact and stated that the Joint Chiefs of Staff would provide comments on the military plans and studies prepared by the military committee of the pact (it also established a military liaison group in Baghdad).[40] Essentially, then, what the administration did was encourage Soviet participation in the Middle East at the same time it strengthened its link with the Baghdad Pact, which was designed to keep Soviet influence out of the area. This policy was doomed from the beginning. The only thing that saved it from outright failure was the course of events that transpired in relation to the Suez crisis in the summer-fall of 1956.

The Eisenhower administration seemed to be selective in allowing the Soviets a role in Middle East affairs. At this point it was convenient to do so, considering the failure of the Alpha plan and the recognition that the Arab-Israeli negotiations, such as they were, needed a jump-start, and maybe the Soviets could provide it; however, the administration's two-track policy seemed to indicate that once the Kremlin had played its part in bringing the two sides to the conflict together, it expected the Soviet Union to return to its junior role in the Middle East. After the Suez war, the administration adopted the exclusivist British posture and tried its best to deny the Soviets a major role in the region despite repeated attempts by the Kremlin to peacefully enter the diplomatic picture.

The United States was also at this time (spring-summer 1956) in the process of developing another policy-track toward the Middle East that would have important repercussions for Syria throughout 1957. This was the attempt by the Eisenhower administration (eventually successful by early 1957) to detach Saudi Arabia from Egypt, or more specifically, King Sa'ud from Nasser, and effect a rapprochement between Iraq and Saudi Arabia. The object was to weaken and isolate Nasser and terminate once and for all

Saudi financing/bribery of groups and individuals throughout the Middle East (especially in Syria and Jordan) who were pursuing policies in the Saudi interest but contrary to American interests.[41] Ambassador Moose stated in June 1956 that it was his belief "that Egyptian activities and influence in Syria would be much less harmful to us if, for whatever reason, the Egyptians were deprived of Saudi financial support."[42] Although Dulles told the British in May that he had not made much progress with Sa'ud,[43] by September, the State Department informed Moose of the following:

> 1) Recognizing the considerable influence which Saudi Arabia exercises in Syria, we have on several occasions pointed out to King Saud the dangers inherent in the Syrian situation and have urged him to use his influence to stop the drift to the left. We now have reason to believe that he is aware of the problem. . . . We believe that this change in Saudi attitude will continue and we shall take every opportunity to encourage King Saud to cooperate in opposing leftist influence in Syria;
>
> 2) A source of instability in Syria has been the conflict of Iraqi and Saudi interests there. We have encouraged and continue to encourage a rapprochement between Iraq and Saudi Arabia which, we believe, would contribute substantially to an improvement of the situation in Syria.[44]

Ironically, the courting of Sa'ud by the United States compounded the difficulties between Washington and London, rooted in their differences over resolutions to the problems between Britain and Saudi Arabia in the Arabian Peninsula (primarily the Buraimi and Omani issues).[45] The United States had been pressuring both sides (especially the British) to resolve the problems peacefully, at first because Washington was interested in not jeopardizing its oil investments (through ARAMCO) and military presence (at Dhahran airbase) in Saudi Arabia, but now there was the added incentive of gaining Saudi support for American policies in the Middle East.[46] As will be seen, the American-Saudi relationship was one of the most significant factors affecting the policy of the United States toward Syria throughout 1957.

Syria's Internal Problems in 1956

The year 1955 was certainly a turbulent one for Syria. In contrast, most of 1956 would be relatively quiescent. The domestic political jockeying would continue as usual, but the anti-Baghdad Pact foreign policy exhibited by the Syrian government had become a legitimate tenet that could not, barring outside intervention, be seriously challenged from within. Events in Syria, of course, would be overshadowed for much of the year by the Suez crisis and the Suez war. The relative tranquility, however, was only the calm before the storm.

The year got off to a rather auspicious start, revolving around the questionable preparedness of the army in the wake of the Israeli attack (Israel claimed it to be a retaliatory raid) during the night of December 11–12, 1955, at Lake Tiberias. The Israelis launched the attack for much the same reason it launched its large-scale raid on Gaza earlier in the year. After the signing of the Egyptian-Syrian defense pact in October 1955, the Israeli government felt it necessary to show that the pact was a militarily ineffective organization and that it was useless for the Syrians to try to confront Israel. On December 13, Syria formally complained to the UN about the Israeli attack, and the issue was discussed in the Security Council between December 16, 1955, and January 19, 1956, when a resolution, co-sponsored by the United States, Great Britain, and France, was passed condemning Israel.[47]

In Syria, there was obvious outrage against the raid coupled with accusations directed at the West; however, there was serious discussion about the alleged poor performance of the army at Lake Tiberias, laying part of the blame with Chief of Staff Shuqayr.[48] There was a report in the January 3 Damascus daily, *al-Hadara* (pro-Ba'th), that an official at the Directorate General of Police had ordered the arrest of anyone who was listening to Radio Israel in public places, claiming that it was "distorting" the events of mid-December. The Syrian government seemed to be trying, unsuccessfully, to conceal the activities of the army in the incident. In any event, the attack had a similar effect on the Syrians as the Gaza raid had on the Egyptians. It accelerated calls for Soviet arms, brought forth statements of solidarity from Egypt, and increased Syrian hostility to the West. All this occurred during the climactic final stage of negotiations between the United States and Syria for an arms agreement, which was set back by the development (and again, might have contributed to the Israeli timing of the raid). Indeed, there is some credence to the assertion that Israel intentionally pushed the Egyptians and Syrians into the arms of the Soviet Union so that it could pose as the anti-communist bulwark in the Middle East and would consequently receive the much-sought-after military aid from the Americans—certainly their propaganda campaign in the United States did nothing to dispel this notion.[49]

The Lake Tiberias incident began what would be months of apprehension, some real, some exaggerated, in Syria of an impending Israeli attack. Various elements would try to exploit this fear to improve their position in the government and pressure the Ghazzi regime to make more concessions on foreign policy. Recognizing the growing turmoil in the Chamber of Deputies, and as a weak attempt to check leftist influence by keeping them in bird's-eye view, Quwatli, on February 15, called for the formation of a National Charter—"a body of generally accepted principles to guide the policies of future governments."[50] The chamber convened a secret session so as not to give the Ba'th a forum in which to rouse public support for their version of the charter.[51] In response, the Ba'th refused to take part and issued a public statement attacking the procedure in the chamber, advocating closer union with Egypt, lashing out in customary fashion at the Baghdad Pact, and threatening to take the issue of continued Israeli activity vis-à-vis the Jordan River waters to the UN Security Council.[52] Nasser, hoping to promote some stability in Syria, applauded Quwatli's National Charter as the true spirit of Arab unity. In a speech on February 19, 1956, Nasser reiterated his support for Syria in the event of an Israeli invasion and declared that he would consider an attack on Syria as an attack on his own country.[53]

By late February-early March 1956, a draft agreement was reached among the parties that resulted in something of a compromise between the right and left-wing elements. It basically reflected the leftist foreign policy orientation adopted ever since late 1954. It stated that Syria opposed imperialism and Zionism, and that it was committed to working for the liberation and unification of the Arab states.[54] In addition, the statement declared Syria's neutral policy in world affairs and claimed that it was free to obtain arms from whatever source it pleased.[55] The Ba'th Party wanted a statement condemning Western imperialism, calling for political union with Egypt, and securing the right to obtain arms from the Soviet bloc—the declaration itself only condemned imperialism in general, called for only a "strengthening" of relations with Egypt, and stated that arms could be obtained from any source.[56] The conservatives wanted a statement condemning communism as the greatest threat to Syria, but it was unsuccessful.[57] Concessions were made on both sides and the final document was ambiguous enough so as not to upset any particular group too much, but the orientation of Syria's foreign policy was still clearly directed by the leftists. Beyond this modest achievement, the process only succeeded in "illuminating the disunity of the conservatives" as they were again unable and unwilling to pull their forces together in order to pick up on Quwatli's lead and meet head-on the challenge posed by the leftists.[58]

There were subtle indications at this time (spring 1956) of the latent antagonisms between the Communist Party and the Ba'th Party over the extent of relations with the Soviet Union and the spread of communism in Syria—differences that would come out into the open in 1957 after their need to cooperate against Western imperialism had diminished. As one journalist aptly noted, "Communism as an open political force is not dangerous in most of these countries. The danger lies in the fact that the nationalists think they can cooperate with the Communists as long as it suits them and then drop them."[59] The Ba'th Party, ever since its establishment, had been wary of the loyalties of the communists, believing that they were more beholden to the Soviet Union than to the dictates of Arab unity and anti-Zionism. Realizing this potential breech, Khalid Baqdash, upon his arrival in Damascus after attending the 20th Congress of the CPSU in Moscow, stated that "we the communists have always worked for the national union to preserve and defend the independence against foreign pacts and conspiracies. To realize the national union we stretch out our hands, as we have always done, to all parties and tendencies and in particular to the ASRP. We are ready to extend our hands to all nationals regardless of their parties, whether from the Nationalist Party or from the Populist Party."[60]

During the summer of 1956, the differences between the Ba'th Party and the Communist Party were more perceptible over the issue of union with Egypt. The only problem, from the American perspective, was that the Populists and Nationalists were as or more divided than ever, precluding the possibility of exploiting the subtle weakness exhibited by the leftists. In addition, the events surrounding the Suez crisis, including the "Iraqi coup" attempt, compelled the Ba'thists and communists to bury their differences for the time being in the face of a direct assault from the outside.

The Ghazzi cabinet resigned on June 2, 1956, after months of incessant internecine fighting between the various factions of the chamber that led to the resignations of several cabinet members in late-May. Quwatli first offered Lutfi al-Haffar the opportunity to form a government, but after vocal opposition from the Ba'th (supported by the army), the task of forming a government fell to Sabri al-'Asali.[61] This he accomplished, and on June 14, Prime Minister 'Asali announced his cabinet, which had a definite leftist orientation. The Ba'th had secured two portfolios, that of minister of foreign affairs with Salah al-Din Bitar and minister of national economy with Khalil Kallas.

Meanwhile, Soviet Foreign Minister Shepilov travelled to Damascus and met with Syrian officials from June 22–27, 1956. The visit was obviously an effort by the Kremlin to shore up the Soviet position in Syria in the wake of Syrian (and other Arab) recriminations against Moscow for issuing its equivocating statement of April 18 in which it offered to cooperate with the West for a Middle East peace settlement. While in the country, Shepilov expressed on numerous occasions the Soviet Union's support for Syria and its intention to continue providing financial and military aid as well as diplomatic support in the UN (i.e., a readiness to use its veto in the Security Council).[62] On July 3, Syria announced its recognition of communist China. The Soviet foreign minister was indeed successful in reestablishing Syrian confidence in the Middle East policy of the Soviet Union. On August 20, Syria signed a cultural agreement with the Soviets. A Soviet parliamentary delegation consisting of seventeen ministers arrived in Damascus on September 4, travelling across the countryside and visiting industrial and agricultural sites.[63] And on October 1, 1956, the Soviet news agency TASS opened an office in Damascus under the name Bulletin d'Information de L'Agence TASS Damas. There also was an increase in economic and trade agreements with the Eastern bloc countries as well as an intensified effort by the Czechs to outbid Western concerns to build a proposed oil refinery at Homs (an issue that would become salient in 1957).[64]

Quickly, however, a problem arose over the Ba'th's insistence that 'Asali include in his ministerial speech a statement proclaiming a "theoretical union" of Syria and Egypt open to other Arab countries who had not joined a Western sponsored defense pact, again in an attempt to isolate Iraq and possibly to insure, by placing themselves in the bosom of Nasser, a paramount position in the country in the face of any advances by the communists *and* conservatives.[65] The Ba'th ministers in the Chamber of Deputies threatened to resign if he refused, most likely forcing the downfall of his regime and a call for new elections that undoubtedly would have been dominated by the leftist and pro-Egyptian elements. Army officers under Sarraj supported the Ba'th position.[66] Accordingly, on June 27, 'Asali declared in parliament that "we shall embark on a consolidation of our ties with Egypt through immediate talks which we hope will lead to a common policy, to which the other liberated Arab countries will be invited to adhere, so that we may achieve a comprehensive Arab unity."[67] In keeping with the spirit of his statement, 'Asali, along with Bitar and Minister of State Muhammad Ayesh, travelled to Cairo on July 2 to speak with Nasser about the prospects of union.[68] Upon the conclusion of the meeting three days later, 'Asali announced the formation of a three-man ministerial committee (himself, Bitar, and Populist Party Minister of Interior Ahmad Qanbar) to conduct the unity negotiations with Egypt.[69] On the same day, the chamber adopted a resolution approving the plans for union.[70]

Nasser, however, was lukewarm about integrated union with Syria. He was not anxious to be burdened with the problems of the Syrian economy and felt that he would gain very little politically or militarily over and above what he was already enjoying without union. The Egyptian leader was also concerned about the reaction of the Saudis, who themselves might feel isolated by a union (because of the nature of their oil economy and political structure, the Saudis were in no way interested in joining a Syrian-Egyptian union — they were merely aligned with Egypt at this time because it suited them to do so vis-à-vis their relationship with Iraq).[71]

Nasser was a captive to his own rhetoric of generating enthusiasm throughout the Arab world for Arab unity and therefore was forced to drag his feet when the issue arose in specific terms. The Egyptian press started to intimate that unity at this time was not in the best interests of either country. Salah Salim was quoted in *al-Sha'b* of July 2 that "unity must be achieved in stages without wishful thinking." A July 7 *Akhbar al-Yawm* editorial stated that union was a "cherished dream requiring time and effort," and "if this generation is not ready for it than it will occur with the next or the one after that." The Syrian communists were not particularly thrilled about the idea of union with Egypt either, knowing Nasser's past history of brutal repression of the communists within his own country. Accordingly, the Damascus communist daily, *al-Sarkha*, printed on July 2 its doubts that Egypt was ready for union or suitably prepared, stating that "the two systems of government are not similar." It asked the question "how could we unite with Egypt whose system of government is still incomplete. . . . Egypt's President has been elected in a manner well known to the Syrian people and which reminds them of Adib al-Shishakli's elections." Ba'thist leader Akram al-Hawrani shot back on July 7, through his party's organ, *al-Ba'th*, that Syria was in danger of "foul play" from the likes of Israel, Britain, and Turkey, with the implication that it needed union with Egypt more now than ever in order to enhance the country's ability to withstand the imminent assault. The initiative was wholly that of the Syrians,[72] specifically the Ba'th, and apparently caught Nasser somewhat off-guard, especially since he was occupied for the most part with the evolving Suez crisis – this also meant, of course, that he had to handle the union question delicately in order not to alienate the Syrians, whose support he so desperately needed at that critical juncture. The other parties in Syria tended to give the Ba'th at least pro forma support for the union idea in order to gain some credit in the eyes of the Syrian public for espousing a very popular notion.

Nasser's lukewarmness for the idea, however, along with the acceleration of the Suez crisis, buried for the moment the plans for the proposed union, although public support for it in Syria increased tremendously following Nasser's nationalization of the Suez Canal Company in July and his country's stand against the combined British, French, Israeli attack in October–November. Nasser's nationalization was in response to Dulles' withdrawal of the American offer to help finance the Aswan High Dam project in Egypt, which in itself was an attempt to lure Egypt away from the Soviets after the arms deal in September 1955. Why Dulles withdrew the offer is the subject of some debate, but it was probably a combination of things: in response to Nasser's recognition of communist China, opposition in Congress to the offer from Israeli supporters and southern legislators whose economies would be hurt by increased cotton production in Egypt, and the realization that the secret Arab-Israeli peace efforts (the Anderson mission) had come to naught. The British and French, who jointly held the shares in the Suez Canal Company, saw the nationalization as the excuse they needed to get rid of Nasser, someone who they felt was in great measure responsible for their reduced status in the Middle East.

The nationalization was legal as long as the shareholders were compensated, which Egypt offered to do. But Britain and France concocted a series of false accusations in their desperate attempt to paint Egypt as an obstruction to peace. But Egypt successfully countered these claims. Dulles, meanwhile, made a futile attempt to arrange a peaceful resolution; futile because Britain and France wanted no part of it. Finally, in what may have been the last grand leftover of classic nineteenth century European imperialism, Britain and France seduced a willing Israel to invade Egypt, thereby providing the excuse the British and French were looking for, i.e., activating the Anglo-Egyptian treaty clause regarding defense of the Suez Canal that would allow the introduction of troops into Egyptian territory. The whole episode was tragic folly. The Egyptians put up a better-than-expected fight. The Eisenhower administration, although anything but enamored of Nasser by that point, furiously opposed the tripartite action against Egypt, coming as it was comtemporaneously with the Soviet invasion of Hungary. With pressure from the United States, as well as the Soviet Union, and with the ludicrousness of the venture exposed, the British and French humiliatingly withdrew, symbolically signalling the denouement of their colonial dominance. Nasser had won a tremendous political victory while losing in the battlefield. He had stood up to imperialism and Zionism, and he was now the most popular figure in the Arab world. The natural outcome accompanying this support for Nasser was the strengthened position of the Ba'th party in Syria and popular support for its foreign policy position.

Ba'th Consolidation and Suez

The Ba'th felt strong enough within the army at this time to force Chief of Staff Shuqayr to hand in his resignation on July 7, 1956. He was replaced by his deputy, General Tawfiq Nizam al-Din, who was generally considered to be pro-West but was much more amenable to leftist pressure and was characterized as an administrator/politician rather than a soldier.[73] Shuqayr followed a rather independent political line, neither consistently leftist nor conservative. This policy approach allowed him to maintain his position in the face of political turmoil in parliament and in the army, but it also prevented him from securing a bloc of support from any one group.

This only added to the trepidations of some conservative elements in Syria who felt that time was running out if they were to have any chance of reversing the leftist trend. A weak anti-leftist coalition was formed by the leader of the Arab Liberation Movement, Ma'mun al-Kuzbari, with the support of Munir al-'Ajlani's Constitutional Bloc and a "few independents."[74] This development led Dulles to make the following comments:

> We understand that conservative elements in Syria, dissatisfied with the present situation, are considering steps which might be taken to bring about an improvement. We are endeavoring to obtain more information about the activities of these conservative elements. . . . we will be happy to discuss the Syrian situation further with the Turkish authorities.[75]

It also might have led Dulles to conclude that the conservatives in Syria were stronger and more determined than they actually were, thus giving him reason to provide tacit support for Operation Straggle.

Any hope of success by the anti-leftist coalition was dashed by the Suez war and the disclosure of the "Iraqi plot." Anticipating the outbreak of hostilities, Jordan adhered to the Egyptian-Syrian defense pact on October 24, an act soon followed by the entrance of Syrian and Iraqi troops into Jordanian territory ostensibly to protect the Hashimite Kingdom from Israel. Jordan now became a full-fledged player in the contest between Egypt/Syria and Iraq, consequently becoming a player in the international arena as well, and would only emerge in the western camp after months of internal turmoil and direct intervention by the United States. During the Suez fighting itself, Sarraj had ordered the Iraq Petroleum Company's (IPC) pipelines running through the country cut, in defiance of assurances by the government that the flow of oil would continue. And symbolic of the growing influence of the Soviet Union in Syria, at the time of the hostilities at Suez, President Quwatli and his minister of defense were in Moscow visiting with Soviet authorities and most likely discussing additional Soviet military aid.[76]

The Eisenhower administration's assessment of the situation in Syria in the wake of Suez was bleak. It felt that the situation in Syria had to be corrected, with the growing implication that this could best be achieved through covert intervention. Dulles told Under Secretary of State Hoover on November 9, 1956, that his brother at the CIA felt that "Operation Straggle might be carried forward but when the British and French troops are out."[77] The implication was that the United States should unilaterally engage in covert operations aimed at removing the leftist Syrian regime, which was the objective of Operation Straggle. Allen Dulles concluded that:

> Syria is in a critical condition where a Communist Coup might be pulled off particularly if Moscow is able to infiltrate hard core Soviet organizers plus a nucleus of a military force. . . . An overthrow of the Syrian government, and even possibly further Soviet pressures on the present government, could result in a Syrian invitation to Moscow to send troops into Syria ostensibly to protect Syria from Israel. This would lead to Syria's becoming a Soviet base of operations in the area in support of Egypt. Syria thus presents a second vacuum into which the Soviet might move even more openly than in the case of Egypt and where there would be no UN force to cover the situation. Jordan is equally vulnerable but geographically less attractive to the Soviet.[78]

The deteriorating situation in Syria, from the American point of view, began to be associated on the policy level with some plan of action to fill the "vacuum" in the Middle East (before the Soviets did so) after the defeat of the British and French at Suez. Admiral Radford spoke in terms of applying action similar to that which the administration took in the Taiwan crisis, when a Joint Congressional Resolution was passed (January 29, 1955) authorizing the president to use American forces in defense of Formosa and the Pescadores.[79] Radford stated that "some form of Congressional Resolution would be necessary to put the Soviet Union on notice that there is a line beyond which they cannot go."[80] The president and his secretary of state seemed to agree and would subsequently formulate and issue in January 1957 what came to be known as the Eisenhower Doctrine, which thrust the United States directly into the vagaries of inter-Arab politics through the professed vehicle of blocking the advance of "international communism" in the area. It gave the impression of a forward policy in the Middle East. It was also intended to remove some of the criticism the administration had been receiving in the press and from Congress, as well as the consternation of its European and Middle East allies, over the lack of a coherent Middle East policy. The doctrine, however, would involve the United States in a whole different set of problems regarding Syria and the Middle East.

Notes

1. In talks with Dulles in Paris, British officials quoted him as saying that Syria was the nearest thing in the Middle East to a Soviet satellite. (British Embassy-Paris, October 26, 1955, FO 371/115469, PRO.) In August 1955, the Syrian government approved the appointment of a Soviet military attache to Damascus and raised Soviet diplomatic representation in Syria to embassy status in November.

2. 260th Meeting of the NSC, October 6, 1955, Ann Whitman File, Dulles-Herter Series, Box 7, DDEL.

3. Ibid.

4. Ibid.

5. Memorandum of Conversation (October 18, 1955), October 21, 1955, Microform Reading Room, microfiche 217D (1981), Library of Congress.

6. Department of State *Bulletin,* October 4, 1955, p. 604. This comment also reveals Dulles' increasing frustration with Israel, since he was obviously referring to it when he stated Egypt felt itself "endangered."

7. Steven L. Spiegel, *The Other Arab-Israeli Conflict: Making America's Middle East Policy, from Truman to Reagan* (Chicago: University of Chicago Press, 1985), p. 66.

8. 262nd Meeting of the NSC, October 20, 1955, Ann Whitman File, Dulles-Herter Series, Box 7, DDEL.

9. For a description of this initiative, see Spiegel, pp. 66–71.

10. Quoted in Spiegel, p. 67; also see British Embassy-Paris, October 26, 1955, FO 371/115469, PRO. Foreshadowing the formulation of and rationale behind the Eisenhower Doctrine, Dulles commented at this time that it

would be easier for the administration to act by way of a congressional resolution, which only needed a simple majority in Congress. (Ibid.)

11. Record of Meeting between Mr. MacMillan and Mr. Dulles at Geneva, November 9, 1955, FO 371/115469, PRO.

12. 260th Meeting of the NSC, October 6, 1955, Ann Whitman File, Dulles-Herter Series, Box 7, DDEL.

13. British Prime Minister Anthony Eden, a leading voice against appeasement, wrote in March 1956 to Eisenhower: "There is no doubt that the Russians are resolved to liquidate the Baghdad Pact. In this undertaking Nasser is supporting them and I suspect that his relations with the Soviets are much closer than he admits to us. Certainly we should accept, I think, that a policy of appeasement will bring nothing in Egypt. Our best chance is to show that it pays to be our friends." (British Foreign Office, March 5, 1956, FO 371/121271, PRO.) With the implication that it does not pay to be "our" enemies.

14. For text of statement, see Magnus, p. 166.

15. Statement made by Admiral Radford upon visit to Pakistan, American Embassy, Karachi (from Radford) to Department of the Army, December 23, 1955, Microform Reading Room, microfiche 354B (1981), Library of Congress.

16. United Kingdom Delegation to the Meeting of Foreign Ministers at Geneva, October 28, 1955, FO 371/115469, PRO.

17. For example, see British Embassy-Baghdad (no. 784), October 5, 1955, FO 371/115954, PRO; British Embassy-Baghdad (no. 785), October 5, 1955, FO 371/115954, PRO; British Embassy-Washington, October 6, 1955, FO 371/115954, PRO; British Foreign Office, October 7, 1955, FO 371/115954, PRO; British Foreign Office, October 8, 1955, FO 371/115954, PRO; British Foreign Office, October 10, 1955, FO 371/115954, PRO; British Embassy-Baghdad, October 12, 1955, FO 371/115954, PRO; British Foreign Office, October 20, 1955, FO 371/115954, PRO; American Embassy, Damascus, talk with Mikhail Ilyan, October 24, 1955, State Dept. Post Files, Cairo Embassy, 1955, RG84, NARA; British Foreign Office, end of October, 1955, FO 371/115954, PRO.

18. See American Embassy-Damascus, October 24, 1955, State Dept. Post Files, Cairo Embassy, 1955, RG84, NARA. For U.S., UK and Iraqi discussion concerning action against Syria, see Telegram From the Embassy in Iraq to the Department of State, October 4, 1955, *FRUS,* pp. 543–544; Telegram From the Department of State to the Embassy in Iraq, October 6, 1955, *FRUS,* pp. 545–546; Telegram From the Embassy in Iraq to the Department of State, October 11, 1955, *FRUS,* pp. 548–549; Telegram From the Embassy in Syria to the Department of State, January 8, 1956, *FRUS,* pp. 563–564; Telegram From the Department of State to the Embassy in Syria, January 13, 1956, *FRUS,* pp. 365; Memorandum of Conversation, White

House, Washington, January 30, 1956, *FRUS,* pp. 567–568; British Embassy-Washington, October 27, 1955, FO 371/115954, PRO; British Foreign Office, October 28, 1955, FO 371/115954, PRO; Levant Department, February 24, 1956, FO 371/121858, PRO; British Embassy-Teheran, March 10, 1956, FO 371/121858, PRO; British Embassy-Ankara, March 13, 1956, FO 371/121858; and Lloyd to Eden, March 15, 1956, FO 371/121858, PRO.

19. The British would make their own demarches to Ankara to persuade them not to intervene in Syria. After one such meeting, Prime Minister Menderes promised that in the event of an Iraqi move, Turkey would not intervene across the Syrian border. (British Embassy-Ankara, March 13, 1956, FO 371/121858, PRO.)

20. Memorandum of Conversation, White House, Washington, January 30, 1956, *FRUS,* pp. 567–568.

21. British Embassy-Baghdad, October 5, 1955, FO 371/115954, PRO; 260th Meeting of the NSC, October 6, 1955, Ann Whitman File, Dulles-Herter Series, Box 7, DDEL.

22. Telegram From the Embassy in Syria to the Department of State, January 8, 1956, *FRUS,* pp. 563–564.

23. Telegram From the Department of State to the Embassy in Syria, October 25, 1955, *FRUS,* pp. 557–558.

24. Telegram From the Department of State to the Embassy in Syria, January 13, 1956, *FRUS,* p. 565.

25. British Embassy-Washington, October 27, 1955, FO 371/115954, PRO.

26. Conversation between Quwatli and British Ambassador Gardener, British Embassy-Damascus, November 17, 1955, FO 371/115955, PRO.

27. British Foreign Office, October 28, 1955, FO 371/115954, PRO.

28. Ibid.

29. A British official remarked that with the collapse of Alpha, the West was "left without a Middle East policy of any kind," and accurately predicted that the Israelis would become more paranoid and desperate and would soon feel compelled to launch an attack against the Arabs or be "slowly strangled by the unreconciled Arab world, which grows stronger every day in wealth, self-confidence and Soviet arms." (British Foreign Office, March 10, 1956, FO 371/121235, PRO.) Also, see Dietl, p. 96; Neff, pp. 130–131, 133–136, 153, 168–169, 177, 194–195, 197–198; Kenneth Love, Suez: The Twice Fought War (London: McGraw-Hill, 1969), pp. 303–310; and, Eli Ginzberg to Eisenhower, July 17, 1956, Ann Whitman File, Dulles-Herter Series, Box 5, DDEL.

30. Memorandum of Conversation, White House, Washington, January 30, 1956, *FRUS,* pp. 567–568.

31. Communism in the Middle East, Operations Coordinating Board, January 26, 1956, White House Office, National Security Staff: Papers, 1948–1961: OCB Central Files, Box 77, DDEL.

32. "The major impact of the Soviet foreign economic program . . . was in the Middle East, where the Soviets were able to exploit the long-festering Arab-Israeli problem, the Anglo-Egyptian dispute over the Suez Canal, and widespread anticolonial sentiment to strengthen their position in the region." Burton I. Kaufman, *Trade and Aid: Eisenhower's Foreign Economic Policy 1953–1961* (Baltimore: The Johns Hopkins University Press, 1982), p. 65. For more information on the seminal 20th Party Congress of the CPSU, see David J. Dallin, *Soviet Foreign Policy After Stalin* (New York: J.B. Lippincott Company, 1961), pp. 322–334 ("The Twentieth Party Congress and Foreign Affairs").

33. Communism in the Middle East, OCB.

34. Ibid.

35. Quoted in ibid. For the Communist Party's viewpoint prior to Stalin's death, see Khalid Baqdash's speech to the plenary session of the Central Command of the Communist Party in Syria and Lebanon held in January 1951 — see Khalid Baqdash, "Document: For the Successful Struggle for Peace, National Independence, and Democracy We Must Resolutely Turn Toward the Workers and the Peasants," *Middle East Journal* (Spring 1953), pp. 206–221.

36. For text of statement, see "Statement of U.S.S.R. Foreign Ministry on Anglo-American Measures in the Near and Middle East," no date, FO 371/121291; also see *The Times* of February 14, 1956.

37. *The Christian Science Monitor*, April 7, 1956.

38. Ibid. (writer was Joseph C. Harsch).

39. For text of statement, see *The Times*, April 18, 1956; and FO 371/121291, PRO.

40. Progress Report on United States Objectives and Policies with respect to the Near East (NSC 5428), Operations Coordinating Board, May 17, 1956, White House Office, National Security Council Staff: Papers, 1948–1961: OCB Central Files, Box 78, DDEL; also, see British Foreign Office, April 23, 1956, FO 371/121243, PRO.

41. In April, Eisenhower told Dulles that he wanted "to settle differences" with Saudi Arabia and speculated if there was any way the United States could "flatter or compliment" King Sa'ud. (Call from Eisenhower to Dulles, April 10, 1956, Ann Whitman File, Ann Whitman Diary Series, Box 8, DDEL.)

42. Letter From Ambassador in Syria (Moose) to the Assistant Secretary of State for Near Eastern, South Asian, and African Affairs (Allen), June 7, 1956, *FRUS*, pp. 572–573.

43. British Embassy-Paris, May 3, 1956, FO 371/121273, PRO.

44. Instruction From the Department of State to the Embassy in Syria, September 21, 1956, *FRUS*, pp. 591–593.

45. For more on the Saudi-British difficulties over Buraimi and Oman, see subsequent chapter.

46. Memorandum for the President from Dulles, March 28, 1956, Ann Whitman File, Dulles-Herter Series, Box 5, DDEL.

47. The resolution condemned Israel for the attack and warned it not to repeat the offense; however, it was silent on Syria's request to expel Israel from the UN, for UN sanctions against Israel, or for Israeli compensation. It did mention a Syrian infraction of the armistice agreement, something Israel wanted included in the text. (Lodge to Eisenhower, January 23, 1956, Ann Whitman File, Administration Series, Box 24, DDEL.)

48. Shuqayr responded by saying that accusations directed at him were vicious rumors and stated that "the factors which motivated the dissemination of these rumors are the same that instigated particular elements to conspire and contemplate a military coup in Syria with the sole purpose of changing the liberal policy of the country." (*al-Ra'i al-'Am,* December 28, 1955.)

49. As Amos Kenan writes, Israel pursued a policy of "making the West always choose between us and them [the Arabs], and if it is not us, we'll create enough trouble to make sure that it must be us." Quoted in Shibley Telhami, "Israeli Foreign Policy: A Static Strategy in a Changing World, *Middle East Journal,* vol. 44 (1990), p. 401.

50. Seale, p. 257.

51. British Embassy-Damascus, February 17, 1956, FO 371/121864, PRO.

52. Ibid.

53. British Embassy-Cairo, February 20, 1956, FO 371/121242, PRO.

54. British Embassy-Damascus, February 28, 1956, FO 371/121858, PRO.

55. Ibid.

56. Ibid.

57. Mikhail Ilyan was reported to be the most insistent on this point. On the other end of the spectrum, Akram al-Hawrani "bitterly objected" to the inclusion of any provision for combatting communism under the pretext that "certain international considerations do not permit such a thing." (*al-Nasr,* March 1, 1956; also, *al-Akhbar,* March 2, 1956.) According to a member of the ad hoc committee of the National Charter, Hawrani did say that the Ba'th's principles did not "harmonize" with the Communist Party's and thought that communism should be combatted in Syria as a social doctrine, in other words, not as an issue in the regional or international arenas. (Ibid.)

58. Department of State, Office of Intelligence Research, Intelligence Report No. 7282, "Political Trends in Syria," July 2, 1956, RG59, NA.

59. *NYT,* April 4, 1956.

60. DA Intelligence Report, April 5, 1956, Entry 85, Intell. Doc. File, 2014670, RG 319 (Records of the Army Staff), NARA.

61. Torrey, p. 307.

62. British Embassy-Damascus, June 28, 1956, FO 371/121867, PRO; for texts of speeches by Shepilov while in Syria, see DA Intelligence Report, June 22, 1956, Entry 85, Intell. Doc. File, R-473-56, RG319, NARA.

63. British Embassy-Damascus, September 6, 1956, FO 371/121867, PRO.

64. For more on the Homs oil refinery issue, see Memorandum From the Assistant Secretary of State for Near Eastern, South Asian, and African Affairs (Allen) to the Under Secretary of State (Hoover), July 16, 1956, *FRUS,* pp. 582–586; Memorandum From the Assistant Secretary of State for Near Eastern, South Asian, and African Affairs (Rountree) to the Acting Secretary of State, August 31, 1956, *FRUS,* pp. 588–589; and, Memorandum From the Assistant Secretary of State for Near Eastern, South Asian, and African Affairs (Rountree) to the Acting Secretary of State, September 17, 1956, *FRUS,* pp. 589–591.

65. British Embassy-Damascus, June 20, 1956, FO 371/121858, PRO.

66. Ibid.

67. *al-Ba'th* (Damascus), June 28, 1956, as quoted in Seale, p. 258.

68. There was a report from Iraqi officials that Sarraj had visited Nasser in Cairo several days before the 'Asali delegation arrived urging the Egyptian president that he be allowed to overthrow the present regime, but Nasser apparently refused because he felt it was not needed since the 'Asali government was following a pro-Egyptian policy anyway. Nasser also believed that a coup would be destabilizing, possibly inviting outside intervention, especially considering the tense Suez situation. (British Embassy-Damascus, July 3, 1956, FO 371/121858, PRO.) There is no corroborating evidence of this report, but a possible reason for Sarraj's demarche could have been that he was concerned about increasing communist and Soviet influence in the country (his approach was made after Soviet Foreign Minister Shepilov's visit to Syria, June 22–27, 1956) and knew that Nasser might be sympathetic to any attempts to check their advance.

69. Seale, p. 258.

70. For text of resolution, see Seale, p. 258.

71. The Saudi government reportedly sent a letter to Egypt protesting possible union with Syria. (British Embassy-Cairo, July 14, 1956, FO 371/121864, PRO.)

72. British Embassy-Cairo, July 11, 1956, FO 371/121864, PRO; British Embassy-Cairo, July 14, 1956, FO 371/121864, PRO.

73. British Embassy-Damascus, July 8, 1956, FO 371/121858, PRO.

74. Torrey, p. 312.

75. Instruction From the Department of State to the Embassy in Syria, September 21, 1956, *FRUS,* pp. 591–593.

76. In attendance at a meeting with Quwatli were such Soviet military luminaries as Defense Minister Marshal Zhukov, Chief of Staff Marshal Sokolovsky, and Assistant Chief of Staff General Antonov. (British Embassy-Moscow, November 5, 1956, FO 371/121867, PRO.)

77. Call from John Foster Dulles to Hoover, November 9, 1956, Memoranda of Telephone Conversations, Dulles Papers, DDEL.

78. Memorandum for the Acting Secretary of State from Allen Dulles, November 10, 1956, Microform Reading Room, on microfiche, Library of Congress.

79. Memorandum of Conversation, Department of State, Washington, November 10, 1956, *FRUS,* pp. 597–598.

80. Ibid.

7

Prelude to the 1957 Crisis

The focus of political attention in Syria by 1957 was in the foreign policy arena. With the pro-Nasser hysteria in the Arab world following the Suez war the most popular political positions could not help but fall within this sphere. The leftists continued to promote anti-imperialist and anti-Zionist themes. They had, however, no cogent domestic political program and therefore relied on doctrinaire enunciations having little applicability to reality. In addition, they still had to rely on individuals who by anyone's definition were rich feudal landowners (like Khalid al-'Azm); therefore, they conveniently chose to concentrate on foreign policy issues. Events in 1957, such as the enunciation of the Eisenhower Doctrine in January (passed by Congress in March), the application of the doctrine in April in support of Jordan's King Hussein, Israel's reluctance to withdraw from the Sinai without strong American assurances,[1] the Gulf of Aqaba question,[2] and finally, the 1957 American-Syrian crisis itself, gave the Syrian people plenty of reason to support the popular foreign policy platform espoused by the leftists.

The leftist elements in Syria used the post-Suez atmosphere to their advantage in order to consolidate power. They also benefitted from and exploited the November 24, 1956, announcement of the discovery of the British-Iraqi plot to overthrow the regime (Operation Straggle).[3] On December 2, 1956, the government charged and arrested those who were accused of participating in the plot, although most of the conspirators had already fled the country (which considerably depleted the leadership of pro-West elements in Syria). On December 11, the Syrian government, spearheaded by Ba'thist leader Akram al-Hawrani and Khalid al-'Azm, announced the formation of a parliamentary National Front pledged to follow an anti-West, neutralist, and pan-Arab policy opposing "plots against the State, imperialism, and the Baghdad Pact."[4] The great majority of deputies in parliament supported the National Front, which signaled the formation of a strong left-wing coalition that would support the country's Ba'thist-inspired foreign policy and provide the unity necessary to withstand the danger posed by outside powers.

The result of this political maneuvering in Syria was that by the time the Eisenhower Doctrine was announced in January 1957, the Syrian government, in the foreign policy arena, had already solidified its official neutralist line with implied hostility to the United States. There could be only one reaction to the Eisenhower Doctrine: rejection.[5] As far as the Syrians were concerned, the doctrine was totally inappropriate because it focused on what Washington saw as the major threat to *its* interests in the Middle East (i.e., the expansion of Soviet influence) and not on what the Arabs perceived to be *their* main problem — Israel. The only aggression the Arabs had experienced of late was that of Britain, France, and Israel at Suez, and a covert operation in Syria sponsored by the British and the Iraqis — nothing emanating from communist or Soviet sources. In addition, any regional interpretation of the doctrine concluded that it was anti-Nasser, and thus contrary to the popular wave of support in the Arab world for Egypt in the wake of Suez. To the Syrians, the doctrine was a unilateral action by the United States in its attempt to assume the "imperialist" mantle of Britain and France, and with the recent American interventions in Iran and Guatemala fresh in the minds of Syrian leaders, the next assault would emanate from Washington.

It was symbolic of the lack of solidarity within the National Front, however, that the reaction of leading Syrians to the Eisenhower Doctrine was mixed — they did not know whether to reject it outright or leave the door open for possible compromise.[6] With the expressed aim of the doctrine targeting "international communism," many Syrians of known leftist orientation proclaimed to the world that their country was not communist and was in no danger of becoming communist. One of the founding members of the Ba'th Party, Michel 'Aflaq, stated in early 1956 that "communism is strange to Arabs just as the capitalist system is strange to them. They will not embrace communism just as they do not embrace capitalism. . . ."[7] They did not want the Eisenhower administration to make the faulty assumption that Syria had fallen within the Soviet orbit.

The conservatives in Syria, however, had not given up hope of a return to power. Despite the paralytic divisiveness within the conservative opposition (between the Populists and the Nationalists, and between the right-wing and left-wing factions in each of the two parties), the year was marked by several attempts to force a showdown with the leftist regime.

The Showdown in Syria

The Eisenhower Doctrine would not be the vehicle of return for the right-wing elements in Syria as it had been for pro-West forces in Jordan in April 1957 or Lebanon in 1958 — it couldn't be. Instead, the first challenge of the conservatives came with the trial and sentencing of those accused of conspiring with foreign powers in the "Iraqi plot." The military trial began in Damascus on

January 8, 1957, in which forty-seven Syrian political figures stood accused (eighteen in absentia). The president of the court-martial proceedings was a man regarded in the West as a communist sympathizer, Colonel 'Afif al-Bizri, who would also figure prominently later in the year. The trial was exploited by the regime to further weaken the conservative forces, this time backed by a vociferous mob and by the press, both emotionally charged by the prospect of crowning their victory over foreign intrigue by humiliating their lackeys. On February 26, eleven Syrians and one Lebanese were sentenced to death (six of them in absentia), three were acquitted, and thirty were given prison sentences.[8] The Iraqi government approached the United States to intercede with the Syrians on behalf of the accused, who had been subsidized by the Iraqis and were generally in favor of union with Iraq, but the State Department, which did not to appear to be interfering in Syrian affairs, used it as an opportunity to find out how much influence its new ally in the region, King Sa'ud of Saudi Arabia, actually had in Damascus.

For two years the Eisenhower administration had worked long and hard to recruit King Sa'ud as a counterpoise to Nasser in the Middle East in order to limit Soviet/communist influence in the region. "Winning over" Sa'ud had essentially been a corollary to the Eisenhower Doctrine. The administration was able to announce Sa'ud's conversion to the pro-West camp upon the king's dramatic visit to the United States in early 1957.[9]

One of the objectives of the Eisenhower Doctrine was to block the alliance Nasser had built to isolate Iraq, then the only pro-West and Arab Baghdad Pact member. To do this, the Americans sought to isolate Nasser, then at the zenith of his popularity in the Arab world following the Suez war — and to halt any further increase in Soviet influence in the Middle East. To accomplish this task, they had to find an Arab leader who could rival Nasser in prestige and who could convince some of the other Arab states to become more pro-West, if not join the Baghdad Pact outright. Because of Saudi Arabia's growing oil wealth and its central position in the Islamic world, the Eisenhower administration chose Sa'ud to be this rival to Nasser and systematically set about augmenting his stature in the region.

The Syrian trial verdicts afforded the United States an opportunity to see if Sa'ud was true to his word. On March 3, 1957, the United States Embassy in Jedda reminded Sa'ud of the discussions he had had in Washington about the dangers of communist influence in Syria. The trial proceedings and verdicts were proof, according to the White House, that Syria was quickly being entrapped in the Soviet snare.[10] The king favorably responded by promising to do what he could to commute the death sentences. Three days later, the Syrian government announced that the death sentences of the five in custody had been commuted to life imprisonment.

It seems as though Sa'ud's intervention had been the decisive factor, and no doubt it was a key element, but the Syrian government had also been under pressure from many Arab leaders appealing for clemency for the accused. Syrian leaders such as Defense Minister Khalid al-'Azm and Prime Minister Sabri al-'Asali, had also not lost sight of the fact that they did not want their country to appear to be a "communist-dominated" state, something the Soviets were interested in as well, since they did not want to bait the United States into applying the Eisenhower Doctrine. The Syrian leadership was also sensitive to the prospects of retribution carried out by the families and friends on behalf of the more prominent among the accused.[11] For these reasons, commutation probably would have been decreed without Sa'ud's intervention. But whatever the case, the State Department came away from this episode with the idea that Sa'ud did indeed carry weight in Syria and the rest of the Arab world. It was probably more than he actually deserved.

Further apparent evidence of Sa'ud's new-found commitment to the United States, to which the Syrian conservative opposition was paying particular attention, came at a four-power meeting between the leaders of Jordan, Egypt, Syria, and Saudi Arabia held in Cairo in late February 1957. Two of the topics under discussion were Sa'ud's visit to Washington and how to respond to the Eisenhower Doctrine. Arab correspondents covering the conference reported that Sa'ud had refused to sit at the same table with Khalid al-'Azm, who, as a result, absented himself with a diplomatic illness. Sa'ud also insisted that the Syrian foreign minister, the Ba'thist leader Salah al-Din Bitar, be excluded from top-level meetings.[12] The United States Embassy in Cairo also reported that strong differences arose over the wording of a joint communique, whose first draft Sa'ud rejected, and at one point he reportedly "thumped the table saying he looked westward while at least Syria looked eastward."[13] Jordan's King Hussein supported Sa'ud.[14] In the end, however, under pressure from Nasser, Sa'ud agreed to wording in the final communique that reflected Nasser's neutrality and said nothing about the threat of communism in the area.

Sa'ud's position in the Arab world at the time rested on his ability to persuade the United States to force Israel into making concessions regarding withdrawal from the Sinai, a solution to the Suez Canal sovereignty question, to the Gulf of Aqaba dispute, and to the Palestinian refugee problem; success would have significantly improved Sa'ud's standing in the region. Sa'ud informed the conference members in Cairo that he had secured American support for Israeli withdrawal, recognition of Egyptian sovereignty over the Suez Canal, and a canal solution based on UN Security Council resolutions. So when Eisenhower personally intervened to pressure Israel to withdraw from the Sinai in early March, there was much more at stake for the administration than simply trying to uphold the authority of the United Nations; it was part of the administration's plan to build up Sa'ud's prestige and popularity in the Middle East so that he could more effectively pursue American interests.[15]

In Cairo following the four-power conference, an American diplomat remarked, "If after this meeting [the] United States doesn't fulfill what Saud thinks are its promises, the King could react very dangerously. He has staked his reputation and honor on [the] United States and could switch completely if he feels betrayed."[16] The United States managed the Israeli withdrawal from the Sinai; it did little else. The conference also showed that Sa'ud was still ultimately subordinate to Nasser, or more to the point, to Nasser's popularity in the Arab world and his ability to cause problems for the king in Saudi Arabia. Sa'ud succumbed to Nasser's pressure regarding the wording of the final communique, something that would presage Sa'ud's continued unwillingness to depart from the Arab nationalist line — a vital element that helped shape events surrounding the 1957 American-Syrian crisis.

Moving Against Sarraj

Despite apparent cracks in the armor of the American-Saudi relationship, the conservative opposition in Syria was encouraged by Sa'ud's actions. This despite the fact that the leftist regime seemed to have consolidated its position. For example, on March 17, 1957, the Syrian government approved a contract with a Czechoslovakian firm after a long bidding war with an Anglo-American concern called Procon to build an oil refinery in Syria. The offer was made primarily on anti-West politics, as many of the leftist politicians readily admitted. The debates in the Chamber of Deputies over the awarding of the contract and the terms of the contract were often heated and split along conservative and leftist lines. Their was a particularly "violent dispute" over the issue in late February between Akram Hawrani and Ahmad Qanbar (of the right-wing branch of the Populist Party), with Qanbar pointing out the economic deficiencies of the Czech offer and the inferiority of its equipment.[17] Hawrani's retort was to emphasize the political aspects of the issue, which clearly demonstrated how East-West politics became entangled in what should have been a strictly internal economic concern. The United States strongly considered breaking precedent by offering to subsidize Procon so that it could lower its bid below the Czech offer.[18] Before the United States could act, however, the contract was awarded to the Czechs.

The conservatives in Syria, however, saw as positive signs Sa'ud's performance at the conference in Cairo, the commutation of some of the death sentences, and the fact that leftist politicians and army officers in Syria continued to deny that Syria was becoming a communist state. Allen Dulles commented that these signs were "evidence of rejection within Syria of the increasing trend toward a decidedly leftist, pro-Soviet government and forces within the country which have been basically anti-leftist apparently took heart."[19] The Eisenhower Doctrine was also interpreted by pro-West elements in Syria (and throughout the Middle East) as a sign that the United States was finally going to give them more then just palliative support. Indeed, Syria was high on the minds of Dulles and Eisenhower when they formulated the doctrine.[20] The stage seemed to be set for a move by the conservatives — with support from external sources.

The "move" would come in the form of action within the army against the head of Syrian intelligence, Colonel 'Abd al-Hamid Sarraj. The opening salvo was fired in early March 1957 when, according to the Beirut daily *Le Soir*, Akram al-Hawrani attempted to replace Ma'mun al-Kuzbari (head of the Arab Liberation Movement, the party of former President Adib al-Shishakli)[21] with a Ba'thist at the Ministry of Social Affairs, which controlled the trade union movement.[22] The ALM shot back on March 13 by publishing an article accusing leftist elements in the government of violating censorship regulations imposed under martial law during the Suez episode.[23] On March 15, Lt. Colonel Amin Nafuri (of the army general staff), with the support of the ALM and other sympathetic officers, put together a transfer list for certain army personnel in "key" posts in an attempt to remove leftist officers from "positions of strength."[24] At the head of the list was a transfer order for Sarraj. Chief of Staff Nizam al-Din subsequently approved and signed the transfer list. According to several reports, President Quwatli also supported the action, ostensibly out of resentment against army interference in civil affairs and as a result of the leftists' repeated attempts to replace him. Reflecting this stand, the right-wing Damascus press began printing articles on March 19 praising Quwatli for his leadership.

On March 16, all Syrian officers off duty in Amman, Jordan, who were generally pro-Sarraj, were summoned back to their units.[25] The army units in the north also tended to support Sarraj while those in the south toward the Jordanian border tended to be anti-Sarraj. The Pakistani legation in Damascus, which generally relied on the American embassy for its information, reported that Sarraj was offered first the job of military attache in Moscow and then a post in Cairo, but he refused both.[26] Supporting Sarraj were Hawrani and Khalid al-'Azm, and they in turn demanded the resignation of Nizam al-Din.[27]

Another anti-leftist group of Syrian officers, led by Colonel Umar Qab-bani, was also reported to be anti-Sarraj and willing to move against him.[28] This potential cabal was known as the "Damascene Group." The Eisenhower administration preferred this group over the Nafuri one because its leaders were said to have been determined to keep the army out of politics. The administration also realized, however. that any hope of success against Sarraj depended upon the formation of a coalition between the two groups, and it subsequently undertook "strong efforts" to do just that. But characteristic divisions between the two army groups hindered cooperative efforts despite having similar goals.

Sarraj, known as one of the shrewdest players in Syrian politics, lived up to his reputation. Apparently, one of the primary aims of the anti-Sarraj groups was to expose Sarraj as the real power in Syria, provoking a confrontation which would bring on a "decisive showdown."[29] But Sarraj astutely sensed what was going on and decided not to play into the hands of the opposition, and consequently put up "surprisingly little resistance to his transfer."[30] Instead, he encouraged other Ba'thist officers on the transfer list to resist more openly and took some necessary military measures, such as the recalling of the off-duty officers in Jordan. There were also reports that pro-Sarraj factions in the Syrian army had surrounded the two chief towns in the Jebel Druze area with tanks[31] – a logical maneuver since the Druze had frequently acted as a starting point for anti-regime action (including the failed Iraqi coup attempt in 1956) and a depot for arms smuggled across the Jordanian border. Sarraj was also secure in the knowledge that Ba'thist officers were in control of the armored units at the Qatana and Qabun military camps on the outskirts of Damascus, whereas the other large armored division, controlled by the Nafuri group, was situated at Dera'a on the Jordanian border and therefore in a tactically weaker position.[32]

What Sarraj did was covertly manipulate the situation by not overtly manipulating the situation – he did not submit to a showdown. As Allen Dulles wrote on March 22: "One major problem in the current behind-the-scenes struggle is the lack of a sufficient provocation for a decisive showdown . . . " and that Ba'thist forces "apparently feel that prolonging the deadlock will result in a compromise solution favorable to their interests and are making no move toward a showdown."[33] Even if their was a showdown it is unlikely the anti-Sarraj forces could have triumphed, due primarily to the lack of coordination between the Nafuri and Damascene factions. Their cooperation would have been a prerequisite for Quwatli to come out into the open any more than he already had by possibly calling for the formation of a new cabinet, which, after Sarraj's no-play maneuver, would have been another attempt to force that elusive "showdown." Instead, a compromise solution was reached as the days passed and the raison d'etre of the anti-Sarraj forces faded. *Le Soir* reported that Egyptian General 'Abd al-Hakim Amir arrived surreptitiously in Damascus to broker the compromise, allowing some of the officer transfers to take place but keeping Sarraj at the head of the Deuxieme Bureau.[34]

The role of the United States in this episode is unclear. Certainly the Eisenhower administration was alarmed over the situation in Syria and would look very favorably on action that would lead to the removal of Sarraj and the ascendancy of more moderate elements in the army that would allow Quwatli and 'Asali to pursue a more pro-West policy. One version of the origin of the anti-Sarraj action had King Sa'ud responsible; another had King Hussein instigating the action following the discovery of a plot against his life organized by Sarraj's Deuxieme Bureau.[35] No evidence has been found that lends credence to either assertion. If these claims were true, the United States probably played some role in the affair. It is interesting to note that during the episode, the American military attache in Damascus sent detailed information to Washington on the Syrian "order of battle," including sketch maps of all the important Syrian army camps and depots, the dispositions of various units, and a sketch of the important Qatana military base outside Damascus showing the concentration of artillery units.[36] This might have been routine, but it also would have been useful information for the anti-Sarraj forces.

If the United States did "discreetly" encourage the anti-Sarraj factions, the timing of the incident coinciding with James Richards' tour of the Middle East was most likely not an accident (Richards' mission was ostensibly to explain the Eisenhower Doctrine to Arab leaders in an attempt to gain converts and offer various sums of economic aid intended to help countries resist communism).[37] Indeed, the leftist and communist press in Syria highlighted this point, alleging that this crisis was brought on by the Richards mission. The Syrian government had informed the United States Embassy in Damascus that if Richards wanted to visit Syria he would be welcome; however, the United States informed the Syrians that Richards would only travel to Syria with a formal invitation from the Syrian government. None would be forthcoming.

It is certainly not difficult to imagine the Eisenhower administration supporting an army coup against Sarraj that would install a government more disposed to cooperate with the United States. The United States could then replace the Soviet Union as Syria's patron by offering economic and military aid as stipulated under the doctrine. This would reduce, for the time being, Soviet influence in the Middle East; additionally, it would isolate and weaken Nasser, possibly forcing him to come to terms with the United States. Syrian leaders seemed to be thinking along the same line as the pro-government press focused its attacks on the Eisenhower Doctrine, with 'Asali commenting at one point that Syria would not tolerate any American attempt to impose the doctrine on it.[38]

If this was the administration's intent, and even if the anti-Sarraj forces were successful, there is no assurance that Syria would have overnight turned to the United States. The majority of Syrians were still vehemently anti-West and pro-Nasser despite the machinations at the top of the political pyramid. There were still powerful civilian leaders such as Hawrani and 'Azm who had strong ties with portions of the army and certain areas of the country. In addition, once in effective power the anti-Sarraj leaders could have followed the path of many of their predecessors and become instantly lukewarm to the ideas espoused prior to the coup and the external actors who had supported their effort.

Even though the move by the anti-Sarraj forces was unsuccessful in its ultimate aim (i.e., getting rid of Sarraj), American and British officials expressed some satisfaction that the leftist elements in Syria got their "wings clipped" somewhat. Ambassador Moose remarked that the surprising thing about the whole incident was that after having failed to oust Sarraj, Nizam and Quwatli retained their positions, presumably indicating that the anti-Sarraj forces were still a viable commodity. He also stated that the Ba'thists were shaken a bit by what they found out to be less than overwhelming support both in and out of the army.[39] It was clear that the cracks in the politico-military structure in Syria had only been papered over, a fact which would become more apparent as the year progressed.

The May 1957 Syrian By-elections

The next trial of strength in Syria occurred with the by-elections to fill four vacancies in the Chamber of Deputies caused by the convictions in the Iraqi conspiracy trial.[40] The elections were scheduled for May 4, but the conservatives, led by Populist party member Ahmad Qanbar, precipitated a parliamentary battle over the issue of martial law, which had been in place since the Suez war. The legitimate charge levelled against the government was that it was using martial law to rid itself and the army of its opponents and suppress the anti-government press. The right-wing elements were understandably concerned that the government would again exploit martial law conditions in order to secure victory for its candidates in the by-elections. On April 8, Prime Minister 'Asali responded to the charges saying that martial law was needed because of the dangers Syria faced from "imperialist aggression."[41] The government had been reporting sightings of unidentified aircraft flying over Syrian airspace dropping leaflets inciting the public against the regime. The opposition accused the government of inventing these aircraft in order to justify its continuation of martial law. There were also reports of Turkish troop movements along the Syrian border; again the riposte by the opposition being that they were convenient fabrications.[42] Although events would soon provide 'Asali with ample justification for the continuation of martial law later in the month during the Jordanian crisis, the government agreed to lift it in the four areas where the seats were vacated: Damascus, Homs, Suwayda, and the Jabal al-'Arab.

Coalitions were formed prior to the elections pitting the conservative opposition (Populists, Muslim Brethren, Arab Liberation Movement, conservative independents, right-wing Nationalists) against the left (Ba'thists, Communists, leftist independents, left-wing Nationalists), thus producing a clear distinction for voters. In three of the four areas the leftist candidate won. The fourth area, Jabal al-'Arab, was in the Druze region, where party politics and affiliations were subordinated to tribal associations. The voting results between the leftist winners and the conservative runners-up were much closer than expected,[43] especially in Damascus where Riyad al-Malki (brother of the assassinated 'Adnan al-Malki) narrowly defeated a Muslim Brethren leader, Mustafa al-Siba'i.

Over half of the eligible electorate failed to vote in the election, possibly due to a feeling of resignation that the government-backed candidates would be victorious. There were several reports of government troops intimidating right-wing supporters, distributing leaflets supporting left-wing candidates, and busing leftist voters to the polls.[44] Even Premier 'Asali openly interfered in the Damascus election by announcing his support for Malki. In addition, *L'Orient* reported on May 8 that Quwatli openly admitted voting for Malki, helping to turn the tide in his favor; this indicated that Quwatli, after opposing the leftists in March and failing, was not about to do it again. Recriminations against the government by the conservatives naturally fell upon deaf ears. Significantly, the Soviet embassy in Damascus was said to have "emphatically" intervened in the election by encouraging communist candidates to *withdraw* from the elections in Homs and in Damascus in favor of more moderate left-wing candidates.[45] The Kremlin continued its indirect approach in order not to contribute to conditions that might compel the United States to intervene more directly.

Some in the West tended to look at the bottle as half-full in relation to the election results, pointing out that despite apparent interference by the Syrian government the right-wing candidates did make a good showing; if the conservative parties would only cooperate they could make a successful push against the leftist regime. There were those who saw signs of moderation on the part of Syrian leaders as an indication that they were feeling isolated and vulnerable after "losing" Jordan to the West as a result of the Jordanian crisis.

The Jordanian crisis of April 1957 was the culmination of the struggle over the political direction of Jordan; it was a microcosm of the overall divisions in the region, and was viewed by many as a weather vane in the Arab world following Suez. Syria and Egypt actively supported those elements in Jordan aligned against the Baghdad Pact and British influence (and military presence) in the country. Riots occurred in December 1955 in Amman that forced the young King Hussein to call for the formation of a new government that resulted in a significant increase in leftist and nationalist representation. One of its demands was that Egypt, Saudi Arabia, and Syria jointly offer to replace the annual British subsidy in order to free Jordan from its dependent status (an agreement consummated in January 1957). This anti-Western and pro-Egyptian trend was confirmed in parliamentary elections just prior to the Suez war in October 1956. The pro-Egyptian National Socialist Party became the strongest in the Chamber of Deputies, with its leader, Sulayman Nabulsi, charged with forming a new government. The Suez war only solidified Nabulsi's position, and there were calls for union with one or more of Jordan's Arab neighbors.

King Hussein, however, became increasingly concerned over the pro-Egyptian and pro-Soviet drift of his government and warned Nabulsi of the negative effects of communist infiltration (using the word "communist" was obviously intended for American consumption). Events came to a head on April 10, 1957, when he dismissed Nabulsi from office. Relying on the loyalty of bedouin officers, Hussein boldly appeared at the Zerqa army base appealing for support from the Jordanian army. The pro-Nabulsi commander of the Jordanian army, Major-General Ali Abu Nuwar, was then arrested on April 14 (subsequently released to the Syrians). By late April, martial law had been declared and leftist leaders were taken into custody. The United States Sixth Fleet sailed into the eastern Mediterranean as a show of support, and King Sa'ud, in a move that reflected his new pro-American position, came out openly on the side of King Hussein. On April 28, as Hussein and Sa'ud were meeting in Riyadh, the United States granted Jordan $10 million in aid to assist it in its struggle against communism.[46]

Some focused on the success in Jordan as a turning point in the balance of power in the Middle East that would have some sort of a ripple effect in Syria.[47] At the regional level, the Iraqis also seemed to think the situation in Syria was moving in their favor. They agreed that King Hussein's stand had greatly encouraged the right-wing elements in Syria, particularly in the army, and speculated that in the near future they would have an opportunity to improve their position.[48]

Others, however, viewed the results of the May elections as further indication that Syria was falling within the Soviet orbit despite continued proclamations by Syrian leaders that their country was simply neutralist and not communist. Ambassador Moose gave the following assessment in light of the election results:[49]

Pro-Western and moderate elements continue to lose ground to increasingly entrenched ASRP-Communist-fellow traveler-opportunist vanguard of [the] proletariat which [is] using self-induced isolation to snuggle up close to Soviet protector in economic, military, political affairs. Battle against Israel now phrased in terms of battle against imperialist US and its imperialist satellites with Soviet Union depicted as only source of strength. USSR policies of establishing influence over military by arms deal and over politicians by support in UN and outside against Zionism and colonialism — imperialism — have been effective. Syria has willfully become [a] base for anti-American propaganda, leftist penetration of labor, sabotage and Communist activity throughout [the] area. . . . opposition shows no sign of competent and courageous leadership nor of spirit of sacrifice and hard work in [the] ranks.

In response to the above telegram, Secretary of State Dulles sent the following message to Ambassador Moose:[50]

> We [are] particularly concerned over evidence [of] growing Soviet influence. . . . USSR at least endeavoring [to] covertly establish Communist domination [in] Middle East and . . . may have succeeded in one case — Syria.
>
> We believe our actions with regard [to] Syria should be within context [of] relations which are correct but neither friendly nor helpful. Our present thinking is that we should continue [to] maintain minimum official contacts with GOS [Government of Syria] while endeavoring [to] discreetly encourage elements opposed [to] present GOS policies but in general avoiding giving [the] impression we attach great importance to our position in Syria or GOS reaction to US acts.

Turkish officials agreed with this pessimistic (and paranoid) view. We have already discussed Turkey's strategic concerns regarding its northern neighbor, the Soviet Union, but what caused trepidations in Ankara was the possibility that it could be strategically outflanked if a communist state came into being on its southern border. The Turks would take the lead among their fellow NATO and Baghdad Pact allies in urging outside intervention to administer "corrective measures" upon the Syrian regime. The Turkish ambassador to Syria, Adnan Kural, usually a moderate, was himself saying in May 1957 that there was no possibility of changing the Syrian regime without assistance from the outside, preferably from Iraq. Kural felt that the success in Jordan did not appreciably strengthen right-wing forces in Syria; indeed, he thought the incident only strengthened the leftist regime by giving credence to their claim of being threatened by imperialist powers. He added that Quwatli was helplessly weak (claiming he failed to back Nizam al-Din at a critical moment during the "transfer" incident in March) and that the first priority had to be to eliminate Sarraj.[51]

Jordan also took a strong line vis-à-vis the Syrian regime. This, of course, was to be expected following American assistance to Hussein during the Jordanian crisis in April 1957 and the fact that Syria and Egypt supported the opposition elements, and may in fact have instigated the crisis.[52] The pro-government press, accordingly, launched a war of words with the Syrian regime that would last into the summer.[53]

Sarraj interpreted the leftist victories on May 4 as an opportunity to consolidate power, knowing now that the regime could not be removed through the instrument of elections and sensing that the right-wing forces must be in disarray following the results. To solidify his hold on the government, Sarraj and some of his staunch left-wing supporters in and out of the army formed toward the end of May a Revolutionary Command Council (RCC), modeled after Nasser's RCC.[54] The group consisted of four army officers and four civilians. On the military side, the members were Sarraj, 'Afif al-Bizri, Ahmad 'Abd al-Karim of G-1, and, as an example of the opportunism and vagaries which often plagued Syrian politics, Amin al-Nafuri, the same man who instigated the anti-Sarraj movement in March. The civilian members of the RCC were Akram al-Hawrani, Khalid al-'Azm, Secretary General of the Foreign Ministry Salah al-Din Tarazi, and left-wing Nationalist Party Minister of Public Works Fakhir al-Kayyali. According to Torrey the RCC's objectives consisted of the following:[55]

> The group's goal was to control the country's foreign affairs and national policies outside the scope of the cabinet or parliament. Their objective was not to seize the government, at least for the present, but to allow President Quwatli to remain in office. The government was to be a facade behind which the RCC was to exert its influence.

Rumors of the formation of the RCC filtered through to the West, raising fears that it would attempt to once and for all rid the regime of dissident pro-West elements.[56] Reflecting the Eisenhower administration's concern over the course of events that had transpired in Syria, an American intelligence report entitled, "Possible Leftist Coup in Syria," stated the following:[57]

> According to a [reliable] source . . . a coup by leftist and Communist Army officers and politicians in Syria is being planned for the near future. The conspiratorial group [obviously a reference to the RCC] is reportedly receiving support from Nasser. It plans to dissolve parliament, purge the Army of rightist elements, and to declare an immediate union with Egypt. Allegedly the USSR has promised that it will support the leftist regime with troops and material, if needed, and in the event of intervention by Syria's neighbors.[58] (insert mine)

The report also stated that the motivations for a leftist coup originated from the regime's perceived isolation in light of the Jordanian crisis, the rapprochement between Saudi Arabia and Iraq (discussed below), and the victory of pro-West elements in parliamentary elections in Lebanon in mid-June 1957, the latter judged in the West as a major defeat for Nasserism.[59] Accordingly, it states that the leftist elements would want to initiate a coup before the conservatives did. The report went on to say that the likelihood of direct Soviet intervention to assure the success of a leftist coup was slight. If report was true, Sarraj merely duplicated his attempt of June 1956, when he reportedly tried to convince Nasser to sanction a coup d'etat that would ensure a Syrian-Egyptian union. As you will recall, Nasser supposedly gave Sarraj a negative response. Sarraj was now taking matters into his own hands, especially since he was essentially in control. He had good reason to be nervous. In addition to the events in Jordan and Lebanon that resulted in Syria being totally surrounded by pro-West regimes, there was still the legitimate suspicion (if not factual knowledge) that the United States was continuing its covert efforts to overthrow the government – under these circumstances, Sarraj understandably tightened the ranks of his inner circle and prepared himself for future "showdowns."

This flurry of reports about the existence of an RCC, the deepening commitment of the Soviet Union in Syria, and the prospects of a leftist coup may have forced the State Department (or rather John Foster Dulles) to reassess the type of action it would recommend vis-à-vis Syria. The last thing the Eisenhower administration wanted to see in Syria was another Nasser, and Sarraj was certainly one of Nasser's proteges; indeed, the term "RCC," so soon after the Suez debacle, was a trip-wire for the administration to act. Dulles may have thought it was time for the United States to become more involved in securing the downfall of Sarraj and his supporters, and may have given the green light to more active clandestine activities. Allen Dulles informed his brother in June that "there is no leadership there [Syria]. . . . we have to start new planning. It is not hopeless."[60]

Meanwhile, the conservative opposition in Syria, desperately trying to find ways to stem the leftist tide, chose the annual parliamentary debate over the budget as the next battle-line. During the course of one particular debate on June 1, 1957, Communist Party leader Khalid Baqdash delivered a provocative speech aimed at the right-wing opposition. In the speech, he sang praises for the Soviet Union and accused the Populist Party of being "lackeys and agents of imperialism."[61] Rushdi al-Kikhia, leader of the Populists, rose up in angry defiance against Baqdash and accused him of selling out the country. Kikhia then resigned from the chamber with 40–50 of his followers threatening a mass resignation on the grounds that they could not operate properly in a parliament dominated by the leftists and where proper parliamentary procedures were not being observed.[62] This might have been an attempt to bring down the government, precipitating the crisis the opposition was looking for in March, but if they were ready then to take advantage of a showdown they now were not, and on June 5, parliament refused to accept Kikhia's resignation, the budget was passed, and the crisis averted. The Populists and their followers in the chamber were persuaded not to follow through with their resignation from a variety of sources either interested in preventing the regime from having a free hand in the chamber or allowing the parliamentary crisis to disintegrate into a national crisis.

As a typical diversionary tactic during a political crisis, the government complained of Israeli violations of the Syrian-Israeli armistice line as a prelude to a possible Israeli invasion.[63] The failure of the right-wing Nationalists to follow the lead of the Populists (or the failure of the Populists to secure the support of the Nationalists) again emphasized the divisiveness and ultimate weakness of the opposition, resulting in another important setback.[64] Parliament recessed until July 20; the leftist regime was still in power and becoming more entrenched by the day.

The Syrian-Soviet Economic Agreement

When parliament resumed, the regime felt secure enough to push through the chamber a government bill exempting the Czech firm building the oil refinery from its payment of taxes. There would again be heated opposition from the right-wing deputies, but the bill passed.[65] The last political convulsion in Syria before the American-Syrian crisis, however, would come in relation to events surrounding the August 6, 1957, announcement by a Syrian delegation in Moscow of an extensive economic agreement with the Soviet Union.[66]

The delegation, led by Khalid al-'Azm, visited Moscow from July 24 through August 6. The agreement basically fell into two parts: 1) the Soviets undertook to provide a large long-term loan to finance major development projects in Syria, and 2) they offered to buy a considerable proportion of Syria's agricultural surpluses.[67] There were also reports of hidden agreements negotiated by 'Azm regarding military aid.

The agreement was hailed by leftists elements as being unconditional (drawing comparisons to conditional American aid) and necessary to help the government reach its economic goals.[68] The right-wing opposition obviously did not view the deal in quite the same light. The Syrian government announced on August 8 its intention to convene an "extraordinary" session of the Chamber of Deputies to pass the Syrian-Soviet economic accord (the chamber had adjourned on August 1 and was not scheduled to meet again in ordinary session until October 17).[69] Populist Party leaders called into question the veracity of the agreement and stated that they were studying its provisions.[70] The Syrian daily *al-Hadara* of August 10 urged the holding of an extraordinary session of parliament "since this session has become a necessity in order to block any attempt aimed at weakening the government's stand toward the successful negotiations held in Moscow."[71] Although this confirmed that there was indeed strong opposition to the accord, the government came to the conclusion that it would be best to keep the issue out of parliament, having recalled the clamor raised by the opposition on the lesser issues concerning the Czech oil refinery contract, martial law, and questions over the budget.

The government announced on August 13 "aggressive" moves by the Israelis in the demilitarized zone and began to move troops to the area. The Turks as well were accused on of massing troops on the northern border.[72] And, of course, there was the announcement on August 12 of the discovery of the American plot to overthrow the regime. On the same day, Syria's

Minister for Propaganda and Information Salih Aqil declared that the plan to hold the extraordinary session of parliament to debate the economic agreement had been canceled.[73]

Among the Syrians recruited by American personnel to participate in the coup were individuals who from the beginning of the operation (probably sometime in June) kept Sarraj and his lieutenants informed of what was going on. It is ironic then that the American plot in essence helped the Syrian regime avoid for the time being public debate on a controversial issue until it could be sure of chamber support for the agreement or escape parliamentary discussion altogether. On August 17, Hasan al-Jabiri, chairman of the political committee of the parliamentary National Front and chairman of the foreign affairs committee, announced that because of the satisfactory manner in which Khalid al-'Azm presented the details of the Syrian-Soviet economic agreement to his committee, he recommended that there was no need for the government to submit the agreement to the Chamber of Deputies for approval.[74] It was reported from Damascus on August 18 that the Syrian cabinet (not the chamber) had met the previous evening and officially approved the Syrian-Soviet economic accord.[75] (The agreement was *formally* signed by Syrian and Soviet representatives in Damascus on October 28, 1957.)

If the Soviet-Syrian agreement was left to progress within the Syrian polity naturally, it might have produced the fissures in the Ba'th-communist front that the United States and its conservative allies in Syria had been looking for all year, since it would have brought out into the open the Ba'th Party's distaste for the communists and the latter's allegiance to the Kremlin (a split which did in fact occur after the American-Syrian crisis). Instead, the bungled American covert operation only brought the leftist groups closer together in the face of external danger (similar to the formation of the National Front following the British-Iraqi plot in late-1956). It even forced the conservative opposition groups to rally behind the leftist government; anything less would have branded them as imperialist underlings in the eyes of the Syrian public. Finally, what had been intended to reduce Soviet influence in the country actually resulted in a tightening bond between Moscow and Damascus, as the latter leaned toward an ally that could help it withstand pressure from the outside—and as it turned out, it made the right choice.

This was also an opportune moment for the regime to purge the government and the army of remaining right-wing elements. First among these was Chief of Staff Nizam al-Din, who on August 15 was replaced by 'Afif al-Bizri (with Amin al-Nafuri appointed as deputy chief of staff). Also resigning was Colonel Muhammad Isma'il, the commander of the Syrian gendarmerie, and many of his subordinates. Nizam was a member of that infamous delegation sent to Moscow and reportedly was very distressed at the depth of the agreement with the Soviets. Upon his return to Damascus, he most likely worked to dilute its significance or scrap it altogether by attempting to bring it to the chamber for debate. When it became obvious that he would not be able to do this, and knowing his days were numbered, he resigned, and probably did so under considerable duress. Many of the officers who were purged on August 15 and 16 were appointed to their ranks during the French mandate and therefore were considered unreliable by the new regime because of their past associations; they were also considered to be incompetent in the military profession because of their lack of military background (most were not graduates of the Homs Military Academy) and the nepotistic manner in which they obtained their positions.[76] A new generation of officers, reflecting the progressive changes that had occurred in the civilian bureaucracy, took their place at the top of the Syrian polity.

The Ba'th Party declared that Syria's administrative structure was "full of shortcomings, weaknesses and corruption" and in urgent need of reform, and it warned that if the government was unable to perform this function, then another one should be constituted that could.[77] And even though there still remained important divisions in the army corps that would later manifest themselves, in the face of adversity the military "often closed its ranks and demonstrated not only a measure of prudence but also a sense of corporate and professional solidarity."[78]

Notes

1. Israel did withdraw from positions held in the Sinai Peninsula and Gaza Strip in March only after weeks of United Nations and American pressure, and, finally, the personal intervention of President Eisenhower.

2. The Arabs claimed it was an Arab gulf and felt they could therefore prohibit Israeli shipping through it. The United States supported Israel's right to use the Gulf of Aqaba by claiming it was an international waterway. (See discussion on this subject below.)

3. For a summary of the charges leveled by the Syrian government, see *al-Nasr* (Damascus), November 25, 1956.

4. Foreign Office Report, "Syria: Annual Review for 1956," November 15, 1957, FO 371/128219, PRO.

5. Official response released January 10, 1957. For text of response see Telegram From the Embassy in Syria to the Department of State, January 11, 1957, *FRUS*, p. 609; also, *L'Orient* of January 12, 1957. In addition, President Sham'un of Lebanon told the British embassy in Beirut that Syrian leaders conferred for two hours with the Soviet ambassador to Damascus before releasing the response (see British Embassy-Beirut, January 16, 1957, FO 371/127740, PRO). Sham'un, however, consistently tended to exaggerate the Soviet threat to his country through Syria.

6. For range of views on response to Doctrine see Weekly Letter on Syria and Egypt, British Embassy-Beirut, February 15, 1957, FO 371/128221, PRO; and, DA Intelligence Reports, January 22, 1957, Entry 85, Intell. Doc. File, R-27-57 and R-28-57, RG319, NARA.

7. DA Intelligence Report, February 19, 1957, Entry 85, Intell. Doc. File, 2040561, RG319, NARA.

8. Telegram From the Department of State to the Embassy in Egypt, February 27, 1957, *FRUS*, p. 613.

9. The conversion was not free of charge, however, as the United States agreed to a new package of economic and military aid to Saudi Arabia, as well as a new agreement favorable to the Saudis on the Dhahran Airbase. See also Memorandum of a Conversation, January 31, 1957, *FRUS*, pp. 441–443, and Memorandum of a Conversation, February 8, 1957, *FRUS*, p. 481, on conversations between Eisenhower and Sa'ud regarding Syria.

10. Telegram From the Department of State to the Embassy in Egypt, February 27, 1957, *FRUS*, pp. 612–613.

11. A report from the British embassy in Washington on March 8 stated that President Quwatli and Prime Minister Sabri al-'Asali, who were at the time in Cairo meeting with other Arab leaders, delayed their return to Damascus and had their families join them in Cairo until the reprieve decision had been made. (British Embassy-Washington, March 8, 1957, FO 371/128221, PRO.)

12. Weekly Letter on Syria and Egypt, British Embassy-Beirut, March 7, 1957, FO 371/128221, PRO.

13. Foreign Reports, letter to John Foster Dulles from Harry Kern, February 28, 1957, John Foster Dulles Papers, Box 118, The John Foster Dulles Collection, Seeley G. Mudd Library, Princeton.

14. Ibid.; also see, Weekly Letter on Syria and Egypt, British Embassy-Beirut, March 7, 1957, FO 371/128221, PRO.

15. Also at stake for the Eisenhower administration was the final passage of the Eisenhower Doctrine, which had been held hostage by the Senate in an attempt to force the president to stop pressuring Israel. The longer the doctrine was held up the less effective it would be as a policy statement because it would be apparent to the world that it did not have the full support of Congress (and to some extent it was already damaged for being held up as long as it was). A settlement of the problem would render Senate objections moot. To pressure the Senate and Israel, Eisenhower appeared on television on February 21, 1957, and personally appealed for the support of the American people on this issue. On March 1, the Israeli government agreed to a "full and complete withdrawal" of military forces. See Dwight D. Eisenhower, *Waging Peace 1956–1961* (Garden City, NY: Doubleday & Company, 1965), pp. 183–189; also see Ralph H. Magnus, ed., *Documents on the Middle East* (Washington: American Enterprise Institute, 1969), pp.

182–185, for statement by Israeli Foreign Minister Golda Meir at the UN on March 1 announcing Israel's intention to withdrawal. On March 9, Congress passed the doctrine.

16. Foreign Reports, Letter to John Foster Dulles from Harry Kern, February 28, 1957, John Foster Dulles Papers, Box 118, The John Foster Dulles Collection, Seeley G. Mudd Library, Princeton.

17. *L'Orient,* February 26, 1957.

18. Memorandum From the Assistant Secretary of State for Near Eastern, South Asian, and African Affairs to the Under Secretary of State for Political Affairs, March 18, 1957, *FRUS,* pp. 614–617.

19. Memorandum for Brig. General Goodpaster from Allen Dulles, "Situation Report on Syria," March 22, 1957, Microform Reading Room, microfiche 26E (1981), Library of Congress.

20. Progress Report on United States Objectives and Policies With Respect to the Near East (NSC 5428), Operations Coordinating Board, December 22, 1956, White House Office, National Security Council Staff: Papers, 1948–1961: OCB Central Files, Box 78, DDEL.

21. The Syrian press reported in late-February that Kuzbari had been pushing within the ALM to formally expel Shishakli and merge his party with 'Asali's Nationalist Party. This move by Kuzbari might have been an attempt to further legitimize his party in the eyes of the public by getting rid of someone who was implicated and sentenced in the Iraqi affair, accumulate allies in the face of Hawrani's attempts to replace him in the cabinet, and/or in anticipation of the episode soon to be described. Of course, Hawrani could have merely been reacting to Kuzbari's maneuvering.

22. As reported in Weekly Letter on Syria and Egypt, British Embassy, April 4, 1957, FO 371/128222, PRO.

23. Memorandum for Brig. General Goodpaster from Allen Dulles, "Situation Report on Syria."

24. Ibid. See also Muhammad 'Umran, *Tajribati fi al-Thawra* (Beirut, 1970), p. 13; and *New York Times,* March 24, 1957.

25. British Embassy-Amman, March 27, 1957, FO 371/128222, PRO. Elements of the Syrian army had been sent to Jordan ostensibly to support King Hussein during the Suez crisis. Due to Israeli disinformation, it was thought at the time that Israel would attack Jordan and not Egypt.

26. British Embassy-Amman, April 3, 1957, FO 371/128222, PRO.

27. *Al-Jumhur al-'Arabi* (Aleppan newspaper) March 26, 1957, as reported in British Embassy-Amman, March 27, 1957, FO 371/128222, PRO.

28. Information on this group's activities from Memorandum for Brig. General Goodpaster from Allen Dulles, "Situation Report on Syria."

29. Report on Syria, British Embassy-Beirut, March 21, 1957, FO 371/128222, PRO. Information from United States Major Neil, who shared

with the British embassy in Beirut intelligence reports received from the American military attaches in Beirut and Damascus.

30. Memorandum for Brig. General Goodpaster from Allen Dulles.

31. Weekly Letter on Syria and Egypt, British Embassy-Beirut, April 4, 1957, FO 371/128222, PRO.

32. Memorandum for Brig. General Goodpaster from Allen Dulles.

33. Ibid.

34. Weekly Letter on Syria and Egypt, British Embassy-Beirut, April 4, 1957. The British Embassy reported that the American embassy in Damascus and an independent Syrian source confirmed at least some transfers. (Ibid.)

35. Weekly Letter on Syria and Egypt, British Embassy-Beirut to Foreign Office, March 28, 1957; report comments on various unsubstantiated claims being tossed about in the Arab press.

36. British Embassy-Beirut, March 21, 1957, FO 371/128222, PRO.

37. See Department of State *Bulletin* (March 25, 1957): 480; Ibid. (May 27, 1957): 841–845; Ibid. (June 17, 1957): 969–972; Ibid. (July 1, 1957): 17–19.

38. "Developments of the Quarter: Comment and Chronology," *Middle East Journal,* vol. XI (Spring 1957), p. 188. The Soviets made a similar charge against the United States in relation to the Jordanian crisis, stating that the incident was brought on by American efforts to prepare a favorable ground in Jordan for the Richards mission. (*Izvestia,* April 23, 1957, as reported in British Embassy-Moscow, April 27, 1957, FO 371/127743, PRO.)

39. Discussion with British officials in Beirut (Weekly Letter on Syria and Egypt, British Embassy-Beirut, April 18, 1957, FO 371/128222, PRO).

40. The four convicted were Munir al-'Ajlani (Constitutional Bloc), 'Adnan al-Atasi (Populist Party), Fadlallah Jarbu (Constitutional Bloc), and Shaykh Hail Surur (Druze).

41. "Developments of the Quarter: Comment and Chronology," *Middle East Journal,* vol. XII (Summer 1957), p. 305.

42. There is evidence, however, to suggest that the Turks were making threatening noises along the border at about this time and possibly even earlier during the Qatana incident, and at the behest of the United States. A report sent to the Foreign Office by a British official in Ankara on September 26, 1957, referring to the more famous Turkish troop deployments along the Syrian border at that time, made a casual and all-too-believable reference to similar such movements earlier in the year in the following manner: "Would you please refer to paragraph 2 of Morris's letter 1042/189/57G of September 11 to Rose about Turkish military dispositions made on the Syrian frontier last spring *at the suggestion of the U.S.G.*" (emphasis mine). (British Embassy-Ankara, September 26, 1957, FO 371/128242, PRO.) I have not be able to obtain the September 11 memo, but

if true, and there is little reason not to think so, this lends credence to my earlier assertion that the United States might have been acting in coordination with the Qatana uprising and/or subsequent moves by the Syrian opposition. The action also could have been taken at the time of the Jordanian crisis in order to keep the Syrians at bay if they were contemplating military intervention against Hussein. Whatever the case, it does set a precedent for the Eisenhower administration using the Turks to pressure Syria.

43. In Damascus, 20,808 votes to 18,461; at Homs, 19,127 to 15,480; and in Suwayda, 3,671 to 2,160. (Torrey, p. 381, n. 10.) Also see *New York Times,* May 6, 1957.

44. Torrey, p. 353.

45. *Observer Foreign News Service,* no. 122238, April 30, 1957.

46. See Raphael Patai, *The Kingdom of Jordan* (Westport: Greenwood Press, Publishers, 1984), pp. 58–72; also, Benjamin Shwadran, *Jordan: A State of Tension* (New York: Council for Middle Eastern Affairs Press, 1959), pp. 346–358; His Majesty King Hussein of Jordan, *Uneasy Lies the Head* (New York: Random House, 1962), pp. 151–183; and, Stephen S. Kaplan, "United States Aid and Regime Maintenance in Jordan, 1957–1973," *Public Policy,* vol. 23, no. 2 (Spring 1975), pp. 189–217.

47. The American ambassador to Jordan wrote the following after the Jordanian crisis: "A unique opportunity is given the United States to encourage realignment of forces in Near East. It is possible to foresee the countering of Communist activity in Arab world, the shifting of alignments in Syria, close cooperation of Iraq, Jordan and Saudi Arabia, the negation of Nasser's influence and protection of Persian Gulf militarily. With a little rosy tinted optimism one can speculate on so quieting things that eventual settlement of the Palestine problem may be possible." (Telegram From the Embassy in Jordan to the Department of State, May 3, 1957, *FRUS,* pp. 124–125.)

48. British Embassy-Amman, May 1, 1957, FO 371/128222, PRO.

49. Telegram From the Embassy in Syria to the Department of State, May 17, 1957, *FRUS,* p. 618.

50. Telegram From the Department of State to the Embassy in Syria, May 28, 1957, *FRUS,* p. 619.

51. British Embassy-Ankara, May 3, 1957, FO 371/128222, PRO.

52. Telegram From the Department of State to the Embassy in Saudi Arabia, April 25, 1957, *FRUS,* p. 111; Telegram From the Embassy in Jordan to the Department of State, May 3, 1957, *FRUS,* pp. 122–125. Eisenhower, referring to comments by John Foster Dulles on the plots "hatched" in Damascus against Jordan, said at the 323rd meeting of the National Security Council on May 16, 1957, that "these plotters are committing illegalities and crimes behind the scenes, and this rendered it easier for us to counter these moves." (Editorial Note, *FRUS,* pp. 131–132.)

53. For instance, see *al-Difa'* of June 5, *al-Jihad* of June 6, and *Falastin* of June 7, 1957, all criticizing Syria's leftist regime.

54. Torrey, p. 355; also, British Embassy-Baghdad, June 26, 1957, FO 371/128223, PRO.

55. Torrey, p. 356.

56. British Embassy-Ankara, June 21, 1957, FO 371/128223, PRO; British Embassy-Baghdad, June 26, 1957, FO 371/128223, PRO.

57. Memorandum for the Chairman, Joint Chiefs of Staff, "Possible Leftist Coup in Syria," June 17, 1957, Microform Reading Room, microfiche 471B (1981), Library of Congress.

58. On the Soviet promise of military and economic support, see British Embassy-Amman, June 12, 1957, FO 371/128222, PRO.

59. For election results, see *The Christian Science Monitor,* July 1, 1957.

60. Telephone call from John Foster Dulles to Allen Dulles, June, 1957, John Foster Dulles Papers, Telephone Calls Series, Box 4, DDEL.

61. Seale, p. 291; Torrey, p. 356.

62. British Embassy-Ankara, June 7, 1957, FO 371/128222, PRO.

63. *American Foreign Policy: Current Documents,* "The United States Position on the Syrian Complaint of Israeli Violations of the Syrian-Israeli Armistice Agreement," Doc. 284, May 28, 1957.

64. On June 8, 1957, the Syrian government announced it had uncovered an espionage ring backed by the British and with the intent of overthrowing the regime. The charges were generally thought to be fabricated—I have not uncovered any evidence indicating whether the charges were true or false—but it was typical for the government to play-up a potential external threat at critical times in order to strike at the opposition and dilute their charges by calling for solidarity in the face of danger. See George E. Kirk, *Contemporary Arab Politics: A Concise History* (New York: Praeger, 1961), p. 95; and *Oriente Moderno,* vol. 37 (1957), pp. 437, 439 and 571. On July 1, *al-Nasr* announced the uncovering of an American plot to overthrow the government in concert with Syrian exiles, the Iraqis, the Lebanese, and the Jordanians. (Ibid.) Again, I have no evidence of the validity of this charge. Paul Johnson reports that American intelligence officers in Syria had been in contact with senior Syrian officers who were opposed to Sarraj and the Ba'th. No doubt this refers to the episode in March in the failed putsch against Sarraj, but also may hint at the continued attempts by the United States to eliminate Sarraj and led to the incident in August. See Paul Johnson, "The Struggle for the Middle East; Part I: America Takes Over," *New Statesman,* July 6, 1957, p. 21.

65. The opposition's criticism in the chamber was that the government had originally publicly agreed to the Czech offer because it was the cheapest, but the exemption would make it the most expensive. To this, Akram Hawrani replied that it was accepted in the first place for political reasons

and it was only incidental that it was the cheapest offer. (Weekly Letter on Syria, British Embassy-Beirut, July 25, 1957, FO 371/128223, PRO.)

66. See FBIS, August 7, 1957, p. C1 for text of communique.

67. *The Economist,* August 31, 1957, p. 690.

68. On July 27, the Syrian ambassador to the United States, Dr. Farid Zayn al-Din, prepared the Eisenhower administration for the deal by repeating his charges that the United States was applying economic pressure on Syria, especially by dumping cotton and grain surpluses on the international market, implying that Syria must look elsewhere for assistance. (FBIS, July 29, 1957, p. C5.) See Yahya Sadowski, *Political Power and Economic Organization in Syria: The Course of State Intervention, 1946–1958* (unpublished dissertation), 1984, for a detailed discussion of the state of Syria's economy at the time of the agreement; also, see Khaled A. Shair, *Planning for a Middle Eastern Economy: Model for Syria* (London: Chapman and Hall, 1965); and, Edmund Y. Asfour, *Syria: Development and Monetary Policy* (Cambridge, MA: Harvard University Press/Center for Middle Eastern Studies, 1959).

69. FBIS, August 9, 1957, p. C3.

70. Ibid.

71. FBIS, August 12, 1957, p. C6.

72. Weekly Letter on Syria, British Embassy-Beirut, August 14, 1957, FO 371/128223, PRO.

73. FBIS, August 12, 1957, p. C6.

74. FBIS, August 19, 1957, p. C9.

75. FBIS, August 19, 1957, p. C8.

76. DA Intelligence Report, September 23, 1957, Entry 85, Intell. Doc. File, 2059533, RG319, NARA.

77. British Embassy-Beirut, September 3, 1957, FO 371/128 225.

78. Itamar Rabinovich, *Syria Under the Ba'th 1963–1966: The Army-Party Symbiosis* (Tel Aviv: Tel Aviv University, 1972), p. 12.

8

Syria's Rapprochement with Saudi Arabia and Iraq

As expected, relations between Syria and Jordan progressively deteriorated following the Jordanian crisis in April 1957. The animosity between the two regimes was expressed in heated verbal jousting through each nation's press and radio. The situation became so bad that by early August, before the American-Syrian crisis erupted, newspaper and radio coverage in and out of the Middle East was referring to it as the Jordanian-Syrian crisis; it would soon be overtaken by events in Syria by mid-August.

During the summer of 1957 one might also have expected relations to become strained between Syria and the other two monarchies in the vicinity, Saudi Arabia and Iraq. Certainly the Saudis seemed to have been won over to the American point of view by early 1957; furthermore, the pro-West regime in Iraq had only less than a year earlier played a major role in the failed "Iraqi plot" to overthrow the Syrian regime. But in the period that immediately preceded the outbreak of the American-Syrian crisis in August, there occurred a rapprochement of sorts between the Syrian regime and the Iraqis and the Saudis that would decisively affect the course of events related to the incident. Counting on Iraqi and Saudi support vis-à-vis the crisis, the Eisenhower administration was taken aback to discover that it in fact did not have it; this unexpected course of events completely altered the way in which the administration viewed the crisis, compelling it to embark on an alternative, and more dangerous, course of action. An examination of the Saudi-Syrian-Iraqi triangle at this time will also reveal how the different players in the region pursued their own sets of objectives, and how the failure of the United States to recognize these various agendas led to important misinterpretations by the Eisenhower administration regarding the American-Syrian crisis.

Saudi-Syrian Relations Prior to the Crisis

We have already discussed King Sa'ud's conversion to the American cause in early 1957, apparently confirmed by his performance at the Cairo conference in late February and his effort to commute the death sentences in the "Iraqi plot" trials. We have also seen how the White House might have credited Sa'ud with more influence than he actually deserved and how subtle weaknesses in the American-Saudi relationship emerged from these episodes. King Sa'ud established his role as an overseer of American interests in the Middle East by supporting King Hussein of Jordan in his successful bid to reassert power in his own country against leftist and pro-Nasser opponents who were supported by Syria and Egypt. Accordingly, Sa'ud was considered by Syria and Egypt as a traitor to Arab nationalism and an instrument of imperialism; and relations would get worse before they got better.

Sa'ud's support of the Jordanian regime became apparent when Hussein visited Riyadh on April 28, 1957, immediately after he had secured his position in his own country. President Eisenhower personally sent a note of thanks to Sa'ud for his support during this incident.[1] In a joint communique issued after the meeting, Sa'ud and Hussein agreed that "no Arab state should interfere in the internal affairs of any other Arab state," which was obviously aimed at Egypt and Syria.[2] This statement would ironically be used again by Sa'ud to *defend* Syria later in the year during the American-Syrian crisis. The two monarchs would again consult with each other when Sa'ud returned state visit to Amman on June 8, producing another joint communique professing their solidarity.

If Sa'ud was to be a counterpoise to Nasser, a rapprochement between Iraq and Saudi Arabia had to be effected in order to present a unified pro-West front in the Arab world. Because of the hostility (often played out in Syria) between the two ruling houses, the task would not be easy. With British and American coaxing, King Faisal of Iraq and Sa'ud "buried the hatchet." On May 11, 1957, Sa'ud arrived in Baghdad for a state visit. The joint communique that followed condemned communism, Zionism, and imperialism, and promised a "new era" in their relations.[3] On July 3, the first Iraqi ambassador to Saudi Arabia, Shaykh Ibrahim al-Suwayyil, presented his credentials to King Sa'ud.

The Syrian regime, however, was not at all pleased with these developments. Even relations with Lebanon deteriorated, especially after the victory by pro-West elements in the Lebanese parliamentary elections in June. To counter this trend, the leftist politicians began to lash out at Sa'ud and draw closer to Nasser, their one last friend in the area.

The communique issued by Sa'ud and Faisal on May 18 was attacked in Syrian newspapers. Michel 'Aflaq was quoted as saying that "Saudi Arabia is no longer a neutral state."[4] On May 21, Damascus papers reported that right-wing elements had stepped-up their campaign to overthrow the 'Asali cabinet. On the same day, the left-wing paper *al-Nasr* accused Shaykh Yusuf al-Yassin, the Saudi deputy foreign minister and one of Sa'ud's closest advisers, of supporting the right-wing opposition. The Syrian regime again went on the offensive following Sa'ud's state visit to Jordan. Khalid al-'Azm accused Sa'ud of siding with imperialism and American policy for the benefit of Israel. On June 17, the Syrian minister of information pointed out what he thought were the "contradictions" to Arab unity and neutrality of Saudi policy.[5] Syria's leading daily, *al-Ra'i al-'Am,* which was considered the voice of the leftist government at the time, printed on June 18 an attack against the United States for embarking on a policy of conquest in the Arab world and using Sa'ud as its principal "agent" in the Middle East.

In retaliation, the Saudis closed their embassy in Damascus, recalled their ambassador, and froze Syrian assets in Saudi Arabia. Prime Minister 'Asali immediately tried to mend the rift between the two countries.[6] Akram al-Hawrani again inflamed the situation on June 28 when he accused the Saudis of organizing a coup in Syria aimed at replacing the current regime with one which would "come to an understanding with American imperialism."[7] Sa'ud responded by announcing that relations between the two countries would not improve until he received an apology from the Syrian government, 'Azm and Bitar had been removed from their posts, and the newspapers in Syria most critical of Saudi Arabia, *al-Ra'i al-'Am* and the communist *al-Sarkha,* had been closed down.[8]

Despite this apparent animosity, however, by July 4 there were signs of reconciliation. The Syrian leadership realized that it was not in their best interest to totally alienate Sa'ud at this time; Syria was already isolated enough in the Arab world. Bitar, Hawrani, and 'Asali thus began to castigate the United States for its position on the Gulf of Aqaba question, an issue close to the Saudis' hearts and obviously calculated to repair relations.[9] *Daily Star* reported on July 4 that the Syrian government issued a statement saying that it expressed "its respect for the King [Sa'ud], its appreciation of his cooperation in the Arab field, its assurance that the Syrian press does not represent the government's views, its promise to sue any paper which attacks King Sa'ud in the future, and its eagerness to reestablish good and strong relations with Saudi Arabia." Subsequently, the British reported that 'Azm and Bitar had temporarily left Syria – Bitar on a four-day visit to Italy and the Vatican en route to Yugoslavia, and 'Azm to Italy for "medical reasons."[10] In addition, the Syrians were "indulging in a minor adventure on the Israeli border – the surest way to bring round the Saudis to some degree of support of the regime in Syria."[11] The move seemed to have worked; by July 18 the Syrian press had turned its attention to border tensions, and the Arab states, including Saudi Arabia, expressed their support for Syria in the event of Israeli "aggression."[12]

At a press conference on July 30, 1957, Bitar, with a further eye toward mending relations with Saudi Arabia, pledged Syria's support for the Saudis on another issue close to their hearts, the territorial dispute with the British over the Buraimi oasis (see below).[13] Since the Syrians addressed Sa'ud's conditions for normalizing relations to his satisfaction, and even went beyond what was expected by tying in the Aqaba and Buraimi issues, the Saudi ambassador accordingly returned to Damascus on July 31 and commerce between the two countries resumed.[14] By announcing its support for Saudi Arabia on Aqaba and Buraimi, the Syrian government was not only attempting to repair relations with the Saudis, but also striking at the American-Saudi front at its most vulnerable point. The Eisenhower administration was on opposite sides with Saudi Arabia on both issues. Sa'ud recognized this and would use the threat of improving relations with Syria and Egypt as leverage against the United States in an attempt to pressure Washington into settling both matters in the Saudis' favor.

The Gulf of Aqaba Question

King Sa'ud became the Arab spokesman for the Gulf of Aqaba question following Nasser's convenient abdication of that role in the wake of the Suez crisis and the establishment of United Nations Emergency Forces in the Sinai Peninsula. It was a brilliant move by Nasser, because he could now hide his own inability to prevent Israeli ships from passing through the gulf by shifting the blame onto Sa'ud, while at the same time promoting a rift in Saudi-American relations.[15] Sa'ud eagerly assumed the leadership role, pronouncing the Gulf of Aqaba a closed Arab gulf. To emphasize this point, he announced on April 11, 1957, that Israeli ships were forbidden from the gulf; he made the announcement while Ambassador Richards happened to be in Jedda on his "doctrine tour" of the Middle East.[16]

Sa'ud took his role as leader very seriously to show his counterparts in other Arab countries that he could bring the United States around to the Arab point of view vis-à-vis Israel. A United States intelligence report on the Aqaba question, however, warned that in the case of Saudi Arabia, "There may well be an increasing rapprochement with Egypt because of the need and possibility of a united front on an issue on which there is no intra-Arab disagreement," with a "resultant gradual deterioration of U.S.-Saudi relations."[17] It was an accurate assessment. As early as May 20, 1957, Saudi Arabia gave assurances to Egypt that it intended to keep Israel from sending its ships through the Gulf of Aqaba. On July 8, Yassin declared that his country would follow Egypt's "active neutralism" and oppose all foreign pacts.[18] On July 21, trade talks resumed between the two countries. On the same day, the former Saudi ambassador to Britain stated that Saudi Arabia broke off relations with Britain because of violations of the agreement over Buraimi *and* its attack on Egypt at Suez.[19] Egyptian press attacks on Saudi Arabia noticeably diminished, focusing instead on Jordan and on the various disputes in the Arabian peninsula in support of Sa'ud against British interests.

The Buraimi Dispute

The United States also found itself wedged between two friends on the Buraimi dispute. Buraimi was the name given to an oasis in eastern Arabia. The dispute revolved around the delineation of the inland boundaries between the Saudis and the British-supported shaykhdoms in the Persian Gulf. Since the oasis was thought to contain large quantities of untapped oil, the demarcation of boundaries gained added importance in the 1950s. The disputed area was also considered by both sides as a kind of buffer against each other. The Saudis took matters into their own hands and seized the oasis in 1952. The British retook the oasis by force in October 1955 ostensibly to recover the area for its ally, the Sultan of Muscat and Oman.[20]

Buraimi was not the only issue pitting the Saudis against the British. Arab nationalism arrived late to the tribes of the Arabian peninsula, but it did come, and by 1956 manifested itself in a rebellion against the Sultan of Muscat and Oman and an uprising by Yemeni tribes against the British protectorate at Aden. Saudi Arabia and Egypt supported both rebellions. Former British ambassador to Egypt, Humphrey Trevelyan, wrote that Nasser actively supported the rebels in Oman and Yemen, but supported Saudi Arabia's position regarding Buraimi only at Sa'ud's request since the issue was not of real importance to Egypt.[21] But Buraimi was the issue in which the British and Saudis directly confronted each other and consequently caught the United States in the middle.

The British, for their part, had from the beginning been very skeptical of the American plan to build up Sa'ud as a rival to Nasser: "The Americans may have been deceived both about the area of real agreement between Saudi and American policy and the degree of influence which Saud exercises over his Arab colleagues. Saud must know that Egypt is able to make serious trouble for him in his own country."[22] In retrospect this observation seems to have been correct on all counts. The United States underestimated the quid pro quo Sa'ud would require for his support for American policy in the Middle East. This fact was not lost upon American embassy officials in Jedda, who began to see the subtle chinks in the armor of the American-Saudi partnership and warned the State Department in April 1957 that "it was clear [that the] Palestine question, Aqaba, Buraimi and in general, old issues of Zionism and imperialism loom large in Saudi thinking and could easily affect our relations quite seriously."[23] Sa'ud knew he had to support the Arab nationalist line in order to compete with Nasser for leadership in the Arab world, and the Eisenhower administration failed to realize that its strategy of building up the king could actually backfire. Washington pressed London to come to terms with the Saudis regarding Buraimi and told Riyadh that it was doing what it could to bring the two sides together; but publicly it took no stand, which irritated Sa'ud and the British.[24] As a result, relations between the United States and Saudi Arabia became strained during the summer of 1957, hardly a situation conducive to cooperation during the American-Syrian crisis.

Sa'ud had placed himself, or was led into, the position of championing Arab nationalism because of his stand on, inter alia, the Buraimi and Aqaba issues. He could not easily back away from this position in support of American policy objectives that ran counter to Arab nationalist ones. Foreign Minister Bitar reported on August 6 that a cable from Sa'ud declared he "is fully prepared to help in solving the crisis between Syria and Jordan" that had been brewing over the course of the summer.[25] The Saudi ambassador to Syria stated that the king was determined to see that Arab ranks remain unified.[26] Sa'ud had shifted from supporting Hussein against Syria in April to offering mediation between the two countries by August, a blow to Hussein and a foreshadowing of Sa'ud's mediation during the American-Syrian crisis. The United States Embassy in Amman reported on August 12 that external pressures on Jordan were increasing, but "help expected from sister Arab states is not forthcoming." The embassy also observed that Sa'ud "appears more quiescent in his support of Hussein and more tolerant of Syrian extremism. Iraq also appears to be leaving Hussein to hold the bag."[27]

Iraqi-Syrian Relations Prior to the Crisis

Iraq had been a cornerstone of British interests in the Middle East since World War One, clearly evidenced by the fact that it was the only Arab country to join the Baghdad Pact. The West certainly thought it could count on Iraqi support during the American-Syrian crisis, especially considering the recent animosities between Iraq and Syria stemming from the "Iraqi plot" in 1956 and the fissures created in Syrian society for over a decade revolving around the issue of possible union with Iraq. But when Loy Henderson, Eisenhower's special envoy to the Middle East, went to Turkey in late August 1957 to sound-out America's friends in the region regarding the situation in Syria, he found the Iraqis wavering. The Americans and the Turks expected Iraq to take the lead among the Arab states in response to the Syrian government's actions. This wavering by the Iraqis destroyed any notion of an all-Arab response and compelled the White House to seek alternative courses of action.

Why did Iraq waver? The primary reason lies in the resignation of Premier Nuri al-Sa'id on June 8, 1957, and the assumption of power by 'Ali Jawdat al-'Ayubi on June 17. Nuri was permanently stained in the eyes of the Iraqi public and the rest of the Arab world because of his close association with Great Britain. His reason for resigning was ostensibly to strengthen the cabinet, but he was probably responding to the civil unrest that had intensified in the aftermath of the Suez war and would eventually burst into rebellion in July 1958, resulting in the overthrow of the monarchy itself.

'Ali Jawdat was known and respected as being independent of the British and more sensitive to public opinion than his predecessor. His first term as premier came at the request of a group who had approached the regent 'Abd al-Ilah and asked him to replace Nuri al-Sa'id with someone who was more palatable to Syrians so that union between Iraq and Syria could be achieved. Jawdat assumed the premiership in December 1949, but all hopes of union were dashed when Adib al-Shishakli overthrew the pro-Iraqi Syrian regime later in December (indeed, the replacement of Nuri was one of the signals to Shishakli that he had better move fast). Despite this turn of events, Jawdat immediately set out to improve relations with Egypt and Syria. He concluded a secret agreement with Egypt (later overturned by the regent) that pledged not to interfere in Syrian affairs for a period of five years.[28] Although his attempt was scuttled, this agreement suggested that he would not interfere in the affairs of other Arab states, something that would certainly make him popular in Iraq and in the ruling circles of Syria and Egypt. He retained this attitude when he assumed power the second time.

Jawdat told British officials in Baghdad in June 1957 that he had instructed the Iraqi representatives in Cairo and Damascus to inform their hosts that Iraq was intent on pursuing good relations with them. He emphasized that Iraq's policy toward membership in the Baghdad Pact was dictated by its geographical position at the eastern end of the Arab world near the Soviet Union; it contained no "hidden designs" against other Arab nations.[29] Jawdat wanted to create some breathing room for his regime by reducing hostile Egyptian and Syrian propaganda. He also was cognizant of the fact that the oil pipelines of the Iraq Petroleum Company ran through Syria, and he did not want the Syrians to destroy them, as they had done during the Suez war. With this in mind, Jawdat made a concerted effort to improve relations with his Arab neighbors.

By early July 1957, the Syrian press was much more moderate in tone toward the new Iraqi government than toward the old, "almost free from the vicious attacks which were regularly aimed at the government of Nuri al-Said."[30] There were also reports of Iraqi troops being withdrawn from the Syrian and Jordanian borders; in addition, the Iraqi government announced for the first time its participation in the annual Damascus International Fair in September.[31] On July 14, the jamming of broadcasts by the Voice of the Arabs, Cairo Radio, and Damascus Radio was suspended; Jawdat also announced that he would reverse a previous decision by the Iraqi government and allow Iraq to participate in a consumer-goods fair sponsored by Egypt.[32] Bitar welcomed Iraq's new posture in a July 29 press conference, saying that Syria "asks only that other Arab governments follow an independent nationalist Arab policy" uncommitted to foreign interests.[33] At a meeting in Baghdad on August 7, Jawdat and the Syrian minister to Iraq agreed to raise diplomatic representation between the two countries to embassy level. Syria also used the occasion to formally invite the Iraqi minister of economy and development, Dr. Nadhim al-Pachachi, to the Damascus International Fair.[34]

The United States and Britain, although realizing the damage Suez had done to their positions in Iraq, did not approve of the moderate tone Jawdat had taken toward Syria and Egypt. Throughout the summer, British officials warned the Iraqi premier of the dire consequences his new foreign policy might have. They pointed out that any weakening of Iraq's position vis-à-vis Syria would be "most damaging" to King Hussein.[35] They also reminded him that the current left-wing leaders in Syria would do everything they could to "upset" the regimes in Jordan, Saudi Arabia, and Iraq, and any sign of conciliation toward them would be construed as a sign of weakness.[36] In response, Jawdat continued to proclaim Iraq's intention to cooperate with the West, but behind the scenes, he set about transforming Iraq into a good Arab nationalist state — not exactly what the United States expected when Henderson arrived in Istanbul. Consequently, Iraq balked at taking the lead in response to the situation in Syria in August. It is therefore not surprising that when King Saʻud visited Damascus on September 25, 1957, at the height of the American-Syrian crisis, the next day ʻAli Jawdat arrived to do his part for Arab solidarity. In this context, it is also not surprising that the British, Turks, and Americans all clamored for the return of Nuri al-Saʻid to Iraq as premier. Jawdat, however, would stay in power until December 1957.

Notes

1. Letter from Eisenhower to Saud, May 11, 1957, Ann Whitman File, International Series, Box 42, DDEL.

2. *Documents on International Affairs* (Royal Institute for International Affairs, London), no. 10, 286–287.

3. "Developments . . . ," *Middle East Journal,* vol. XII (Summer 1957): 295; also, *Documents on International Affairs,* 286–287.

4. *al-Baʻth,* May 20, 1957.

5. Weekly Letter on Syria, British Embassy-Beirut, June 20, 1957, FO 371/128223, PRO.

6. Quote from Middle East News Agency on June 24, 1957, from Weekly Letter on Syria, British Embassy-Beirut, June 27, 1957, FO 371/128223, PRO. Also see Damascus left-wing paper *al-Ahram* of June 27 on ʻAsali's attempts to mend relations.

7. *Daily Star* (Beirut), June 29, 1957.

8. Weekly Letter on Syria, British Embassy-Beirut, July 4, 1957, FO 371/128223, PRO.

9. *L'Orient*, July 2, 1957 for Bitar; Weekly Letter on Syria, British Embassy-Beirut, July 11, 1957, FO 371/128223, PRO, for Hawrani; and Weekly Letter on Syria, British Embassy-Beirut, July 25, 1957, FO 371/128223, PRO, for 'Asali. Bitar told Ambassador Moose on June 24 and June 27 that the American position regarding the Gulf of Aqaba was "improper and evidence of partiality toward Israel." (Memorandum of Conversations, American Embassy, Damascus, June 24, 1957, *FRUS*, p. 624). Also see FBIS, August 7, 1957, p. C3, for further statements by Syrian officials in support of Saudi Arabia.

10. Weekly Letter on Syria, British Embassy-Beirut, July 4, 1957, FO 371/128223, PRO.

11. Weekly Letter on Syria, British Embassy-Beirut, July 11, 1957, FO 371/128223, PRO.

12. Weekly Letter on Syria, British Embassy-Beirut, July 18, 1957, FO 371/128223, PRO.

13. Anatolian News Agency, July 30, 1957, from British Embassy-Ankara, August 1, 1957, FO 371/128223, PRO.

14. *Al-Sham*, July 31, 1957, from Weekly Letter on Syria, British Embassy-Beirut, August 1, 1957, FO 371/128223, PRO; Telegram From American Embassy in Damascus to Department of State, August 3, 1957, Microform Reading Room, microfiche 71G (1977), Library of Congress; FBIS, July 29, 1957, p. E4.

15. Memorandum From the Secretary of State's Deputy Special Assistant for Intelligence to the Secretary of State, July 17, 1957, *FRUS*, pp. 498–499.

16. For Sa'ud's claims in the Gulf of Aqaba, see ibid; also see Telegram From the Embassy in Saudi Arabia to the Department of State, April 11, 1957, *FRUS*, pp. 489–491; and Letter from the Saudi Arabian government to Secretary of State John Foster Dulles, June 25, 1957, Ann Whitman File, International Series, Box 42, DDEL.

17. Memorandum From the Secretary of State's Deputy, July 17, 1957, p. 499. Also see report from Britain's Foreign Office on July 30, 1957, in anticipation of meeting with John Foster Dulles, expressing similar concerns on the effects of the Aqaba question on Sa'ud's relations with the West: "We are as anxious as the Americans that trouble over Aqaba should not drive King Saud back into Nasser's arms." (FO 371/127757, PRO).

18. Weekly Letter on Syria, British Embassy-Beirut, July 8, 1957, FO 371/128223, PRO.

19. Weekly Letter on Syria, British Embassy-Beirut, July 8, 1957, FO 371/128223, PRO.

20. To underline the importance Britain attached to the Persian Gulf and southern Arabia, see a study by the Royal Institute of International Affairs

published in 1958, entitled, *British Interests in the Mediterranean and Middle East.* In it the following conclusion was made: "With the *exception* of her obligations to the Sheikhs of the Persian Gulf and southern Arabia, there are no longer any specifically and uniquely British interests which would justify large military expenditure undertaken single-handed." p. 101 (emphasis mine).

21. Humphrey Trevelyan, *The Middle East in Revolution* (London: The MacMillan Company, 1970), pp. 71–72.

22. British Foreign Office Report, "Middle East: The Nature of the Threat and Means of Countering it" (in preparation for Bermuda Conference with the United States), March 8, 1957, FO 371/127755, PRO; British Foreign Office Reports in preparation for Anglo-American talks on June 12–14, no dates, "Measures to Ensure Continued Access to Middle East Petroleum Resources," FO 371/127756, PRO; and, "Saudi Arabia and Buraimi and Their Relations to Kuwait," FO 371/127756, PRO.

23. Telegram From the Embassy in Saudi Arabia to the Department of State, April 11, 1957, *FRUS,* p. 492.

24. The British press attacked what it thought was an equivocating American stance on Buraimi. They also blamed Washington for the crisis in Oman, accusing it of either supplying the rebels directly with arms or "allowing" Sa'ud to funnel American arms to the rebels. (See *Sunday Express,* July 21; *Daily Mail, Daily Telegraph* and *Manchester Guardian* of July 22; and the *Times,* July 23). At the official level, however, the British and Americans successfully tried to minimize the differences in policy vis-à-vis Buraimi, especially so soon after the open breach in relations during the Suez crisis and the public mending of relations at the Bermuda Conference. See Coral Bell, *The Debatable Alliance* (New York: Oxford University Press, 1964), pp. 42–43. For summary of conversations between Eisenhower, Dulles, MacMillan and Lloyd at Bermuda Conference see, Bermuda Conference Records, "Middle East: General Questions," March 21, 1957, FO 371/127755, PRO; and for summary of U.S.-UK policy regarding the Middle East see, Foreign Office Report, July 11, 1957, FO 371/127757, PRO.

25. FBIS, August 7, 1957, p. C4–5.

26. Ibid.

27. Telegram From the Embassy in Jordan to the Department of State, August 12, 1957, *FRUS,* p. 158.

28. Seale, p. 89.

29. British Embassy-Baghdad, August 13, 1957, FO 371/128249, PRO.

30. DA Intelligence Report, July 9, 1957, Entry 85, Intell. Doc. File, 2052166, RG319, NARA.

31. Ibid.

32. "Developments . . . ," *Middle East Journal,* vol. XIII (Autumn 1957): p. 420.

33. Telegram from American Embassy in Damascus to the Department of State, August 3, 1957, Microform Reading Room, Microfiche 71G (1977), Library of Congress.

34. FBIS, August 9, 1957, p. C5. Pachachi, his entourage, and a number of Iraqi journalists had all travel and accommodations paid for by the Syrian government and were treated with "much courtesy" while in Syria. (British Embassy-Baghdad, Sept 20, 1957, FO 371/128249, PRO.)

35. Foreign Office Report, "Situation in Syria," August 13, 1957, FO 371/128223, PRO.

36. British Embassy-Baghdad, August 13, 1957, FO 371/128249, PRO.

9

The American Riposte

The 1957 American-Syrian crisis officially began on August 12, when the Syrian government announced it had uncovered an American plot to overthrow the regime. The next day, Damascus Radio broadcast that the "Syrian Government would be grateful" if three members of the American diplomatic contingent in Damascus left Syria within twenty-four hours.[1] The secretary general of the ministry of foreign affairs, Salah al-Din Tarazi, informed the United States Embassy in Damascus that in order to "preserve good relations between Syria and the United States it was necessary . . . to declare them persona non grata."[2] Washington responded in kind on August 14 by declaring the Syrian ambassador to the United States and his second secretary persona non grata.

The covert operation was apparently masterminded by the second secretary to the American legation in Damascus, Howard Stone, who had become somewhat notorious for his role in similar activities in Iran, Guatemala, and the Sudan. Reportedly, the objective was to return Colonel Adib al-Shishakli and his associate Colonel Ibrahim al-Hussayni to power after "getting rid" of the likes of Sarraj, Bizri, Hamdum, and Nafuri.[3] The Populist Party would then be placed in control of parliament. In order to accomplish this, the United States needed the support of military officers in the Syrian army; however, Stone and his associates, who apparently had the authority to do whatever they wanted in Syria, were careless in their choice of Syrian accomplices. Among the Syrians Stone had recruited were several officers who either worked for Sarraj or upon hearing about the details of the plot decided to divulge its contents to Syrian intelligence. The American plot, in many ways, resembled the British-Iraqi action in 1956 (Operation Straggle) and failed just as miserably; but whereas the British were in no position to react to the Syrian disclosure because of their preoccupation with the fall-out from the Suez crisis, the Eisenhower administration had no such burden. The fact that the Syrian government's initial reaction to the disclosure of the American plot was relatively mild indicated that it was not anxious to confront the United States for fear of providing it with a pretext to intervene in Syria.[4] This also leads one to believe it was the reaction of the Eisenhower administration that elevated the American-Syrian bilateral problem into a regional and international one.

Strategic Considerations

Other than the pro forma statement that declared the Syrian diplomats in Washington persona non grata, the Eisenhower administration was at first stumped on how to respond. Eisenhower and Dulles were also distracted by and preoccupied with their battle with Congress over the Mutual Security bill.[5] Speaking to British officials on August 19, Dulles stated that "he had not yet caught up with the developments either in Syria or Oman, as he had been absorbed in the Mutual Security program and had spent the morning testifying in the Senate."[6] The attention of the British was also partially diverted by the UN Security Council debate over the Omani rebellion.[7] Naturally, the State Department tried to gather as much information as it could on the extent of the problem in Syria. The Syrians, however, had surrounded the American embassy in Damascus with police, making it extremely difficult to gain first-hand information.[8] The administration tried to assess the situation: was it the culmination of Syria's leftist drift that had been observed in recent years or was it a genuine leap toward Soviet/communist domination? In this vein, it should be pointed out that the administration viewed the August 15 resignation of Nizam al-Din from his position as Syrian chief of staff, replaced by 'Afif al-Bizri, as foreboding for its interests and as great an indication of the leftist orientation of the Syrian polity as the uncovering of the plot itself. Eisenhower and Dulles had two policy choices: minimize the fall-out or take advantage of the "showdown" to irreparably weaken the leftist regime.

Eisenhower convened a meeting at the White House on August 14, 1957, to discuss an appropriate response. It was agreed that the United States should declare the Syrian diplomats persona non grata. Eisenhower did this with the full realization that Syria could respond by severing diplomatic relations with the United States. This was a major concern for the administration since the British and French were already without diplomatic representation in Damascus (because of the Suez war) and could leave a "fairly open field" to the Soviets. The president, however, emphasized that strong measures must be taken and if they led to a severance of relations then at least the American public would see the "gravity" of the situation, i.e., rising Soviet influence in the Middle East; by implication, this also meant that the American people would then support subsequent actions by the administration. Despite what would be vociferous opposition from Israel, Eisenhower also spoke in favor of dispatching military aid to Arab allies in the region who could be threatened by Syria; consistent with his actions during the Suez crisis, the president stated that the Israeli attitude "could not be the determining factor in connection with the policy which we decide upon if it were in our interests to provide some heavy equipment."[9] Also on August 14, the State Department sent telegrams to American embassies in Jordan, Iraq, Lebanon, and Saudi Arabia, instructing them to convey to their respective hosts the administration's concern over the course of events in Syria. The memo stated that Syria's accusations were false and that its actions were typical of a communist-controlled state. It described the situation as "extremely disturbing" since it came on the heels of the Soviet-Syrian economic agreement, with the implication that the Kremlin may have orchestrated the maneuver; this again is an example of how American officials in Washington were quick to conclude, without sufficient evidence, that the Kremlin lurked behind every door.[10]

The State Department received memos on August 19 from its embassies in Lebanon, Jordan, Turkey, Saudi Arabia, and Iraq expressing the deep concern of those countries over the developing crisis in Syria.[11] From the beginning King Hussein realized the importance of Saudi Arabia to any regional response and immediately proposed a meeting with Sa'ud to assess the situation, with the possibility of enlarging the meeting to include other key Middle Eastern leaders. Hussein stressed the necessity to impress upon Sa'ud the serious nature of the impending crisis.[12] President Sham'un of Lebanon, who was understandably the most anxious of Syria's neighbors, remarked that he would follow Sa'ud's lead.[13] Iraqi Prime Minister 'Ali Jawdat echoed his counterparts' sentiments but lamented his country's limited ability to reverse the situation in Syria. He pointed out that Iraq had few contacts left in Syria and that the pro-Iraqi factions were virtually powerless (not ruling out, however, the possibility of direct Iraqi intervention). On August 19, however, the Iraqi acting minister for foreign affairs, 'Ali Mumtaz, "clearly discounted" Iraqi military action against Syria, emphasizing his concern over the IPC pipelines.[14] Mumtaz also informed the American ambassador in Baghdad that he hoped that Israel would not benefit from the situation. He went on to state that Israel should be restrained lest all the Arab states turn to the Soviets for support; he also warned the Eisenhower administration to be careful not to make any moves that could be construed as being pro-Israeli.[15]

In Istanbul, also on August 19, Prime Minister Menderes of Turkey met with King Faisal of Iraq and his crown prince, imploring them to take decisive action against Syria; however, he said there was little or nothing Turkey could do to rectify the situation. The Turks, as noted before, were primarily concerned about being confronted by communist states on two borders. Menderes and Faisal agreed that the situation in Syria was indeed very serious, that a strong response was in order, and that the United State should make up its mind what it wants to do.[16] The trend emerging from this meeting was that the Middle East friends of the United States were waiting for and/or urging someone *else* to spearhead retaliatory action against Syria, hopefully with the support of Saudi Arabia, and all were waiting for the Eisenhower administration to formulate a policy response.

Eisenhower and Dulles both felt that the course of events in Syria was unacceptable. The White House believed it "could not afford to have exist a Soviet satellite not contiguous to the Soviet border and in the midst of the already delicate Middle East situation."[17] They were also anxious to take advantage of the trepidations initially expressed by Syria's neighbors, feelings that would subside if the United States did nothing. The administration also knew their friends in the Middle East were looking to it to lead the way, but Eisenhower and Dulles were looking in the opposite direction for a regional response to the crisis. Eisenhower and Dulles were in favor of corrective action in Syria but were hamstrung by the specter of Suez and Hungary; in both cases the administration strongly condemned outside intervention, and it did not want to appear to be second generation imperialists.

That the United States seriously contemplated action against Syria is clear. In a telephone conversation with Chief of Staff General Nathan Twining on August 21, Dulles stated that "we are thinking of the possibility of fairly drastic action."[18] On the same day, Dulles wrote to British Foreign Minister Selwyn Lloyd that "it seems to us that there is now little hope of correction from within and that we must think in terms of the external assets reflected by the deep concern of the Moslem States. . . . We must perhaps be prepared to take some serious risks to avoid even greater risks and dangers later on."[19] British Prime Minister Harold MacMillan commented on August 27 that "this question is going to be of tremendous importance. The Americans are taking it very seriously, and talking about the most drastic measures—Suez in reverse. If it were not serious . . . it would be rather comic."[20]

The desire for a regional response supported by Saudi Arabia, however, was most clearly demonstrated in a letter from Eisenhower to Sa'ud dated August 21: "We believe . . . that it is highly preferable that Syria's neighbors should be able to deal with this problem without the necessity for any outside intervention. In view of the special position of Your Majesty as Keeper of the Holy Places of Islam, I trust that you will exert your great influence to the end that the atheistic creed of Communism will not become entrenched at a key position in the Moslem world."[21] The constraints on the willingness and ability of Sa'ud to carry out American wishes and the misperception by the administration that Sa'ud had great influence in the Middle East eliminated any hope for a regional response. MacMillan wrote Dulles on August 23 that the "essential point is that the other Arabs should expose the pretensions of the present Syrian regime to be good Arab nationalists and should denounce them for what they are, namely Communists and Communist stooges."[22] The problem was that Syria's Arab neighbors, namely Saudi Arabia, did not agree with MacMillan's assessment. Several press reports and comments by Arab diplomats indicated that Sa'ud had visited Cairo around August 20 to confer with Nasser and Quwatli.[23] If this meeting did indeed take place, and it does make sense in view of Sa'ud's subsequent actions, it signaled his abandonment of any American-inspired move and showed just how far he had gone in the other direction to gain power in the region.

Eisenhower gave the first public indications of the position of the United States regarding Syria at a press conference on August 21, 1957. What is important about the conference is not only what Eisenhower said but also what he was prepared to say. Dulles advised the president along the following lines:[24]

I think it important that you avoid any statement or implication that you have as yet determined that Syria is now controlled by International Communism within the meaning of the Middle East Resolution [Eisenhower Doctrine]. On the other hand, I would avoid any statement that you think it is *not* so controlled. ... I think it important that you should say nothing which would encourage Israel ... to stimulate an incident with Syria on the theory that we have judged Syria to be Communist controlled. On the other hand, we would want to keep freedom of action to make such a decision under certain contingencies. We would like to keep the Syrian Government uncertain as to our intentions.

Eisenhower stated that Syria had not yet been found to be under the control of "international communism" and the Eisenhower Doctrine therefore did not yet apply. He also accused the Soviet Union of wanting to control Syria by transforming it into a communist dominated state following the "classic pattern" the Soviets had used elsewhere in the world. The Syrian accusations against the United States were a part of this pattern. Dulles stated that "we do not yet know how far along this pattern [in] Syria has yet gone, but certainly what has already happened is a sign of danger and should be a warning to others who are sought to be lured by the Communist technique."[25]

It was fairly easy to keep the Syrian government confused about American intentions since the Eisenhower administration itself was undecided as to what specific course of action it should take. The ambiguity of Eisenhower's press conference was as much a reflection of an administration in the dark as a strategic move to keep the Syrians nervous.[26] Ironically, a statement by Damascus Radio accurately assessed the administration's attitude: "On the one hand, it wants to impose its influence on Syria and associate it with the foreign policy of American imperialism. But on the other hand, it cannot find an opening through which to move into Syria. ... "[27] The White House had to consider a multitude of factors before a policy decision could be made – the result of being caught off-guard. Administration officials readily admitted time was against them. They knew they had to take advantage of Arab sentiments quickly, but to his credit on many occasions, Eisenhower was never one to act rashly before he examined all of the contingencies and possibilities.

Of paramount importance to the Eisenhower administration was the position of the Soviet Union, i.e., prevent any significant increase in Soviet influence in the area. At the same time, the administration wanted to avoid a conflagration that could pit the two superpowers against one another. The administration also was wary of the possibility that the Kremlin would commit its prestige to the maintenance of the Syrian regime so deeply that it would be forced to react to an American move. Both the Americans and the British agreed that Syria itself (or more precisely, the Syrian army) did not present an immediate military threat to its neighbors.[28] Subversion based out of Syria was judged the primary threat in the area, especially in light of the stockpiling of Soviet weaponry in the country. The United States found itself in a position that would become all too familiar: finding the point where it could maintain its influence and prestige in the region without goading the Soviets into taking more than reciprocal action to protect what they saw as their own position in the Middle East, with the concomitant possibility of global warfare over a relatively minor incident.

In a classic zero-sum game, Eisenhower and Dulles also had to decide if they could take advantage of the existing situation to advance American interests in the region at the expense of the Soviets. This was the advantage of promoting a regional solution to the American-Syrian crisis: the United States would not be directly involved, thereby obviating the need for a reciprocal Soviet response while at the same time getting rid of the decidedly leftist and pro-Soviet Syrian regime. This might have then coalesced the regional friends of the United States into the long-sought-after pro-West regional alliance.

Under no circumstances, however, did Dulles want the Syrian situation to spillover into the Arab-Israeli arena, which would force the Arab states to line up behind Syria and put the United States in a very difficult position. The secretary of state repeatedly sent messages to the Israeli government and personally wrote Israeli Prime Minister David Ben-Gurion, cautioning him against any Israeli action which could be construed as aggression against Syria. Syria, of course, was doing its best to embellish the Israeli threat in order to solidify support from other Arab countries. Dulles wrote a letter to MacMillan on August 22 in which he said: "I think it important that not only Israel but the Western countries should avoid any initiative but that if Syrian developments carried a threat to Syria's Moslem neighbors they should know that they would have our moral support in any defensive measures they might feel called upon to take."[29] Even though this statement was not made public, it does reveal some interesting insights into the rather passive thinking of the administration at the time. Dulles essentially said that the United States would avoid any active intervention unless Syria threatened its "Moslem neighbors" (using the word "moslem" thus includes non-Arab Turkey); even if Syria threatened its "Moslem neighbors," the United States would only offer "moral support in any defensive measures" undertaken by these nations. The passive nature of the American response was viewed by the Turks as inaction, whereas America's European allies described it as reacting "relatively calmly."[30] The "calmness" of the American response was due to a variety of factors: the administration was unprepared to address the situation in a timely fashion and thus had to start from scratch to find an appropriate policy; it was also preoccupied with legislative matters as the current session of Congress came to a close; and Eisenhower and Dulles, among others in the administration, were concerned about Soviet actions in response to any American initiative and wanted to carefully assess all contingencies before taking action of their own.

In addition, the United States, as well as its European allies, were largely in agreement that the Soviets did not intend to rush things in Syria or do anything too provocative. They were fairly certain that the Kremlin feared the effects that an aggressive policy might have on the Arab states (primarily Egypt), all of whom disliked communism and any Soviet interference that would just be a substitute for Western imperialism. It was still far from certain that the Soviets wanted to develop Syria as a military base, "since this would mean committing Russian forces to a country not contiguous with the Soviet Bloc."[31] The Soviet economic agreement with Syria could have been the Kremlin's riposte to the Eisenhower Doctrine. And after observing the political turmoil in Syria following the economic aid agreement, the Kremlin might have wanted to lay low for awhile until the situation stabilized.

Nasser's Concerns About Syria

Gamal 'Abd al-Nasser was quite unsettled about the state of affairs in Syria. The State Department obtained information that the Egyptian president had no foreknowledge of the economic agreement between the Soviet Union and Syria, and he was not very happy about it.[32] A Syrian official informed the Americans in Damascus that Nasser was "disturbed" at not having been more fully apprised of Khalid al-'Azm's negotiations in Moscow.[33] He correctly pointed out, however, that Egypt was in the same position as the Syrian government, since 'Azm apparently was given wide latitude to negotiate a deal and consummated it without consulting his colleagues in Damascus or even in Moscow. It was also reported that Populist Party leader Ma'ruf al-Dawalibi, on a visit to Cairo to commemorate the inauguration of the Egyptian parliament, obtained assurances that Nasser would help prevent a communist takeover in Syria (without specifying how).[34] Nasser reportedly indicated that he needed two months of extensive planning, but the announcement of the Syrian-Soviet agreement altered the equation altogether.[35] The Egyptian president subsequently sent Quwatli back to Damascus on August 25 to "put the brakes on" and prevent Khalid al-'Azm from filling the vacuum in the Syrian president's absence.[36] Quwatli's return was no doubt the main topic of discussion at the reported meeting in Cairo around August 20 between Sa'ud, Nasser, and the Syrian president. Nasser and Sa'ud apparently negotiated with Syrian representatives, the outcome of which produced two conditions for allowing Quwatli to return. One condition was that the dismissals and arrests that had taken place in Syria would remain; the second was that no more dismissals or arrests would take place without the expressed authority of the president.[37] Quwatli's return was a key to maintaining Saudi-Syrian relations, and if he had not been allowed to return, Sa'ud likely would have been in a position to accede to American wishes regarding action against Syria; in fact, it might have been Sa'ud's price quoted to Nasser for the king's hands-off approach to Syria. Nasser, therefore, was not only concerned about the situation in Syria in and of itself, but also preventing the crisis situation from acting as a catalyst to American-Saudi cooperation and the establishment of a stronger pro-West Arab front in the Middle East. Subsequently, it is not surprising that the Egyptian press began to praise Quwatli for his leadership in Syria in a belated attempt to build up the prestige of the beleaguered president.[38]

The Eisenhower administration believed the crisis made Nasser vulnerable, possibly forcing him to be more cooperative with the West. There were those in the State Department who insisted that Nasser still was not completely lost. In a September 9 interview with *al-Ahram,* Nasser castigated American policy, but his speech was "not balanced by correspondingly friendly references to the Russians, and this proved that Nasser, despite his bluster, was worried by the extent to which the Syrians had moved into the Soviet camp and out of his own."[39] Administration officials admitted that Nasser could not be brought around to the original ideas of a MEDO or MEC, but they hoped they could persuade him to play a beneficial role regarding Syria. The American ambassador to Cairo, Raymond Hare, wrote *before* the American-Syrian crisis, referring to Nasser, that "for appearances sake if for no other, sinner should be given [the] opportunity for redemption." He went on to say that "what is needed is a well-labelled escape hatch which Nasser could use in [the] unexpected event he decided to mend his ways . . . " while not giving the "idea that we are going soft on Nasser or that we are in any way letting down friendly governments of [the] area."[40] With the crisis, Hare confirmed reports that Nasser was irritated over the Syrian deal with the Soviets and its possible negative effects upon Egypt, and he advanced the idea that it was an exploitable situation that might allow the United States to use Nasser's perturbation over Soviet influence in Syria to open a channel. The Eisenhower administration, therefore, may have also reacted cautiously to the Syrian incident and promoted a regional response to give Nasser another opportunity to "see the light" and move closer to the United States.

We also see a clear distinction in policy approach between the Eisenhower administration and Nasser. The Egyptian president, like Sa'ud, responded to the Syrian problem at the regional level, taking into consideration his regional interests. The United States, on the other hand, examined the situation from the international level, with its own position in the Middle East and that of the Soviet Union paramount in its calculations. Although dismayed over events in Syria, it would have been a fatal blow to Nasser's claim to Arab leadership if he acted against a sister Arab state, especially as outside pressure mounted upon the Syrian regime. This much was clear from the September 9 interview with *al-Ahram* cited earlier, in which he repeatedly stated that the real objective of the Eisenhower administration was to "lighten the burden of Israel, shift attention from it, and direct Israel to achieve other objectives in line with the interests of American policy."[41] Nasser wanted to make sure that the focus of attention in the Middle East did not sway from the one enemy that provided him with his prestige and stature. He also did not want the Middle East to become a cold war battleground where he would become just another pawn in the superpowers' diplomatic games. He had worked hard for Syria and was not about to let it slip away as a result of superpower diplomacy. Nasser ended the interview by stating that Egypt "stands on Syria's side unconditionally. Regardless of pressure being brought to bear upon Syria, one thing must not be forgotten, namely that all Egypt's political, economic, and military potential supports Syria in its battle. Indeed, it is our battle—the battle of all Arab nationalists."

American-Saudi Divergence

We have already noted the pivotal position King Sa'ud assumed in the Middle East by the summer of 1957, a role largely attributable to the fact that this was the way the United States wanted it. The 1957 American-Syrian crisis was the type of situation the Eisenhower administration envisioned when it promoted Sa'ud as its bulwark against Soviet expansionism in the Middle East. As we have seen, however, relations between the Saudis and the Americans at the time were less cordial than they had been earlier in the year.

Secretary of State Dulles said that the American position vis-à-vis Syria was complicated by its support for Israel and its differences with Sa'ud.[42] Correspondence between Tel Aviv and Washington, combined with hindsight, indicate that the possibility that Israel would take military action against Syria was never a factor during the crisis. This cannot be said of the differences with Sa'ud. Neither Dulles nor King Hussein received a direct reply from Sa'ud to messages they had earlier sent him requesting his assessment of the Syrian situation. Instead the United States Embassy in Jedda received a secondhand note from Saudi officials stating that, while the king viewed the situation in Syria as alarming, he expressed "great pleasure" at what turned out to be a false report that the Lebanese were offering to mediate between the Syrians and Americans.[43] In other words, Sa'ud was implying that he favored diplomacy over force.

Dulles was reluctant to press Sa'ud on individual problems until he could more accurately gauge the king's attitude, thus he did not specifically urge him to use his influence in Damascus.[44] The secretary of state knew the relationship with Saudi Arabia had changed considerably since Sa'ud's earlier actions at the Cairo conference and with the trial verdicts. As it turned out, Sa'ud's apparent laissez faire attitude toward Syria was a decisive factor that prevented the United States from organizing a regional response to the crisis.

Confirmation of Sa'ud's stance came in the form of two notes that the State Department finally received from the king himself on August 25 (the same day that Quwatli returned to Damascus). One dealt with the Gulf of Aqaba question and the other with the American-Syrian crisis. While their contents are still unknown, they were described as being "couched in extremely tough language," suggesting Sa'ud was placing the blame for the events in Syria squarely on the United States.[45] In response to the king's notes, the State Department wrote to its embassy in Jedda the following:[46]

> "We find [it] very disappointing indications you have received of King's attitude toward developments in Syria. . . . In interests [of] Saudi Arabia and in those of all NE [Near East] states we are anxious that [the] King use his political and moral authority to rally opposition in area to present Syrian regime and to facilitate generating of pressures designed to isolate Syria and to work toward an improvement of situation in that country.

The American ambassador in Jedda also emphasized to the king the danger of communism and Soviet influence in the Middle East and tried to play down the American relationship with Israel. He was unable to persuade Sa'ud.

The Henderson Mission

Responding to strong requests from its allies in the Middle East for action, Eisenhower decided to send Deputy Under Secretary of State for Administration Loy W. Henderson to Turkey to meet with the leaders of what the United States thought would be an anti-Syrian coalition. He arrived in Istanbul on August 24, 1957, and met with Menderes, King Hussein of Jordan, and Iraq's King Faisal, then went to Lebanon to meet with President Sham'un; he then returned to Turkey to talk with Crown Prince 'Abd al-Ilah of Iraq, the Iraqi army chief of staff, and Menderes, before arriving back in Washington on September 4. Henderson was one of the architects of the Truman Doctrine in 1947 and played an instrumental role in the overthrow of the Mossadegh regime in Iran in 1953—he was considered the "Middle East man" for the Eisenhower administration.[47] The decision to send Henderson was a fateful one, as his presence in the Middle East instantly raised the tension in the American-Syrian crisis to new heights.

Henderson's instructions reportedly were to relay to those who gathered in Turkey the administration's view on the situation in Syria and get their assessment of the crisis. In addition, Dulles instructed Henderson along the following lines:[48]

> In your discussions you should of course bear in mind U.S. policy of supporting the principles of the UN and opposing unprovoked military intervention in any country. At the same time the United States must be fully alert to obvious dangers of situation in which Syria, under increasing Soviet influence, is receiving large amounts of military goods obviously exceeding those required for Syria's defensive needs. We must take into account any legitimate military planning required by Syria's neighbors to be prepared to protect themselves from any Syrian aggression. Indeed, it is the purpose of the Middle East Doctrine to assist countries in the area to develop their economic and military strength, to resist communist threats and to make clear the preparedness of the United States to come to the assistance of any of them requesting such aid which is the victim of an attack by a country under the control of international communism.

Henderson, while acknowledging the administration's deep concern over the affair, emphasized that the United States was prepared to give "appropriate support to Syria's Moslem neighbors in case Syrian provocations would force them to take some kind [of] defensive action." He pointed out that the United States was not "urging any particular type of action" but felt that they "could best decide among themselves what they could and should do." Henderson added that no action should be taken that could not be justified under the United Nations Charter (i.e., not another Suez-type operation).[49]

All the participants agreed that the Turks should not engage in any fighting against Syria since it would force the Arab states to unite in support of Syria against a non-Arab foe (especially one burdened by the history of the Ottoman empire). Jordan and Turkey believed Iraq should take the lead in a regional initiative. The conferees discussed a wide range of options to counter the Syrian threat, from diplomatic pressure, to using Syrian exiles, to direct military intervention. In the process, an assessment was made of the fighting capabilities of the Jordanians, Iraqis, and Syrians. It was pointed out that while Syria probably possessed a greater quantity of armaments than either Jordan or Iraq, the latter two far surpassed it in military organization and training.

Eisenhower wrote that "it was thought that if on the west, south and north of Syria, Lebanon, Jordan, and Turkey should each mass its own troops along the Syrian boundary, that country would be required so to disperse its own forces as to facilitate successful Iraqi military operations from the east."[50] He felt that by massing troops on their borders, the Syrian people would see other Arab states "helping out" and might themselves turn against the regime.[51] The president thought, however, that if the Iraqis intervened and did not achieve a quick decisive victory, the Turks might need to be called into the fray to assist. This, in turn, might be enough to provoke the Soviets to make noises along Turkey's northern border, requiring the United States to come to the aid of its NATO ally (with all the possibilities for direct superpower confrontation).[52] It would also brand Turkey and Iraq, both members of the Baghdad Pact, as instruments of imperialism and lend credence to Nasser's claim that the pact was indeed a shield to protect Western interests. Expecting a regional response, Eisenhower pledged that the United States would do all that it could to keep other countries, i.e., the Soviet Union and Israel, from interfering. To back up his pledge of protection (or insulation), the president authorized the transfer of American aircraft from Western Europe to the American airbase at Adana, Turkey, and ordered the Sixth Fleet to steam toward the eastern Mediterranean. He also placed the Strategic Air Command on a state of alert. Eisenhower remarked that "all we can do under the Middle East Doctrine is to make sure that the Soviets cannot come in, and give assurances to that effect, and also give military aid to our allies."[53]

The president stated at a press conference that the United States had yet to make a determination that Syria was a country controlled by international communism. The administration, however, was reportedly very close to making such a determination, especially if taking this step would facilitate "other important actions to deal with the present situation."[54] State Department officials were quick to point out, however, that a "finding" was only the first part the Eisenhower Doctrine; there also had to be an attack by the labelled country and then a request from the country being attacked for American assistance.

Eisenhower had two majors problems with military intervention in Syria. One was the fact that during the Suez crisis and the Soviet invasion of Hungary, he had supported the principle that "military force was not a justifiable means for settling disputes"; yet "now we were being asked to give our tacit approval to an invasion of one sovereign nation by another."[55] But

Eisenhower was also convinced that Syria was on the road to becoming a Soviet satellite, and he was determined not to allow this to happen. He felt the negative consequences of inaction would outweigh any that might be associated with an active response. The president had to find a way to rationalize this dilemma, first to himself, then to the outside world. He did this by viewing the Syrian situation as inherently different than the Suez crisis. The Arabs, he postulated, were "convinced" that Syria had been clandestinely invaded through infiltration and subversion, whereas during Suez they believed Nasser had acted well within his rights in nationalizing the Suez Canal. Eisenhower decided that Arab action against Syria "would be *basically* defensive in nature, particularly because they intended to react to *anticipated aggression*, rather than to commit a naked aggression".[56] (emphasis mine). It is interesting that the president did not officially attempt to compare military intervention in Syria with the Hungarian incident, for he knew he would be standing on shaky ground.

The sticky question of how to deal with subversion, which critics of the Eisenhower Doctrine had asked when it was announced, had again come to the forefront. The administration was forced to answer it. Now, however, instead of the pretext for implementation of the doctrine being an open attack of one country against another, the administration prepared the way for possible military intervention on the grounds of *anticipated aggression*. All the White House needed was an arbitrary finding that Syria was controlled by international communism, and what would probably have been a prearranged request from the likes of Jordan, Iraq, and Lebanon for American assistance *after* they had moved against Syria. In this fashion, administration officials were sure they could insulate the conflict at the inter-Arab level and prevent a Soviet-American confrontation. As Dulles stated: " . . . it was one thing to use United States military force to drive the Soviets out of a position where they were [Hungary for instance] and another to interpose United States force between the Soviet Union and some new area which they might be intent upon attacking. The first would surely mean general war; the second probably would not."[57] (Insert mine.)

The Eisenhower administration had another problem: no Arab state was willing to assume the leadership role. This was apparent from Henderson's mission. Unexpectedly, he did not have a solid proposal to put forth to the conferees when he arrived in Istanbul. In fact, the British ambassador to Turkey described Henderson as having been "inadequately briefed and rather devoid of ideas."[58] Henderson was devoid of ideas because the administration was devoid of ideas. Rountree told British officials that the State Department would not decide on any policy for "future action" until it received Henderson's findings.[59] The administration expected concrete proposals from the conferees meeting in Turkey. Instead, while its Middle East allies expressed great concern over the events in Syria, this was not "followed by any positive suggestions."[60] The conferees had obviously expected Henderson to arrive with a proposal, but none was forthcoming, and all they could agree upon was that something had to be done soon (within sixty days according to Dulles).[61]

Inter-Arab dynamics was also a mitigating factor against concerted action. Crown Prince 'Abd al-Ilah of Iraq frankly admitted there was no trust between King Hussein and himself, although the United States had counted on Iraqi-Jordanian cooperation if any "effective" action were to be taken against Syria (as an American official pointed out, Iraqi troops would have a much easier time penetrating Syria through Jordan than to traverse the vast desert and roadless space directly across the Syrian-Iraqi border).[62] The Jordanians insisted that Saudi support was the key to the whole situation, but Saudi cooperation did not materialize.[63] Without it, Hussein could only leave Turkey to vacation in Italy and Spain, a move which led Eisenhower to conclude that "contrary to what we had been led to believe . . . [Jordan] did not want to join in any move against Syria."[64]

In addition, the Saudis so distrusted Iraqi ambitions toward Syria that a stream of messages was sent from Baghdad to Riyadh hoping to allay the king's apprehensions. The Turks were also suspicious of Iraq's intentions and were poised to make certain they did not lose their sphere of influence in northern Syria. Finally, the Arab states were not confident that the United States would fully support an Arab initiative. They cited as worrisome the actions the United States had taken against their closest allies during the Suez crisis. Then there were always unpredictable constitutional barriers an American president might encounter.[65] That Henderson came unprepared had done nothing to diminish their worries.

Differences of opinion could also be found within the ruling circles of the Arab world as to the seriousness of the Syrian situation. They had to be wary of the sentiments of the populace, who were largely sympathetic to the Syrian regime. Henderson was reported to have been "shocked" by the negative reaction of the Lebanese press to his visit in Beirut, a reaction that was typical in most Arab states at the time below the government level. Nowhere was this more evident than in Iraq, the country earmarked to lead the charge into Syria. Henderson almost immediately found the Iraqis lukewarm at best to military intervention. There was a split within the Iraqi hierarchy regarding Syria. King Faisal and the crown prince favored aggressive action, while Premier Jawdat and Foreign Minister Mumtaz preferred a diplomatic solution, the latter two being described as "feeble" or "weak," or preferring "drift to action."[66]

Dulles stated that the Iraqis, "who logically should have the initiative were somewhat wobbly, the government was weak and it might be desirable that Nuri Pasha should go back."[67] Indeed, American and British officials, as well as Faisal and 'Abd al-Ilah, were all clamoring for the return of Nuri al-Sa'id to inject some "nerve" into the Iraqi government. Nuri was known to favor a policy of intervention and, in lieu of an invasion through Jordan, preferred his long-held plan of fomenting a tribal uprising in the eastern part of Syria; when the Syrian army was called out to suppress the rebellion the Iraqi army would be waiting.[68] But most Iraqis believed the matter to be strictly an internal Syrian affair. The king and crown prince had to be cognizant of the temperament of the Iraqi people, since their past British ties weakened their positions after Suez. Iraqi press comments on the American-Syrian crisis were divided along political lines; right-wing papers *al-Hawadith* and *al-Sha'b* criticized the regime in Syria while the leftist papers *al-Bilad* and *al-Zaman* attacked the West and supported the Syrian regime. Even *al-Akhbar*, which was considered at the time to be pro-American, issued a stern warning about the inadvisability of the Henderson mission and accused the United States of ignoring the more pertinent and pressing problems of Israeli expansionism and French terrorism in Algeria.[69] But Nuri was unable to effect his return to power "in time," and the Iraqi government's refusal to lead an all-Arab response against Syria was as important to the disruption of the Eisenhower administration's plans as Sa'ud's refusal.

A Shift in Tactics: The Turkish Alternative

Henderson's findings left the White House confused. The president would write in his memoirs, referring to Henderson's trip, that "whereas early information had indicated the possibility of prompt Iraqi military action with the Turks abstaining, there were now hints of a reversal of this arrangement."[70] The administration decided only to accelerate the delivery of allocated military hardware to Iraq, Jordan, Saudi Arabia, Iran, and Turkey in an attempt to bolster their resolve and give the impression that the United States was on the ball.[71] With the failure of the Henderson mission, the administration, and especially John Foster Dulles, reverted to standard post-Second World War cold war thinking. From this point on, it viewed the American-Syrian crisis as it related to the Soviet Union, with all the trappings befitting the "Munich mentality," something which would have a particularly telling impact on the Turks. As Jerald A. Combs writes: "The lesson of Munich came to be applied not only to the Axis during the war [WWII] but also to the Soviet Union and the communist movement in the war's aftermath. Appeasement brought war as surely as aggression, Americans decided. Military force was a necessary and legitimate tool of foreign policy. War might well be the lesser of evils in certain situations."[72] To Dulles, this was one of those "situations."

In a letter to Harold MacMillan discussing Henderson's findings, Dulles wrote the following:[73]

There is nothing that looks particularly attractive and the choice of policy will be hard. We are not completely satisfied with any of the alternatives which have thus far been suggested. There are risks involved in and objection found to all of them. We are continuing to explore other possibilities. . . . I do not by the foregoing mean to suggest that we have reached any conclusion in favor of encouraging positive action. However, Loy Henderson has the impression that the Turks are desperately serious about this situation and I do not think either of our governments wants to try to impose what could be another Munich.

An important meeting took place at the White House on September 7 to discuss the Syrian situation in light of Henderson's trip. An attempt was finally made to draw up some concrete plans to address the matter. In addition to Eisenhower, Dulles, and Henderson, Assistant Secretary of State Rountree, Chief of Staff General Twining, and others of Eisenhower's policy planning staff attended the meeting.[74] The record of the discussion and subsequent policy decisions clearly indicate that the level of analysis vis-à-vis the American-Syrian crisis had shifted from the regional to the international level. It was now based more on preconceptions, theory, and conjecture than the reality of the situation; the administration utilized a level of analysis where it felt most comfortable and where the facts could be made to fit policy.

At the meeting, Dulles circulated a paper of "findings and recommendations" concerning the Syrian situation. He advised the group to view the memorandum "in relation to our over-all relation with the Soviet Union." The secretary of state then went on to paint a rather unseemly picture of the Soviet leader, General Secretary Nikita Khrushchev, comparing him with Hitler. He called Khrushchev "more like Hitler than any Russian leader we have previously seen" and characterized him as "crude and impulsive." Dulles pondered that if the Soviets "pulled this operation off successfully . . . the success would go to Khrushchev's head and we might find ourselves with a series of incidents like the experience with Hitler." Referring to Turkey's serious concerns regarding Syria, Dulles stated that "we certainly do not want to repeat the type of pressures that were used on Czechoslovakia to force them to accept Hitler's demands." In other words, Dulles was determined not to appease the Soviets by allowing them to use Syria as a base to subvert its neighbors one by one. The difference in this case was that the Turks could easily have defeated the Syrians at the time, while the Czechs prior to the Second World War would not have been victorious over the Third Reich had they been "allowed" to resist its absorption by Germany—they needed strong support from the Great Powers, but none would be forthcoming.

The dynamics of the Syrian situation were much different. Dulles equated Khrushchev with Hitler, yet the Turks would only confront the Soviet Union and Soviet expansionism by proxy, which may or may not have invited Soviet reprisals. In this situation, the United States would have fought the Soviets indirectly itself, once removed, since its proxy, Turkey, would be combatting the Soviets' proxy, Syria. If the Soviets invaded Turkey, the United States would then be in a position to either appease the Soviets or attempt to reverse their gains, but only after the administration itself precipitated the chain of events by giving the Turks the green light to intervene in Syria. Fortunately, the preceding scenario remained hypothetical; however, the policy that evolved out of that September 7 meeting had the potential to place the United States in an excruciating dilemma.

Eisenhower was not completely comfortable with the memorandum circulated by Dulles at the meeting. He found a "deficiency" in that it did not "indicate specifically what we aim to do," and he questioned whether "we should not lay out exactly what we will do in the event certain things occur," in other words, he wanted a contingency plan. The president also revealed at the meeting that he had not lost hope in using the Saudi card. He thought the United States should do "everything possible" to stress the "holy war aspect," recalling that Sa'ud, on his state visit to Washington, agreed that the Arabs should oppose communism. Although this line of thought indicates a serious misreading of Sa'ud's position in the Arab world and his motivations, Eisenhower did not seem to push much farther with this idea and basically let Dulles construct administration policy vis-à-vis the crisis.

This policy was elaborated in a telegram signed by Dulles on September 10 and sent to the United States Embassy in Turkey. It reflected decisions regarding the American-Syrian crisis that were "reached at [the] highest level [of] US Government" and instructed the ambassador to "convey them orally" to Prime Minister Menderes under "absolute secrecy."[75] The policy paper consisted of sixteen points, of which the following were the most notable (numbered as they appeared in the telegram):

2. Nations are confronted at periods in history with need to take decisions fundamentally affecting their own destinies. US believes such momentous decisions may be taken *only by nation concerned*. Holding to this belief, US does not consider it can assume responsibility of urging Turkey to follow any specific course of action or inaction.

3. The United States judges that Syria *has become, or is about to become,* a base for military and subversive activities in the Near East designed to destroy the independence of those countries and to subject them to Soviet Communist domination.

4. If the aggressive spirit which is being inculcated into Syria by means of Soviet arms, propaganda, etc., should, *as seems likely,* manifest itself in actual deeds — and some such manifestations have already occurred in Lebanon☐

the United States would hold that a case existed for individual or collective self-defense under Article 51 of the United Nations Charter and that there would be no violation of Article I of the NATO Treaty.

5. The United States believes, however, that Israel should, irrespective of provocation other than large-scale invasion, show restraint so as not to unite and inflame the Arab world against Israel and in support of Syria on the theory that Israel has aggressive purposes and territorial ambitions.

6. The United States further believes that Turkey should not act other than in requested reinforcement of Arab defensive action.

7. If Syria's Moslem neighbors should consider their security endangered by the threat of Syrian aggression and should request from the United States economic assistance and military supplies in connection with a *concrete plan* effectively to meet such aggression, the US would give prompt and sympathetic consideration to such a request. If any one or more of Syria's Arab neighbors, responding to provocation, should act pursuant to Article 51 of the Charter, the United States would, upon request, and pursuant to the Middle East Resolution, extend such countries economic assistance and military supplies; it would support such countries if attacked in the UN SC [Security Council] or the GA [General Assembly].

8. If any of Syria's Arab neighbors were physically attacked by the Sino-Soviet Bloc, the United States, upon request, would be prepared to use its own armed forces to assist any such nation or nations against such armed aggression.

9. If hostilities between Iraq and Syria should result in the closing of the pipelines and the cutting off of revenues from Iraq, the United States would, as a temporary emergency measure, help to mitigate the financial consequences of this to Iraq.

10. If, despite what is said in (6), Turkey should feel *compelled* to react to armed provocations which *implied* a serious threat to its own national integrity and independence, or if Turkey should come to the aid of any of Syria's Arab neighbors engaged in hostilities with Syria, the United States would support Turkey *in the UN*. The US also would not stand idly by if the Sino-Soviet Bloc should attack Turkey, directly or by organized volunteers. In that case the US would honor its obligations under the NATO Treaty, and the Middle East Resolution would also be applicable.

12. If any of Syria's neighbors should become involved in hostilities with Syria, it is a precondition to any US support that it be made clear that such hostilities are not for the purpose of impairing the political independence or

the territory of Syria but are merely for the purpose of restoring Syria to the Syrians.

13. The US will continue to deploy the Sixth Fleet in the Eastern Mediterranean.

14. US has consulted with UK [United Kingdom] which is in complete agreement with this position.

* underlining mine
** Points #1, 15, and 16 were diplomatic atmospherics. Point #11 was sanitized from the record.

Dulles strongly suggested that the administration keep this policy from Congress, fearing that consultations with its members would inevitably wind up in next morning's newspapers. He noted that if this happened, it would make the United States "appear to be the center of decision in the matter — which we certainly do not want."[76] At first the United States wanted a regional response. When it became clear that this was not going to occur, Eisenhower and Dulles decided to adopt the Turkish alternative. And it is quite apparent from the sixteen point plan (in particular points two and ten) that the administration, while not explicitly encouraging the Turks to intervene in Syria, did not tell them not to, and in diplomatic language this is as good as giving the green light. Evidence of this was given by Eisenhower's former speechwriter, Emmet John Hughes, who wrote in his memoirs that Under Secretary of State Christian Herter had "reviewed" with him in "rueful detail" shortly after the 1957 crisis "some recent clumsy clandestine American attempts to spur Turkish forces to do some vague kind of battle with Syria. . . . "[77]

As revealed in point ten, the United States would only intervene in the event Turkey came under attack from the Sino-Soviet Bloc. The administration knew the Turks were extremely anxious about the Syrian situation, and after an anti-Syrian Arab coalition failed to materialize, it advanced the idea about Turkish military action.[78] As a result, Turkish forces on the Syrian border were increased from 32,000 to 50,000.[79] Dulles then called General Twining on September 7 to remind him of the importance of keeping the Strategic Air Command on an alert status, pointing out that the situation regarding Syria had "a considerable amount of danger in it."[80] The Middle East was on the precipice of war.

Assessing the Soviets

Although Syrian trade by 1958 was still largely with the West, the Eisenhower administration had seen a forty-fold increase of communist bloc purchases of Syrian goods between 1954–1958, capped-off by the August 6, 1957, Soviet-Syrian economic agreement.[81] Akram al-Hawrani aptly noted, however, that "Turkey obtained a loan from the Soviet Union and Poland obtained a loan from the United States, yet this did not constitute a dangerous situation from the West's viewpoint, but if Syria obtains a loan from the Soviet Union, imperialist quarters call it alignment."[82] With the leftist regime in power in Syria, the "threatening tone" of the Soviet Union's announcement on August 26 of the launching of its first ICBM, the Soviet-initiated break-up of the disarmament talks that were being held in London, and the Kremlin's Middle East "note" of September 3, 1957 (discussed below), which was "couched in the rudest and most provocative terms of any received during his tenure," Dulles believed a pattern was unfolding that signified "a period of the greatest peril for us since the Korean War."[83]

An intelligence report was prepared for the administration by the intelligence community and the joint staff; it was entitled, "Developments in the Syrian Situation."[84] It was an enlightening but rather confusing report, offering analyses which could support an aggressive or passive posture vis-à-vis Syria and the Soviet Union. On one level, the report stated the following:

> The Syrian relationship with the Bloc appears to differ in important respects from that envisioned in Nasser's doctrine of "positive neutralism." Syria has already accepted a degree of dependence upon the Soviet Bloc and of alienation from the West which gives the Bloc significant political and economic warfare capabilities. Furthermore, the Syrian leaders have gone so far in their hostility toward the West and uncritical trust of the Bloc that they are almost as susceptible to Soviet influence as they would be if Syria were actually a member of the Bloc. Indeed, they probably are *more useful to the Bloc as nationalists than as Communists.* (emphasis mine)

The report went on to state that "in the *absence* of forceful intervention from outside Syria, the presently dominant coalition . . . probably will be able to maintain control for some time. No opposition group *within* the country, civilian or military, is likely to challenge the coalition effectively. Some groups within the country may hope for intervention from the outside." (emphasis mine).

Yet on another level, while acknowledging that the Syrian situation had improved the Soviet position in the Middle East, the report stated that the Kremlin "has shown some caution in accepting commitments in the Middle East" and therefore "believe that the USSR will not wish to treat Syria as a new satellite but will find it expedient to deal with it as an Arab nationalist state and to render economic and political support, as well as military aid, to the presently dominant group." Indeed, administration officials conceded the Soviets had been acting cautiously up to that point. The report also mentioned that it did not find any evidence, "except in the case of Baqdash and perhaps Bizri," that the Syrian government had been under the influence of "communist ideology."

It is not surprising that Dulles chose to follow the more damaging assessment. The administration had long identified Syria as a "soft spot," and it believed the Soviets were now taking advantage of it. Contrary to the distinction Eisenhower made between communists and nationalists at his August 21 press conference, Dulles, supported by this intelligence estimate, now established that it did not matter if the Syrian government was communist-controlled or not, since the nationalists were as useful to the Soviets as the communists (while the Kremlin mistakenly viewed the nationalists as less threatening to the West).[85]

This was not Hungary, where the Kremlin imposed its will. The success of Soviet foreign policy in the Middle East depended on parallel objectives with the nationalist elements without force-feeding doctrinaire communism down the throats of the indigenous populations. From the Eisenhower administration's perspective, it was possible to distinguish between the nationalists and the communists; but now it did not matter what the political affiliation of those identified as taking action deleterious to American interests was; the point being they were supporting Soviet objectives while doing so. This would obviously improve the Soviet position at the expense of the American. The final sentence of the report concurred, "the Soviets are likely to find Syria useful to their interests as a sphere of influence, as an example of the benefits of Soviet friendship, and as a base for operations in the Middle East." This Dulles could not and would not tolerate, and the fact that the nationalists in Syria (namely the Ba'th) tacitly cooperated with the communists only made his job easier in trying to sell to the public and Congress a more forward American policy.

It was the Henderson mission that really engaged the Soviets in the crisis and, in turn, sounded an alarm in the White House. Henderson's trip also had disruptive effects in the Arab world. After the initial flurry of anti-American sentiment following the uncovering of the coup attempt, however, the Syrian and Egyptian press in particular seemed to soften their attitude and purposely left the door open for an American-Syrian rapprochement. It is also possible that they did not want to give the United States any more ammunition to legitimate the use of the Eisenhower Doctrine. In either event, Syrian leaders continued to deny that Syria was under communist/Soviet domination or that certain members of the government were communist.

But when news of the Henderson mission reached Moscow, the Kremlin unleashed a massive diplomatic and propaganda offensive designed to counter what it perceived was an impending American-sponsored move against Syria. Henderson's reputation had preceded him, and indeed, his own reservations about the sagaciousness of his trip were coming to pass. Press and radio statements in the Arab world vehemently attacked Henderson. But even with the Henderson mission, Syrian leaders still attempted to dispel the notion that their country was communist-dominated, stating that Eisenhower had been seriously misinformed about the situation.[86] The Syrian government made a special effort to avoid directly attacking or implicating the United States *government* or Eisenhower personally. Salah al-Tarazi stated he did not accuse the United States government directly of hatching the plot, but said it was "planned by three officials of the American Embassy in Damascus."[87] Syrian Foreign Minister Bitar said: "We hope that Henderson's visit to the Middle East will enable President Eisenhower to become familiar with the real developments in the Middle East. . . . Syria is open to all visitors and to all seekers of the truth."[88] The Syrian government officially stated that it would not "impede the task of this envoy should the purpose of his task be to gain facts and to try to understand the truth about the situation in this area."[89] *Al-Ra'i al-'Am* published a report on August 29 stating that Henderson had come to offer generous financial aid to the Arabs and to improve relations with Egypt and Syria. Apparently anxious to dispel any notion that Syria had fallen under Soviet control, on September 9, Sarraj and Bizri convened a press conference where they made the following points: Syro-Turkish relations were cordial and would continue to be so; Syria would never permit the establishment of foreign military bases within its territory or allow military operations to be conducted from within Syria against Turkey; there were no Soviet officers in Syria; and Syria would never become communist.[90] Sarraj again went in front of the press on September 16, disavowing any communist sympathies on his part or Bizri's—he described himself and Bizri as nationalists. In this interview, Sarraj definitely gave the impression of exasperation and irritation over constant press comments in the West that labelled Bizri and himself as communists. He pointed out that he had been in the army for many years but only recently had the West claimed that he was a communist.[91] The Egyptian press generally followed the same line as the Syrian press, blaming Dulles personally for the American-Syrian crisis rather than Eisenhower or the government. *Al-Ahram* on August 31 accused Dulles of making a unilateral decision to rescind the funding of the Aswan Dam project (that compelled Nasser to nationalize the Suez Canal Company), without consulting Eisenhower. Ishaq Hanna's commentary on September 5 on Egyptian Home Service radio referred to the American coup attempt as "the Howard Stone plot" and the "Loy Henderson international plot," again refusing to directly implicate the American government.

While the Syrians were attempting to calm American apprehensions, Soviet propaganda launched a barrage of articles implicating Henderson as the errand boy for the Eisenhower administration's imperialist plans to attack Syria.[92] Simultaneously, the Kremlin involved itself in the crisis on the diplomatic front, sending on September 3 a "note" to the governments of the United States, Great Britain, and France. The substance of the note was very similar to earlier notes the Kremlin had sent regarding its role in the Middle East (February 11 and April 19, 1957, respectively) in which it called for a four-power declaration on the renunciation of the use of force and interference in Middle Eastern affairs. In form, however, Moscow strongly condemned the United States for its policy in the region, from the Eisenhower Doctrine to the Jordanian crisis to the Syrian incident, while juxtaposing itself alongside the "aggressor" United States as the nation truly interested in promoting peace in the region: "It is difficult to assess such a position of the Government of the USA in any way other than as proof for the fact that the United States is not in the least interested in the lessening of tension in the Near and Middle East and in presenting to the peoples of this area the opportunity to live in peace and quiet and to themselves determine their domestic and foreign policy."[93] The Egyptian and Syrian press unanimously praised the proposal and called the Soviet Union a peace-loving nation.

The propaganda gambit had worked. The Soviets, as they had done at Suez, positioned themselves on the side of the Arab people against actual and would-be imperialist aggression. The United States rejected this note as well, stating that it contained nothing that was not already provided for by the United Nations Charter. Dulles remarked at his September 10 press conference that the Soviet's hands-off proposal regarding the Middle East means "our hands off and their hands under the table." Echoing the administration's sentiments, a September 6 *Washington Post* editorial remarked that "the new Russian proposal for a pledge of non-interference in the Middle East reflects the magnanimity of the thief who has just stolen the chickens. . . . "

A Game of Chess

On September 7, 1957, Dulles issued a statement that reflected the administration's position in light of the Henderson mission.[94] Dulles said that the United States shared the "deep concern" of Syria's neighbors and that the president "affirmed his intention to carry out the national policy, expressed in the Congressional Middle East Resolution . . . and exercise as needed the authority thereby conferred on the President." He announced Eisenhower's authorization to accelerate arms deliveries to the Middle East. Finally, he stated that the president "expressed the hope that the International Communists would not push Syria into any acts of aggression against her neighbors and that the people of Syria would act to allay the anxiety caused by recent events." American press comment generally concurred that the administration had de facto invoked the Eisenhower Doctrine. It also noted that in order to provide an escape route for the Syrian government, the administration was careful not to explicitly state that Syria had fallen under the domination of international communism. Eisenhower and Dulles *publicly* continued to be ambiguous, having invoked a portion of the Eisenhower Doctrine with the arms shipments. Still, they had not labelled Syria as communist-dominated, but at the same time they called upon the Syrian people to act against their own government before it was too late (a point in time that was becoming more nebulous with each passing day). To quote Henry Kissinger, " . . . the test of a doctrine is the marginal case – the situation for which the doctrine does not provide and which has to be improvised under the pressure of events." It was becoming more and more obvious that the Eisenhower Doctrine was failing this test; in fact, any improvisation admitted to the fragility of the original version.

A veiled threat to the Soviet Union was evoked by Deputy Under Secretary of State Robert Murphy on September 9 before the annual conference of mayors in New York. He stated that it would be "unwise to underestimate the industrial and military power of our country and to misinterpret our determination." Of course, everyone was just guessing at the level of "determination" of the administration anyway since its policy had been confusing and contradictory up to that point. It would be wrong to assert that this was the intention of the administration in order to keep the Syrians and Soviets guessing. The record shows that this ambiguity was a reflection of confusion within the policymaking apparatus in its attempt to fit the American-Syrian crisis neatly into the constraints of the Eisenhower Doctrine and the post-Suez, anti-imperialist mood of the White House. This was combined with the necessity to minimize or reduce Soviet gains in the region, a goal that was felt to be obtainable under the more free-wheeling active posture befitting the Munich mentality.

The position of the United States became more distinct on September 10, 1957. Dulles gave a press conference in which he considerably downplayed the danger of the Syrian situation, in stark contrast to the administration's earlier statements.[95] Answering questions, Dulles brought American policy back in line with the original interpretation of the Eisenhower Doctrine as it applied to the Syrian case, i.e., there must be the three "findings" before there would be direct armed intervention by the United States. He went on to state that "at the present time I don't think it likely that those three things will occur." He further expressed the feeling that he believed the "situation probably will work out." The press recognized very quickly that the situation in Syria had not changed so much in the three days since Dulles' more alarming remarks on September 7 (or Murphy's comments the night before) and asked him why he had downgraded the threat. Dulles essentially responded in two ways. First, he invoked the words of another world leader whose position he obviously hoped to emulate. Dulles recalled that India's Nehru had said on September 2 that the situation in Syria was "dangerous and explosive." "Now, he [Nehru] is a somewhat detached and philosophical observer. . . . " Second, he delivered a very ambiguous analysis of the American-Syrian crisis:

> The situation internally in Syria is not entirely clear and fluctuates somewhat. While I have not discussed this with the President I would think that in a situation which is still somewhat borderline the President would not make a finding unless there were other events which called for it so that the finding would be contemporaneous with the other events. Now, as you know, there are in the world some of these borderline situations. There are some countries which are, beyond the peradventure of doubt, under the domination of international communism and others where it is not so clear. In cases where it is not entirely clear and where the situation is somewhat obscure from the standpoint of who is exercising authority at the moment, I would think that the President . . . would not make the finding until it was of practical significance to do it rather than an academic exercise.

Dulles immediately cautioned, however, that "there could be developments within the next week or so which would make clear beyond a doubt that Syria was dominated . . . by international communism." Was this just a cover for the unpredictability of the events in Syria or was it a possible presaging of a Turkish invasion which he had essentially sanctioned?

The evidence suggests it was not coincidental that Dulles' "16 points" telegram to Ankara was sent on the same day as his press conference. Newspapers tended to report, following Dulles' statements on September 10, that the Eisenhower administration was bidding a hasty retreat after discovering that Syria was *not* spiraling into the communist orbit as previously suspected.[96] With his mollifying remarks on the 10th, Dulles might have been attempting to indicate an abdication of American responsibility in any effort to correct the Syrian situation. It did not mean that the administration had abandoned the idea of corrective action in Syria. One does not talk the way Dulles did at the September 7 White House meeting and all of a sudden, without any visible improvement in Syria, state that the situation could now be resolved though peaceful measures. A September 11 conversation between Dulles and Senator Mansfield was recorded as follows:[97]

> He [Dulles] said that the newspapers had generally regarded his comments at his press conference yesterday as indicating he felt that the tension was lessening somewhat and that he was less worried about the situation than he had heretofore been. The Secretary said that in fact the contrary was true. He felt the tension was mounting and he had tried in his press conference not to say anything which would add to that tension. The Secretary said that he

was concerned by what appeared to be an increasingly truculent and reckless attitude on the part of the Soviet Union.

It was certainly a press conference with a hidden purpose. Dulles wanted to put the peaceful intentions of the United States on record (in the face of the propaganda victory the Soviets were enjoying as a result of their September 3 note), give notice to Moscow that the United States was not prepared to militarily intervene in Syria, and while doing so, provide a feint for what he thought might be a Turkish and/or Arab initiative, essentially hoping to relax tensions at the international level, yet at the same time, confine any impending conflict in the area to the regional level. All the while he would assume the position favored by Nehru, that of a "philosophic observer" of forthcoming events.

September 10 was also a pivotal date for Soviet involvement in the crisis. At the same moment the United States *appeared* to be backing off, the Soviets decided to go in the opposite direction. Soviet Foreign Minister Andrei Gromyko, who replaced Shepilov in June, entertained a press conference in which he made some rather bold statements directed at the United States and Turkey. By implication, he accused Washington of orchestrating the conspiracies against the Syrian regime and explicitly warned Turkey, as the West's "gendarme" in the Middle East, by asking, "How would Turkey like it if troops of a foreign state [i.e., the USSR] were concentrated on her frontiers?," and added that "it would be dangerous for Turkey to be guided by the advice of those [i.e., the United States] who want to compel her to carry out their adventurous plans for unleashing war in the Near East," and if Turkey should follow this path, it may end up "in an abyss." Gromyko went on to attack the Eisenhower Doctrine in pro forma fashion and asked the United States why, if it was so concerned about Syrian aggression, it did not take the issue to the UN Security Council. Taking its cue from the Kremlin, the Soviet press began to portray Turkey as the "agent" or "axis" of American foreign policy.

On September 11, Soviet Premier Bulganin addressed a note to Prime Minister Menderes warning him of the possible dire consequences if Turkey should invade Syria and pointed out that the Soviet Union "cannot remain indifferent to these events." He went on to state in a not-so-veiled threat that "considering the current international situation and particularly the development of military techniques, the danger of local military conflicts being converted into a large-scale conflagration of war has become much more pronounced. . . . Once started, military action in such an area could easily become a broad conflict." Dulles, in other words, would not have the insulated conflict he had hoped for. The Soviets were using his own medicine of brinkmanship against the United States.

The Soviet Union obviously examined the Syrian situation under a worse-case scenario, especially after Henderson's trip to the Middle East, and were guarding against the possibility of an invasion of Syria by some combination of Arab states and/or Turkey with the support of the West. In practical terms, Syria was not that important to the Kremlin, but with the crisis coming so soon after the new foreign policy elucidated at the 20th Party Congress, its actions were under a microscope by the rest of the Third World (or at least it thought so), and therefore it was prepared to take a very strong stand in this instance to protect its prestige in the Middle East and elsewhere. Moscow was well aware of Turkish troop movements along the Syrian border, stepped-up American military aid, the activities of the Sixth Fleet in the eastern Mediterranean, and it remembered the recent actions of the United States vis-à-vis the Jordanian crisis. The Soviet Union also assumed that Henderson's mission was more than just a fact-finding trip.[98] The Kremlin hoped to preempt any intended action against Syria by raising the stakes of its response – it wanted the West to at least think that it would be more than just reciprocal. At the same time, Moscow launched a worldwide propaganda barrage depicting Syria as an innocent victim of imperialist aggression, gaining points all the while for standing beside her against "colonialists." Encouraged by this support, the press in Syria and Egypt intensified its criticisms of American policy.

Dulles, of course, was not about to take the Kremlin's attacks and threats lying down – the United States had its own prestige to preserve, as well as the vitality of NATO and the Eisenhower Doctrine. Describing the Soviets as "getting pretty nasty,"[99] Dulles termed Gromyko's statements as "perhaps the bitterest attack ever made by a Soviet official on the U.S."[100] He felt that Moscow was "putting the screws on Turkey very hard."[101] He believed a sharp response was in order, primarily to assuage those who had been gravely disappointed by the propitiating tone of his remarks at the September 10 press conference. Iraqi Foreign Minister 'Ali Mumtaz bluntly told a British official that his country was getting "fed up with the Americans" for what he thought was the vacillating and often baffling policy of the Eisenhower administration.[102] Mumtaz pointed out that at the meetings in Istanbul, Henderson anxiously pressed the Iraqis to take action against Syria as soon as a pretext could be found that would hold up to scrutiny in the Security Council; then, all of a sudden, the United States seemed to disengage itself from the policy they tried to initiate.[103]

To counter the Soviets, Dulles first sent out the official American riposte to the September 3 Kremlin Middle East note. The text stated that the United States found the Soviet note to have been "highly offensive in tone and cynically distorts United States objectives and actions in the Middle East. It is clearly designed to serve only Soviet propaganda purposes rather that to promote peace and stability in the Middle East." Of course, Dulles was correct in the preceding assumption, but to the administration's dismay, Moscow had already won the popularity contest in the region by appearing to be on the side of peace. It then went on to blame the Kremlin for the "present aggravation of tension" in the area, stating that Soviet arms shipments to the Middle East had been the real cause for setting in motion the chain of events that precipitated the American-Syrian crisis.

In a State Department press statement on September 12, Dulles directly addressed Gromyko's remarks with at least as much acrimony as that which was displayed by the Soviet foreign minister:

> The United States deplores the statement made by Soviet Foreign Minister Gromyko on September 10. Its falsifications and its importance seemed deliberately calculated to break those bridges of understanding which still sustain our hopes for peace. His blustering attack on the Eisenhower Doctrine is similar to past attempts to frighten the free nations from taking action to reinforce their freedom. This language recalls that which was used by the Soviets in regard to the Marshall Plan, the Truman Doctrine, foreign aid to Greece and Turkey, NATO, the foundation of the German Federal Republic, the Japanese peace treaty and the South East Asia Security Treaty. We had hoped for better things, but it seemed that the Soviet Communists are in all respects confirmed reactionaries who can only replay the old wearisome tunes of which the world has grown so tired. The Soviet denunciations of the past did not halt the quest for greater security in greater freedom. The present denunciation will not halt measures to provide security against Soviet communist entrapment.

In other words, Dulles said that the United States would not be intimidated. The American-Syrian crisis had thus expanded to the level of a potential superpower confrontation.

Notes

1. FBIS, August 14, 1957, p. C1. The three American diplomats were: Military Attache Lt. Colonel Robert Molloy, Second Secretary Howard Stone and Vice-counsel Francis Jetton.
2. Memorandum From the Assistant Secretary of State for Near Eastern, South Asian, and African Affairs (Rountree) to the Acting Secretary of State, August 13, 1957, *FRUS*, p. 633.
3. Syrian Bill of Indictment, FBIS, October 1, 1957, p. C6.
4. This did not prevent the Syrian press from lashing out at the United States; *al-Nasr* of August 15, 1957, stated, "American imperialism has no intention of letting Syria alone, securing the means of its safety, and letting it attain its national aims by means unanimously approved by its people. American imperialism is working continuously to hatch an uninterrupted

chain of plots, despite the continued failure which awaits all links of this criminal chain." The fact that *al-Nasr* was the voice of Khalid al-'Azm proves the above comment to be more than just mere hyperbole; it was an attempt to keep the American "danger" alive in the minds of the Syrian public in order to justify the Soviet-Syrian economic agreement, for which 'Azm was primarily responsible.

5. Letter from Dulles to Eisenhower, August 23, 1957, Ann Whitman File, Dulles-Herter Series, Box 7, DDEL.

6. Memorandum of a Conversation, Department of State, Washington, August 19, 1957, *FRUS*, pp. 243–246.

7. See Memorandum of a Conversation Between the Deputy Under Secretary of State (Murphy) and the British Ambassador (Caccia), Department of State, Washington, August 17, 1957 (on Omani situation), *FRUS*, pp. 238–239; Memorandum of a Conversation, Department of State, Washington, August 19, 1957 (Oman), *FRUS*, pp. 243–246; and Memorandum of a Conversation, Waldorf Towers, New York, September 16, 1957, 1 p.m., (Oman), *FRUS*, pp. 247–248.

8. Notes of the Secretary's Staff Meeting, Department of State, Washington, August 19, 1957, 9:15 a.m., *FRUS*, p. 639.

9. For a summary of discussion, see Memorandum of a Conversation, White House, Washington, August 14, 1957, *FRUS*, pp. 635–636.

10. Telegram From the Department of State to the Embassy in Jordan, August 14, 1957, *FRUS*, pp. 636–637: "Syrian action is merely latest and most convincing evidence of willingness GOS promote instability in NE by endeavoring sow suspicion and distrust throughout area, thereby advancing Soviet interests."

11. Daily Top Secret Summary, August 19, 1957, *FRUS*, pp. 638–639.

12. Ibid.

13. British Embassy-Beirut, August 21, 1957, FO 371/128224, PRO.

14. British Embassy-Baghdad, August 21, 1957, FO 371/128224, PRO.

15. Ibid.

16. Telegram From the Embassy in Turkey to the Department of State, August 21, 1957, *FRUS*, pp. 642–644. Menderes' statement included: "In present situation unless USA takes definite position and decisions, nothing can be done. Up to now USA has been very cautious, very diplomatic – she has been bound by diplomatic forms and theory. . . . We are awaiting 'solid decision' in order to be able to take appropriate measures." Later in statement Menderes noted the "important" position of Saudi Arabia regarding the situation.

17. Memorandum of a Conversation, Department of State, Washington, August 19, 1957, 3:45 p.m., *FRUS*, pp. 340–341.

18. Dulles telephone call to General Twining, August 21, 1957, John Foster Dulles Papers, Telephone Calls Series, Box 7, DDEL. Specification

of various courses of action are either still classified or were destroyed – the latter was the case with a "talking paper" outlining possible responses, destroyed on August 22, 1957. (Memorandum of a Conversation ..., August 19, 1957).

19. Dulles to Selwyn Lloyd, August 21, 1957, Ann Whitman File, Dulles-Herter Series, Box 7, DDEL.

20. Harold MacMillan, *Riding the Storm 1956–1959* (New York: Harper & Row, 1971), pp. 279–280. MacMillan went on to inform his cabinet on August 28, however, that "the problem is not to discourage the Americans, if they are really serious and will see through any action to the end; at the same time not to stimulate them to do something which (if it goes half-cock) will be fatal." (p. 280).

21. Eisenhower to King Saud, August 21, 1957, Ann Whitman File, International Series, Box 42, DDEL.

22. British Foreign Office, August 23, 1957, FO 371/128224, PRO. Same letter reproduced in, Harold MacMillan, *Riding the Storm 1956–1959,* p. 279.

23. British Embassy-Amman, August 22, 1957, FO 371/128224, PRO.

24. Memorandum for the President from Dulles, August 20, 1957, Ann Whitman File, Dulles-Herter Series, Box 7, DDEL.

25. Ibid.

26. British Embassy-Beirut, August 29, 1957, FO 371/128245, PRO.

27. FBIS, August 22, 1957, p. C1.

28. British Embassy-Washington, August 22, 1957, FO 371/128224, PRO.

29. Dulles to Harold MacMillan, August 22, 1957, Ann Whitman File, Dulles-Herter Series, Box 7, DDEL.

30. For instance, see British Embassy-Paris, August 23, 1957, FO 371/128224, PRO.

31. British Foreign Office, August 20, 1957, FO 371/128224, PRO.

32. British Embassy-Washington, August 21, 1957, FO 371/128224, PRO. Lebanese Foreign Minister Charles Malik also heard of reports from his sources that Nasser was less than sanguine about the deal. (British Embassy-Beirut, August 19, 1957, FO 371/128223, PRO).

33. American Embassy, Damascus to Department of State, August 17, 1957, Microform Reading Room, microfiche 71G (1977), Library of Congress.

34. Ibid.

35. Ibid.

36. British Embassy-Amman, August 26, 1957, FO 371/128224, PRO; and British Embassy-Washington, August 24, 1957, FO 371/128224, PRO.

37. British Embassy-Ankara, September 6, 1957, FO 371/128226, PRO.

38. For instance, see the September 2, 1957 *al-Akhbar, al-Jumhuriyya, al-Ahram,* and *Rose al-Yusuf.*

39. British Embassy-Cairo, September 12, 1957, FO 371/128237, PRO.

40. Hare to Secretary of State, August 24, 1957, Subject Series, State Department Subseries, Box 1, DDEL.

41. Following this line of thought, the Egyptian press and Cairo's Voice of the Arabs emphasized the Israeli link to American policy in the Middle East.

42. British Embassy-Washington, no. 1625, August 24, 1957, FO 371/128224, PRO.

43. Ibid.

44. Ibid. Also, see British Foreign Office, August 23, 1957, FO 371/128224, PRO.

45. Memorandum of a Conversation With the President, White House, Washington, August 28, 1957, 10:30 a.m., *FRUS*, pp. 659–660.

46. Telegram From the Department of State to the Embassy in Saudi Arabia, August 27, 1957, *FRUS*, pp. 500–502.

47. The State Department established on August 23 a "special handling category for cables and memoranda concerning sensitive aspects of policy or operations related to the Syrian situation" in order to "control the dissemination of information" vis-à-vis American policy toward Syria. (Editorial Note, no date, *FRUS*, p. 651.) In a telephone conversation with the deputy director of the CIA, General Cabell, Dulles pointed out that Henderson would be sending back communications that "should not get into anybody's files" and asked the general if he had the "facilities" to handle it. Cabell answered in the affirmative, stating he could rapidly file any message marked "eyes only" for the secretary of state. (Dulles Telephone Call to General Cabell, August 22, 1957, John Foster Dulles Papers, Telephone Calls Series, Box 7, DDEL).

48. Telegram From the Department of State to the Embassy in Turkey, August 23, 1957, *FRUS*, pp. 650–651.

49. Telegram From Consulate General . . . , August 25, 1957, op. cit.; Telegram From the Consulate General in Istanbul to the Department of State, August 26, 1957, 5 p.m., *FRUS*, pp. 656–657; Telegram From the Consulate General in Istanbul to the Department of State, August 26, 1957, 6 p.m., *FRUS*, p. 658.

50. Eisenhower, *Waging Peace*, p. 198.

51. Summary notes on Legislative Leaders Meetings, August 27, 1957, Ann Whitman File, Legislative Meetings Series, Box 2, DDEL.

52. Eisenhower, *Waging Peace*, p. 199.

53. Summary Notes on Legislative Leaders Meetings, August 27, 1957. DDEL.

54. British Embassy-Washington, August 24, 1957, FO 371/128224, PRO.

55. Eisenhower, *Waging Peace*, p. 198.

56. Ibid.

57. Memorandum of Conversation between Senator William F. Knowland and Dulles, August 30, 1957, John Foster Dulles Papers, General Correspondence and Memoranda Series, Box 1, DDEL. Another pretext for military intervention into Syria was discussed between Henderson and George Middleton, the British Ambassador to Beirut, while the under secretary was visiting Lebanon on August 28. Middleton records that in his conversation with Henderson they both agreed that "one way of putting pressure on Syria would be to seek assurances about future Syrian intentions as regards the uninterrupted transit of oil and civil aviation across her territory. The enquiry about Syrian intentions might be framed in such a way as to needle the Syrians into taking some foolish action which would justify intervention in the internal affairs of that country; this was a doubtful gambit as the Egyptians and Russians would no doubt both advise against it. But it was just worth exploring." (British Embassy-Beirut, August 31, 1957, FO 371/127743, PRO.) As far as I can tell, nothing came of this suggestion, but it does provide some insight into the frame of mind of the administration's "Middle East man," which was probably an accurate reflection of the willingness of Eisenhower and Dulles to precipitate an incident calling for application of the Eisenhower Doctrine.

58. British Consulate-Istanbul, August 25, 1957, FO 371/128224, PRO.

59. British Embassy-Washington, August 23, 1957, FO 371/128224, PRO.

60. Ibid.

61. British Embassy-Ankara, September 6, 1957, FO 371/127743, PRO; Memorandum of a Conversation Between the President and the Secretary of State, White House, Washington, September 2, 1957, 3 p.m., *FRUS*, pp. 609–670.

62. Ibid.

63. British Embassy-Amman, August 28, 1957, FO 371/128225, PRO.

64. Eisenhower, *Waging Peace,* pp. 200–201.

65. See, for example, Nuri al-Sa'id's concerns expressed to British officials in, British Foreign Office, September 6, 1957, FO 371/128225, PRO.

66. See British Embassy-Beirut, August 31, 1957, FO 371/127743, PRO; Telegram From Consulate General in Istanbul to the Department of State, September 2/3, 1957 – midnight, *FRUS*, pp. 670–672; British Embassy-Washington, August 26, 1957, FO 371/128227, PRO; and, Memorandum of a Conversation With the President, White House, Washington, September 7, 1957, 10:07 a.m., *FRUS*, pp. 685–689.

67. Memorandum . . . , September 2, 1957.

68. British Foreign Office, September 6, 1957, FO 371/128225, PRO.

69. British Embassy-Baghdad, August 29, 1957, FO 371/128234, PRO.

70. Eisenhower, *Waging Peace,* p. 200.

71. For an itemization of the military hardware sent to these countries, see Special Staff Note, Prepared in the White House, September 20, 1957, *FRUS,* pp. 714–715.

72. Jerald A. Combs, *American Diplomatic History: Two Centuries of Changing Interpretations* (1983), p. 197. Also on this subject, see Les K. Adler and Thomas G. Paterson, "Red Fascism: The Merger of Nazi Germany and Soviet Russia in the American Image of Totalitarianism, 1930s–1950s," *American Historical Review* (April 1970), 75, no. 4.

73. Letter From Secretary of State Dulles to Prime Minister Macmillan, September 5, 1957, *FRUS,* pp. 681–682.

74. For this and subsequent references to meeting, see Memorandum of a Conversation With the President, White House, Washington, September 7, 1957, 10:07 a.m., *FRUS,* pp. 685–689. Also at the meeting were: Secretary Quarles, General Whisenand, General Cabell, Mr. Wisner, General Cutler, and General Goodpaster.

75. For this and subsequent references, see Telegram From the Department of State to the Embassy in Turkey, September 10, 1957, *FRUS,* pp. 691–693.

76. Memorandum of a Conversation . . . , September 7, 1957.

77. Emmet John Hughes, *The Ordeal of Power: A Political Memoir of the Eisenhower Years* (New York: Atheneum, 1963), pp. 253–254.

78. Nuri al-Sa'id told the British that at the meetings in Turkey he gathered the impression that if no one else took action against Syria, Turkey would. (British Foreign Office, September 11, 1957, FO 371/128227, PRO.)

79. Eisenhower, *Waging Peace,* p. 203. *New York Times* of September 15 reported that Turkey was massing troops along Syrian border with a number of "incidents" occurring.

80. Dulles Telephone Call to General Nathan Twining, September 7, 1957, John Foster Dulles Papers, Telephone Calls Series, Box 7, DDEL.

81. Harry B. Ellis, *Challenge in the Middle East: Communist Influence and American Policy* (New York: The Ronald Press Company, 1960), p. 162. For a cogent analysis of Soviet economic influence in the Middle East, see Joseph S. Berliner, *Soviet Economic Aid: The New Aid and Trade Policy in Underdeveloped Countries* (New York: Praeger, Inc., 1958).

82. FBIS, August 21, 1957, p. C7.

83. Memorandum of a Conversation . . . , September 7, 1957, *FRUS.*

84. For this and subsequent referrals, see Special National Intelligence Estimate, SNIE 36.7–57, "Developments in the Syrian Situation, September 3, 1957, *FRUS,* pp. 674–680.

85. A 1956 State Department report stated the following: "Syria, at this time, cannot be termed a Soviet satellite. In contrast to the European satellites of the USSR, Syria does not have a Communist or Communist-dominated regime put in power directly or indirectly through the agency of

the Soviet army, maintained against the wishes of its people and controlled in its actions by the USSR. It is a state that, under an independent, non-Communist government follows a popular, nationalist course which happens to coincide with Soviet aims of preventing extension of the Baghdad Pact and, as far as possible, eliminating Western influence in the Near East. Soviet and Communist support of the Syrian Government are thus given with the aim of strengthening this policy line, but the pursuance of the line as such is not dependent on Soviet control or aid." Department of State, Office of Intelligence Research, Intelligence Report No. 7282, "Political Trends in Syria," July 2, 1956, RG59, NA.

86. See for instance, FBIS, September 4, 1957, p. C5.

87. FBIS, September 4, 1957, p. C7-8.

88. FBIS, August 27, 1957, p. C5-6.

89. FBIS, August 30, 1957, p. C2.

90. DA Intelligence Report, September 17, 1957, Entry 85, Intell. Doc. File, 2058810, RG319, NARA.

91. DA Intelligence Report, September 23, 1957, Entry 85, Intell. Doc. File, 2059505, RG319, NARA.

92. For example, see FBIS, September 10, 1957, Significant Foreign Radio Reportage (TASS summary of *Izvestia* and *Red Star* articles). See Oles M. Smolansky, *The Soviet Union and the Arab East Under Khrushchev* (Lewisburg, PA, Bucknell University Press, 1974), pp. 59–74, for citations of Soviet press articles dealing with Syrian crisis.

93. British Foreign Office, September 3, 1957, FO 371/127736, PRO.

94. For text of statement, see The White House, "Statement by the Secretary of State re Syria," September 7, 1957, John Foster Dulles Papers, Box 116, Seeley G. Mudd Library, Princeton.

95. For text of press conference, see Department of State For the Press, no. 507, September 10, 1957, John Foster Dulles Papers, Box 116, Seeley G. Mudd Library, Princeton.

96. For example, see *NYT,* September 15, 1957.

97. Memorandum of Conversation, September 11, 1957, John Foster Dulles Papers, General Correspondence and Memoranda Series, Box 1, DDEL.

98. In Bulganin's September 11 note to Menderes, he stated that "it is known that it was Henderson's task to organize a plot against Syria and devise a means to overthrow the Syrian National Government . . . To achieve an armed attack against Syria, certain American quarters would like to utilize primarily such Middle Eastern countries as Jordan, Iraq and possibly others." The Soviets may also have learned of American plans from leaks out of the Henderson meetings in Turkey. Nuri al-Saʻid suggested as much by telling British officials that the Iraqi ambassador

to Turkey could not be trusted. (British Foreign Office, September 11, 1957, FO 371/128227, PRO.)

99. Telephone call from Senator Knowland to Dulles, September 11, 1957, John Foster Dulles Papers, Telephone Calls Series, Box 7, DDEL.

100. 336th Meeting of the NSC, September 12, 1957, Ann Whitman File, NSC Series, Box 9, DDEL.

101. Telephone call from Knowland to Dulles, September 11, 1957.

102. British Foreign Office, September 12, 1957, FO 371/128227, PRO.

103. Ibid.

10

Regional Diplomacy
of Sa'ud and Nasser

While the United States and the Soviet Union were indulging in their super-power standoff, diplomacy shifted back to the regional level as Saudi Arabia reentered the scene. King Sa'ud saw the crisis as an opportune moment to become leader of the Arab world. On the more practical side, he also wanted to salvage his assets in Syria and pull it again toward the Saudi orbit and away from Nasser's. Iraq was unable to do this because its government was un-redeemably regarded as a lackey of imperialism, in addition to the fact that it had lost most of its assets in Syria as a result of the exiles and trial verdicts following the exposure of the "Iraqi plot." But Sa'ud had distanced himself from Washington sufficiently to act the part of an Arab nationalist leader, and he was totally at odds with the British.

Sa'ud's first step was to rehabilitate Syrian President Shukri al-Quwatli, who had been financially beholden to the royal family (as well as to Nasser) for some time. To effect this and remain on amiable terms with the real power in Syria, the Saudis continued to exchange niceties with the Syrian government. But Sa'ud had considerable leverage working in his favor, of which no doubt the Syrians were well aware: he held the key to American-sponsored regional action against Syria. Sa'ud's refusal to cooperate with the Eisenhower ad-ministration vis-à-vis the crisis left the United States with the vexing problem of how to galvanize an Arab response. Knowing this, the Syrians, no doubt with the encouragement of Nasser, did everything they could to maintain their link to Sa'ud so as not to push him irretrievably into the American corner. All the protestations by Syrian leaders stating that they were not communists and that their country was not communist-dominated were directed as much to the Saudis (and the Egyptians) as the Americans. This Saudi-Syrian friendship was definitely a marriage of convenience. The Damascus International Fair in early September 1957 provided a conduit for the Syrian regime to exchange contacts with the Saudis and the Iraqis. At the fair, the Saudi finance minister, Muham-mad Surur al-Sabban, commented that Saudi-Syrian relations had never been better than at that moment.[1]

En route to receive "medical treatment" in West Germany, Sa'ud made a dramatic 24-hour stopover in Beirut on September 7, 1957, to consult with various Lebanese officials. The Syrians, who earlier probably would have viewed Sa'ud's mediatory efforts as unwarranted interference in Syrian affairs, now publicly welcomed this visit as something that would be, as Syrian Minister of Education Hani al-Siba'i stated, "beneficial to us and will remove the harm facing Syria."[2]

While in Lebanon, Sa'ud visited Shaykh al-Sabah, the Kuwaiti ruler, at the latter's summer resort at Shtura near the Syrian border. It was heavily rumored (but denied by both sides) that while at Shtura, Sa'ud surreptitiously met with a high-ranking Syrian official, possibly 'Asali or Quwatli.[3] There is no doubt that Sa'ud communicated with the Syrian leadership while in Lebanon, especially considering the somewhat coordinated sequence of events soon thereafter. Almost overnight, the Lebanese, Jordanian, and Iraqi governments started to back away from their earlier condemnation of Syria and began to make noises in support of the Syrian regime. On September 10, the pro-West Jordanian foreign minister, Samir al-Rifa'i, exclaimed that Israel was Jordan's number one enemy and rejected any notion that one Arab state would invade another, emphasizing that the arms Jordan received from the United States would be used only for self-defense (against Israel).[4] Jamil Midfa'i, the Iraqi Senate leader, was quoted as saying that "any aggression against Syria would be aggression against Iraq and every Arab country."[5] The Saudi ambassador to Syria stated on September 10 that his country would "spare no effort to support, back, and aid" Syria should it be the target of aggression.[6] On September 12, a Saudi official commented that "Saudi Arabia will not stand with hands folded in the event of any aggression against Syria."[7] On the same day, Sa'ud sent a note to Eisenhower urging patience and forbearance in dealing with the Syrian situation, and he claimed that reports of the Syrian threat had been exaggerated.[8]

Recognizing this swift turn of events, the Syrian regime, on September 15, astutely sent public notes to the governments of Jordan, Lebanon, and Iraq asking each of them if they had in fact informed Loy Henderson in August that they were "seriously concerned" about events in Syria and the threat it posed in the region, as Henderson had reported to Eisenhower. The Arab commentator Ahmad Sa'id remarked that the notes put the "imperialist underlings," as he called them, in quite a dilemma, for if they admitted that they had expressed their concerns to Henderson then they would "openly declare their hostility to Arab nationalism," but if they denied it, then they would "embarrass" the United States.[9] The quandary was apparent in the Iraqi government response. It denied that developments in Syria had caused it any anxiety and pointed out that Henderson did not specify *which* Middle East governments had expressed concerns, only that he "sensed" concern in the area over communist "penetration." The Iraqi government remained party to Arab pacts and voiced its readiness to assist Syria against any outside danger.[10] An Iraqi official declared that Iraq "is fully convinced that Syria will never contemplate aggression against any Arab state. . . ."[11] Jordan and Lebanon sent similar replies.

One reason for the Iraqi turnabout was the effectiveness of the Syrian and Egyptian propaganda campaign in Iraq. The Jawdat government was already sympathetic to the Syrian regime, but during the crisis it came under increasing pressure, internally and externally, to come out openly in support of their beleaguered Arab neighbor. The British ambassador in Baghdad admitted that leading Iraqis "realize the dangers of the Syrian situation, but they do not command the support of public opinion. This is still shaped largely by Egyptian and Syrian propaganda making out that this is an Arab-Israeli issue . . . ," and as a result, the Iraqi chief of staff "found it necessary" to withdraw Iraqi troops from the Syrian border in the face of questions about why Iraq was keeping so many troops there.[12] The British distraughtly remarked that the Iraqis "are doing nothing to educate their own or world opinion about Syrian subversive activities, either against themselves or against Jordan and the Lebanon. The result is that world opinion is swallowing the Russian and Syrian line of an innocent Syria merely reacting to the hostile behavior of her neighbors."[13] The British embassy in Baghdad even suggested having the Turks communicate to the Iraqi government the text of an alleged (and wholly bogus) Syrian-Soviet agreement reportedly discovered by the Turkish government that would have confirmed all of the worst fears of Soviet-Syrian expansion and subversion in the Middle East.[14] The British thought this might "stiffen" the resolve of the Iraqis while falling "in line with a policy of keeping the Syrian pot boiling."[15]

The Eisenhower administration, for its part, also recognized that it was losing the propaganda battle being waged in the Middle East. United States Information Service posts in the region reported "widespread acceptance" of the following propaganda lines: that Syria only turned to the Soviets for aid after the United States refused to grant it unconditional aid, that American imperialistic intentions were responsible for the current tensions, and that Washington favored Israel over the Arabs.[16] In response, the State Department and the United States Information Agency revamped their psychological propaganda campaign in the Middle East, focusing on two major objectives: 1) point up the gravity of the communist effort in Syria, and 2) show that American policies support and protect legitimate Arab nationalist aims.[17] The report to the president stated that "Middle East posts have been instructed to use every resource to pursue this campaign, to give it top priority, and to devote to it maximum available initiative, imagination and talent. It is anticipated that the scope of government effort will be similar to that undertaken in countering the Communist drive in Guatemala."[18]

The State Department and USIA recognized that it would be very difficult to successfully carry out this program and realized it could only be implemented indirectly since a "frontal, all-out assault" would only increase hostility toward the United States; nevertheless, they hoped for some of the success that similar operations had experienced in Guatemala and Iran, but this was a case of too little, too late. The United States had failed to convince the Arab world (other than those who conveniently chose to accept the American version) that Syria was communist-dominated, a threat to its neighbors, or a springboard for Soviet subversion. The pro-West Arab leaders, therefore, already vulnerable following Suez, were unable to resist the popularity of Arab nationalist themes. King Sa'ud had laid the groundwork for his scheme; he had mollified Syria's Arab neighbors and endeared himself to the Syrian regime. For the time being, Sa'ud's star was outshining Nasser's, and there was even talk of convening an Arab summit meeting to discuss the Syrian situation in Riyadh, not Cairo.

As the climax to his diplomatic effort, Sa'ud appeared at the Damascus airport on September 25, 1957, to consult with Syrian officials (Iraqi Premier 'Ali Jawdat arrived the following day). Sa'ud also dispatched Crown Prince Faisal to Washington on September 23 to confer with Eisenhower and Dulles, obviously aimed at maintaining cordial relations with the United States. Faisal's visit also was a warning flare. He probably pointed out that Saudi Arabia and the United States had similar objectives vis-à-vis Syria but differed on the means to achieve them, while making it perfectly clear that the king preferred the crisis to be resolved through mediation and not force; he did not want the crisis to irrevocably divide the Arab world, which would weaken Sa'ud's position in the region. From the record of the discussion at the White House it is clear that the administration developed its Middle East policy on a completely different level than the Saudis. While Faisal kept emphasizing that Israel was the most immediate threat to the Arabs, Eisenhower and Dulles repeatedly tried to convince him that international communism was the number one danger in the Middle East.[19] An earlier note the president had sent to Sa'ud, in an attempt to convince the king of the sagaciousness of American policy, had obviously failed.[20] The administration even reiterated to Faisal its earlier pledges that it would not tolerate Israeli expansion or aggression at the expense of the Arabs; indeed, as part of its revamped psychological campaign in the Middle East, any Israeli government criticisms of the United States were highlighted in order to bolster the administration's image in the Arab world.

Echoing the sentiments of other Arab leaders, Crown Prince Faisal stressed that the Syrian situation should be dealt with "a great deal of patience and wisdom." Following the meeting, Faisal told *al-Ahram* on September 25 that Saudi Arabia would defend any Arab country against outside aggression, regardless of its source, and stated that Eisenhower was "greatly astonished" by his remark that Syria posed no threat in the area, contrary to the information the president had received from Henderson. Before the United States could dissuade Sa'ud from pursuing his diplomatic solution, he handed the Eisenhower administration a fait accompli by showing up at the Damascus airport.

In Syria, Sa'ud saw all of regime's top brass in meetings described as taking place in "an atmosphere of sincere friendship, good faith and complete frankness." While Sa'ud and his Syrian hosts agreed that they should work together to reduce tensions in the region, they disagreed most likely on the make-up of the Syrian hierarchy and Sa'ud's probable insistence that communist/Soviet influence in Syria be kept to a minimum. Quwatli assured both Sa'ud and Jawdat that Syria was not and would never be communist, and that it had accumulated stocks of Soviet arms to defend itself against Israel.[21] Sa'ud and Jawdat reportedly warned the Syrian leadership that if their country did indeed become communist, that the other Arab states would be forced to discard their ties with Syria and "strongly" oppose it.[22]

While in Damascus, Sa'ud also wanted to assess the positions of 'Asali and Quwatli. He wanted to make sure his assets in Syria were viable, i.e., able to block the communists and Nasserists. If they were mere puppets of Sarraj, Bizri, and Hawrani, then some alternative course of action might then be in order. The Syrian leadership seemed to have obliged Quwatli's and 'Asali's pretensions to power for the benefit of Sa'ud and attempted to quell rumors of increased communist influence. While Jawdat could not precisely ascertain Quwatli's position, he did comment that at a cabinet meeting the Syrian president spoke with an "air of authority" and the other cabinet ministers had all agreed with what he had said.[23] He added that Bizri did not even open his mouth at the cabinet meeting and that if he and Sarraj were truly running the show, they gave no indication of it. The Iraqi premier also discovered that many parliamentary ministers were having "misgivings" over the extent of Soviet popularity in Syria, rooted as it was in the Kremlin's support in the United Nations. The ministers expressed their opposition to the further spread of communism in their country. Jawdat and Sa'ud agreed that this was all the more reason to boost the position of Quwatli and other anti-communist politicians in Syria and in the rest of the Arab world.[24] In fact, the quid pro quo for continued Saudi and Iraqi support for the Syrian regime was probably Quwatli and 'Asali staying in power (and definitely Khalid al-'Azm being excluded from power; as you will recall, he became rather loathsome to the Saudis for his disparaging remarks over the summer, and he also supported a closer relationship with the Soviets).

After the meetings, the diplomatic niceties continued to flow back and forth between Damascus, Riyadh, and Baghdad. The Saudi ambassador to Damascus, Shaykh 'Abd al-Aziz ibn Zayd, stated that Sa'ud's visit was "the greatest proof of the inseparable fraternity between the two countries."[25]

Another Saudi official stated that there was "no inclination toward communism in Syria and that the accusations made by Western circles and the press against Syria are untrue and only point out the bad intentions of the Western states and their attempts to reimpose their influence in this area."[26] Jawdat was quoted as saying that "Iraq absolutely supports Syria against any aggression" and that he "is not disturbed about sister Syria arming herself."[27] The Baghdad press followed suit and generally supported the premier's statements.[28] Jawdat had succeeded in portraying himself as a true Arab nationalist, quelling for the time being domestic criticism of the government for having isolated Iraq in the Arab world. Finally, on September 26, Sa'ud issued a statement on his talks with Syrian leaders:[29]

> On this occasion, I would like to declare without obscurity and ambiguity and with sincerity for which I am known by my Syrian brethren in particular and the Arabs in general that I denounce any aggression against Syria and against any other Arab country from wherever it comes. I shall resist with my Syrian brethren and the Arabs any aggression committed against them and against their independence whatever its source may be. I do not think that any Arab will sink so low as to harm any other Arab.

The fact that Sa'ud and Jawdat met with Syrian representatives while two Soviet warships (the cruiser Zhdanov and the destroyer Svobodny arrived on September 19) were anchored off the Syrian coast at Latakia as a show of force in response to the presence of the Sixth Fleet, only added insult to injury from Washington's perspective. Whether or not it was intended, Sa'ud's visit at that particular moment symbolically confirmed Syria's contention that it was not Soviet or communist-dominated. As a gesture to the United States, however, and as a reminder to his new Syrian friends of his potential leverage, Sa'ud spoke for a few minutes with the American charge d'affaires in the presence of Quwatli just before boarding his plane upon leaving Damascus on September 27. The subject of the conversation is not known, but its message was clear.

On October 6 the Saudi government denied its acceptance of the Eisenhower Doctrine, countering what had been assumed in diplomatic circles since Sa'ud's visit to Washington, even though the king never officially announced his country's adherence to it.[30] The denial was the result of regional diplomatic jousting with Nasser, a match the Saudis would eventually lose. The day before, Nasser had announced that he would not attend the summit conference that Sa'ud had been planning because he would not participate in a forum with countries that had accepted the doctrine. Sa'ud wanted the meeting while he was riding high; Nasser did not at a time when he was not at the top. The Saudi announcement regarding the doctrine was an attempt to remove this obstacle. In Washington's eyes, however, Sa'ud had virtually come full circle and perhaps serendipitously, Nasser had forced Saudi Arabia's further estrangement from the United States. This was a given, however, for Nasser had long set the standard for Arab nationalist leadership, and any pretender to this position had to detach himself from the West.

Sa'ud's diplomacy had an immediate effect on Jordan, which had been somewhat reluctant to come out in support of Syria. At the opening of the Jordanian parliament on October 1, King Hussein delivered a speech regarding the Syrian situation that can be classified as moderate compared with his earlier pronunciations. He clearly recognized Jordan's increasing isolation in the Arab world. The king continued to attack Syria and Egypt for their refusal to pay the subsidies they agreed to provide Jordan after the British ended their subsidy; however, he veered away from his usual emphasis on "international communism" and stressed his requirements for military aid in order to defend his country against the "Zionist menace."[31] He also rejected participation in any foreign pacts (i.e., the Baghdad Pact) and indicated his resistance to submit to any alien doctrine (i.e., the Eisenhower Doctrine); additionally, he opened the door to Syria by promising friendship for "those who befriend us."[32] Sa'ud encouraged Hussein along this line by sending him a message that discussed ways to mend Syrian-Jordanian relations.[33] Hussein accepted Sa'ud's suggestion that if Syria ceased its propaganda attacks against the Jordanian regime that he would reciprocate, and implied as much in his parliamentary speech.[34] Within a week, the press attacks between Amman and Damascus dropped off considerably. Sa'ud had succeeded in mediating a detente between Syria and its Arab neighbors, and for the time being, he was the most dynamic figure in the Arab world.

Nasser's Response

Sa'ud's ascension in the Arab world was something Nasser was not prepared to accept, especially since it was at his expense. As early as September 11, Nasser was scheming with Syrian officials to steal Sa'ud's thunder. Nasser, along with his commander-in-chief, 'Abd al-Hakim Amir, and the chief of staff of the joint Egyptian-Syrian command, Hafiz Isma'il, met with Sarraj and Bizri in Cairo.[35] In retrospect it is clear that at this meeting the plans were drawn up for a dramatic move to reestablish Nasser's preeminence in the Arab world. Nasser also intended to build up the pro-Nasser army/Ba'th faction in Syria through Bizri and Sarraj in order to check Saudi advances through Quwatli and 'Asali, as well as Soviet influence through Khalid al-'Azm and Khalid Baqdash. Nasser thus began a diplomatic offensive that at first was subtle so as not to appear to be in conflict with Sa'ud's popular mediation efforts. In addition, Nasser was well aware of the Saudi monarch's relationship with the Americans and probably realized that he too would benefit from Sa'ud's mediatory efforts, for the Egyptian president did not want to be in a position where he would be forced to come to Syria's aid against fellow Arab states, least of all Turkey or the United States, or play second fiddle to the only country really capable of protecting Syria, the Soviet Union. Nasser would cleverly allow Sa'ud to commit himself to a peaceful resolution before he made his move.

In the meantime, Nasser tried to maintain his distance from Saudi policy. In a statement to an Associated Press correspondent (subsequently broadcast on Cairo Radio on the September 27), Nasser said he had no objection to meeting with Eisenhower to discuss Middle East problems, so long as the initiative came from the American side.[36] Asked if this was his attempt to mediate the American-Syrian crisis, he responded that he did not believe in mediation and that he preferred direct negotiations between American and Syrian authorities.[37] On a more practical level, Nasser reportedly offered Bizri and Sarraj at the September 11 meeting the use of Soviet trained Egyptian technicians to help in training the Syrian army in the use of Soviet armaments. Nasser apparently urged the Syrian officers to use Egyptian rather than Soviet technicians in order to avoid unnecessary tension with the West (i.e., not get closer to the Soviets).[38] In addition, Nasser announced on September 27 that Egypt would resume normal trade with the West, particularly with France, setting an example which he hoped Syria would follow in order to stem the slide into the Soviet orbit through economic strangulation. With this step, Nasser hoped to strengthen the Ba'th position in Syria by encouraging action that would benefit the Syrian business sectors, many of whom (especially in Aleppo) were moderate to conservative and/or independents (in which case it would be undercutting 'Azm's constituency as well) and generally opposed to the Ba'th's socialist policies.

Sa'ud, meanwhile, attempted to extend his diplomatic gains at the Arab games in Beirut on October 10, 1957. The Beirut paper *al-Hayat* reported on October 5 that Bizri and Sarraj had left Syria to meet with Sa'ud in Riyadh (both Syrians subsequently denied the meeting). The paper stated that the purpose of the trip was to "restate Syria's position to King Sa'ud with a view to warning the Saudi sovereign against any demarches by Syria's enemies during his forthcoming talks in Beirut." If the meeting did in fact take place, it might well have been an information gathering exercise to confirm how long Sa'ud was going to be in Lebanon and find out if he was planning any more diplomatic surprises. Sa'ud reportedly wanted to convene a meeting of Arab leaders while in Beirut and asked Nasser whether he would attend, and if not, whether he would object to one being held in his absence. Nasser certainly viewed with distaste any meeting held at Sa'ud's behest, and if he could not postpone such a meeting, the least he could do would be to embarrass Sa'ud.

This Nasser did by sending troops to the Syrian coastal city of Latakia on October 13 to defend Syria against Turkish "aggression," as the Turks had been steadily building up their forces along the border. The contrast of Sa'ud at a sports event and Nasser sending Egyptian troops to the aid of a sister state threatened by outside forces did not go unnoticed, as was most certainly Nasser's intention. Helped by a massive propaganda campaign, Egypt became the Arab state that matched words with deeds and honored its commitments. *Al-Ahram* printed on October 14 that the action showed that the defense agreement between Syria and Egypt (signed November 1955) was not "merely ink on paper . . . it is a reality." The headquarters of the joint Syrian-Egyptian command in Cairo announced that it had been sending "basic elements" of its armed forces to Syria since the middle of September.[39] The Syrian press hailed the arrival of Egyptian troops, while Damascus Radio simultaneously intensified its charges against Turkey for its "provocations" and "aggressions" on the border. On October 17, Syria placed the army on alert and arms were distributed to civilian groups (the Popular Resistance Organizations); it would have seemed even more awkward than it already was to have Syrian troops not in a state of readiness at the exact same time that Egyptian troops were helping Syria face the imminent threat from Turkey. Had the threat been real, of course, Nasser would not have sent his troops. The Soviet Union had already warned against any action vis-à-vis Syria, so in a sense Nasser was operating under a Soviet defense umbrella. That it was more of a political than a military move is born out by the fact that only about 2,000 Egyptian troops landed at Latakia, which was a woefully inadequate number for the task.

Serendipitously, the troop landing also upstaged a meeting (set up by the Americans and the British) on the Jordanian-Iraqi border on October 13 between Hussein and Faisal, who attempted to improve relations between Jordan and Iraq. Middle East radio broadcasts at the time highlighted Egypt's move, except for Lebanon's and Jordan's, which continued to emphasize Sa'ud's visit to Beirut and the Hussein-Faisal meeting. Nasser had turned the tables on Sa'ud and had won a tremendous propaganda victory.

In addition to upstaging Sa'ud and regaining the diplomatic initiative in the Arab world, Nasser had other reasons for sending Egyptian troops to Syria at this particular time. He wanted to take advantage of the opportunity to place Amir in the position of commander-in-chief of the Syrian-Egyptian joint command. This, along with Egyptian troops on the ground in Syria, put Nasser in a position to regain his influence in the country, manipulate the political process, and protect his army-Ba'thist assets. It also prevented Bizri's advancement in the Syrian power structure through the vehicle of the joint command — Nasser reportedly did not trust Bizri and shared the American view that he was a communist.[40] In addition, the move was designed to solidify support for Akram al-Hawrani, who was up for election on October 14 as speaker of the Chamber of Deputies against the incumbent Nazim al-Qudsi, a leading member of the Populist Party (which was the single biggest party in the chamber, although disunited). Nasser preferred to see Hawrani victorious, and the timing of the Egyptian troop landing was intended to help his election chances. In view of the fact that Hawrani won by only a slim majority, Nasser's timely assistance could have been a decisive factor in the election. It was important to Nasser to have Hawrani in the position of speaker of the chamber, for it was ex-officio the vice-presidency of the Syrian Republic, and if the president becomes ill or is away, the speaker undertakes his functions.[41] With Quwatli in his seventies and often ill (real or diplomatic), this position assumed added significance. Hawrani, as a leader of the Ba'th Party and the key to its link with the military, had essentially become the number two figure in Syria, and he was therefore in the catbird seat for the next presidential election. In this way, Nasser and his Syrian supporters could continue to keep the "Russian millionaire" Khalid al-'Azm from his long-time ambition.

As mentioned, Nasser was intent on securing the Ba'th position in Syria.[42] In this fashion, he could enhance the ability of the Ba'th to withstand and reverse growing Soviet influence in Syria and solidify the country's attachment to Egypt. The fact that the Egyptian troops immediately moved inland toward Aleppo only proves this to be the case. The district of Aleppo had traditionally been the stronghold for the Populist Party. It was also a region of growing communist influence, which was the case with most of northern Syria. Though Aleppo was also a center for Hawrani's Ba'thist followers, the region as a whole was generally anti-Egyptian (the Populists, of course, were mostly pro-Iraqi). Municipal elections were scheduled to be held throughout Syria on November 18, with Aleppo being a very hotly contested area. As far as the Ba'th or Nasser were concerned, the situation took a turn for the worse on October 8, when the Populist Party announced it was boycotting the elections ostensibly because it felt that it was inappropriate to hold elections while the country was threatened by outside forces. In reality, however, it was the legitimate fear that it would be overwhelmed by the leftist parties; therefore, they wanted the elections postponed.

The Ba'th considered that a conservative boycott might very well result in election victories for the "better organized" communists, which would have been especially true in Populist-dominated Aleppo.[43] The communists were about the only ones in Syria who wanted the municipal elections held as scheduled. Seventy communist candidates had registered for the vote by October 11, compared with 75 for the much more numerous Nationalists and 35 for the Ba'th.[44] Nasser and his Ba'thist allies believed that they could help their cause in Aleppo by staging a dramatic "rescue," with the possibility of changing the view of most Aleppans toward Egypt and thus providing more votes for Ba'thist candidates. It is not surprising that the

Egyptians and Baʻthists exaggerated the Turkish threat, giving plenty of air-time to the purported Turkish battle-cry "on to Aleppo." Nasser and the Baʻthists, as well as the conservatives, were clearly concerned about communist advances in Syria and the concomitant increase in Soviet influence. The Baʻth had allied itself with the communists to combat imperialism and the old-guard Syrian politicians; when they succeeded, with proportionately more power accruing to the communists as Syria's relationship with the Soviet Union tightened during the crisis, the Baʻthists decided to unofficially split from the communists and utilize Nasser's own willingness to prevent Syria from falling under the yoke of the Kremlin.[45] All of this maneuvering proved to be unnecessary, however, as ʻAsali, bowing to pressure from all sides, indefinitely postponed the elections in early November, thus buying more time for the Baʻth to figure out a way to prevent their one-time allies from leap-frogging in front of them.[46] The landing of Egyptian troops returned Nasser to prominence in Syria, which made Baʻthist control and union with Egypt more palatable to many and inevitable to all.

The Egyptian troop landing at Latakia took Saʻud totally by surprise. Quwatli made a point to send a message to the king admitting that he too was caught off-guard.[47] On October 14, Quwatli feebly attempted to support Saʻud by publicizing a telephone call he made to the king in which he expressed "his immense gratitude and thanks for the generous sympathy which His Majesty has shown . . . , which has affected deeply the souls of the Arab people in Syria."[48] At a loss, Saʻud could only offer to put his armed forces at Syria's disposal, but this was hopelessly outshone by Nasser's initiative, and it was clear to all that the latter was now dictating the pace and direction of the regional diplomatic game. Evidence of this came on October 16, when King Hussein informed the ambassadors of Turkey, the United States, and Britain that Jordan fully supported Syria in the event of an attack and that Syria's independence should be maintained. Iraq publicly restated its support for Syria; even the Lebanese reportedly gave Syrian officials assurances that they would offer assistance in case of an attack.[49]

In diplomatic circles in the West, however, many viewed Saʻud's diminution in a positive light. They felt that now Saʻud would finally realize the "uselessness" of Quwatli and the whole diplomatic track upon which he had embarked.[50] The king would then be forced to cooperate more with the West's attempts to rectify the situation in Syria and support Hussein and Faisal. There were those that all along believed that the internal factionalism in Syria would eventually disrupt the government's ability to conduct foreign policy and would eventually cause the regime to shoot itself in the foot; the latest rebuff to Saʻud was a case in point. As one British official put it: "If left to themselves, there is a good chance that the Syrians and their friends will do some of our work for us in their dealings with the rest of the Arab world, as indeed they have already done in alienating Saud by not telling him about the arrival of Egyptian troops."[51]

But Saʻud was not yet ready to abandon his carefully constructed strategy. He told the American ambassador in Lebanon that the West must accept Arab nationalism and that it was his "firm policy to guide and restrain this nationalism within reasonable limits and to bring all Arab states to friendly cooperation with the west."[52] Saʻud realized he now needed "all the prestige possible among his own and other Arab peoples" to succeed; therefore, he continued to press the Eisenhower administration to relent on the Gulf of Aqaba issue in order to provide him with that prestige: "if the United States could force Israel to turn back its invasion of Egyptian territory and the Gaza Strip to help Egypt, which under its present government was scarcely a friend to the United States, then America should prevent Israeli use of Aqaba to help Saudi Arabia, which was a true friend of the United States."[53] Saʻud and Eisenhower, however, had been on different policy wavelengths before the American-Syrian crisis erupted, and there was no reason to expect that the two would all of a sudden start seeing eye to eye on the issue. The administration had become wary of Saʻud's motives and did not lose sight of the fact that Nasser's adept move had effectively limited Saʻud's usefulness to "correct" the situation in Syria. Saʻud, for his part, had committed himself too deeply and would continue along his diplomatic path hoping against hope that his assets in Syria would not allow his efforts to go in vain.

Saʻud responded to Nasser's move on October 20 by officially offering to mediate the Syrian-Turkish dispute. To this point Saʻud had not officially announced his role and had referred to the Syrian situation in general terms without specifying which countries threatened Syria. Saudi radio broadcast that both Turkey and Syria had immediately accepted the king's offer, adding that "at this grave moment everyone is looking toward His Majesty King Saud" to resolve the tense situation.[54] Radio Damascus immediately issued a denial that Syria had accepted Saʻud's offer, stating the government would never accept mediation and that the proposal had not been discussed with Syrian officials. The next day in Washington, the State Department said it welcomed Saʻud's offer. At the United Nations, Turkey officially accepted Saʻud's services, whereas the Syrian delegation to the UN stated that Syria did not reject his offer but that reports of mediation were "not in conformity with the facts."[55] The ambiguity surrounding the Syrian acceptance or non-acceptance of Saʻud's offer of mediation reflected the on-going splits within the Syrian polity. Apparently, Quwatli had accepted the offer and either promised Saʻud something which he could not deliver or was hoping the Saudi monarch's fait accompli would force the Syrian leadership to accede.

But the landing of Egyptian troops at Latakia, which bolstered the position of the Baʻth and committed Egypt to Syria's defense, essentially negated the leverage Sa'ud had obtained vis-à-vis the crisis only a few weeks earlier; therefore, the regime, or more specifically, Sarraj, Hawrani, and Bizri, did not feel compelled to accept Sa'ud's offer. After the initial denial, the government realized that it would not be wise to offend Sa'ud too much and subsequently retracted their blunt statement made on October 20 and issued the less harmful but more confusing message at the UN on the 21st before settling for a more polite and diplomatic denial on October 23, stating that there was no need for mediation and that all that was required for a resolution of the crisis was the withdrawal of Turkish troops from the border areas.[56] Cairo radio only broadcast the Syrian denial, while featuring reports that Egypt's "bold" move was the primary reason that the "imperialists" had not attacked Syria.

The information disseminated from Cairo also focused on linking Israel and Turkey together (with American support) in an alleged plot against Syria, reporting that Israeli Chief of Staff Moshe Dayan had paid a visit to Turkey to discuss such plans. Not only did Nasser effectively portray Egypt as the savior of Syria and Arabism against Turkey and the imperialists, but also against public enemy number one, Israel, which compelled other Arab states to follow his lead. In addition, a Turkish delegation (led by Minister of State Fatin Rustu Zorlu) visited Saudi Arabia on October 24 as part of Turkey's acceptance of Sa'ud's mediation; however, it cast the king in a negative light in the Arab world to be seen as personally negotiating with the country that Egypt had effectively portrayed as an aggressor and imperialist tool. Sa'ud had various constraints upon his diplomatic maneuvering, namely he did not and could not make the United States too uncomfortable, and his efforts were slow and plodding; he had to walk a tightrope to maintain a balance between Arab nationalist forces on the one hand and the West and pro-West elements in the Arab world on the other. Nasser, however, did not have this constraint, and this allowed him to take the bold and decisive step of sending his forces into Syria. Nasser also had the military wherewithal to do so; Sa'ud did not, and the only role the king could play was that of a mediator. Sa'ud tried to use diplomacy rather than force to resolve the Syrian situation. In many ways, he was attempting to accomplish the same thing the United States was, i.e., reduce Soviet influence in Syria. But he also tried to pull Syria into the Saudi orbit, which would have propelled him to the top in the regional battle for Arab leadership. Sa'ud's fatal mistake was that he could only accomplish this at Egypt's and Nasser's expense. This compelled Nasser to respond to the challenge in a way that Sa'ud could not.

Sa'ud's offer of mediation, in and of itself, came to nothing, with the question of acceptance or non-acceptance being debated between Damascus and Riyadh for another week before it faded completely into memory.[57] The effect of Sa'ud's proposal, however, was much more keenly felt in the United Nations than in the Middle East. In fact, the regional chess match between Sa'ud and Nasser caused a good deal of confusion in the diplomatic game being played at the international level at the United Nations.

Notes

1. FBIS, September 5, 1857, p. C8; also quoted in *al-Insha'* (Damascus), September 5, 1957.

2. FBIS, September 9, 1957, p. A4; the Syrian minister of justice, Ma'mun al-Kuzbari, added that "we believe this visit is for the good (of) the Arabs considering His Majesty's attitude toward the recent plot against Syria and the generous feelings and noble efforts which the King manifested to repel harm from Syria." Ibid.

3. FBIS, September 9, 1957, p. F3.

4. FBIS, September 11, 1957, Significant Foreign Radio Reportage.

5. British Embassy-Baghdad, September 16, 1957, FO 371/128227, PRO.

6. FBIS, September 11, 1957, Significant Foreign Radio Reportage.

7. FBIS, September 16, 1957, p. A1.

8. *NYT,* September 15, 1957.

9. FBIS, September 16, 1957, p. A2.

10. FBIS, September 23, 1957, p. A4. For text of Iraqi reply, see British Embassy-Baghdad, September 26, 1957, FO 371/128249, PRO.

11. Ibid.

12. British Embassy-Baghdad, September 24, 1957, FO 371/128229, PRO.

13. British Foreign Office to Istanbul, September 25, 1957, FO 371/128228, PRO.

14. British Embassy-Moscow, September 13, 1957, FO 371/128241, PRO. The agreement reportedly had the Kremlin undertaking "to give political aid to Syria for creation of a 'greater Syria' by gaining territory from Turkey, Iraq, Lebanon, Jordan and Israel." The Turks criticized the Iraqis for their apparent abandonment of the plan agreed upon in Istanbul, accusing them of "pulling the rug" out from underneath their feet as well as Hussein's. (British Embassy-Ankara, October 4, 1957, FO 371/128231, PRO).

15. British Foreign Office (from R.M. Hadow), September 21, 1957, FO 371/128241, PRO.

16. Department of State Circular re Syria, September 25, 1957, White House Office, Office of the Staff Secretary, Subject Series, State Department Subseries, Box 2, DDEL.

17. Arthur Larson to Eisenhower re Syria, September 28, 1957, White House Office, Office of the Staff Secretary, Records 1953–1961, Subject Series, State Department Subseries, Box 2, DDEL.

18. Ibid. The CIA had successfully implemented an extensive propaganda and psychological campaign (following to some extent that which was implemented in Iran during the overthrow of Mossadegh) directed at the

ruling regime in Guatemala. The campaign led the regime to believe that the American-sponsored Guatemalan rebel forces were much larger and better equipped than they actually were. The government of Jacobo Arbenz Guzman thought it was faced with insurmountable odds and thus withdrew without a fight, even though only a small portion of its army could have defeated the rebels. See Richard H. Immerman, *The CIA in Guatemala: The Foreign Policy of Intervention* (Austin: University of Texas Press, 1982), pp. 163–168.

19. For this and subsequent references to this conversation see, Memorandum of a Conversation, White House, Washington, September 23, 1957, 11:30 a.m., *FRUS*, pp. 505–507.

20. Eisenhower to Saud, September 12, 1957, Ann Whitman File, International Series, Box 42, DDEL.

21. British Embassy-Beirut, October 1, 1957, FO 371/128230, PRO; see also British Embassy-Beirut, October 2, 1957, FO 371/128238, PRO. Information provided by Lebanese acting foreign minister, Jamil Makkawi, who also was present at the Damascus talks with Sa'ud and Jawdat.

22. Information from Premier Jawdat, British Embassy-Baghdad, September 30, 1957, FO 371/128249, PRO.

23. British Embassy-Baghdad, September 30, 1957, FO 371/128249, PRO.

24. Ibid.

25. FBIS, September 26, 1957, p. C3.

26. FBIS, September 26, 1957, p. C4.

27. FBIS, September 27, 1957, p. A2.

28. For example, see September 27 *al-Akhbar* and *al-Hurriyah* and September 28 *al-Zaman* and *al-Hawadith.*

29. For text of Sa'ud's statement see *L'Orient,* September 27, 1957; and FBIS, September 27, 1957, p. C6.

30. Jordanian papers published the following statement by a Saudi official: "In a recent commentary the BBC stated that Saudi Arabia has accepted the Eisenhower Doctrine for the Middle East. In fact, Saudi Arabia has not accepted the plan and has not received financial aid from any source. However, this attitude will not reflect on her cordial relations with the United States." (British Embassy-Amman, October 6, 1957, FO 371/127155, PRO).

The British commented: "We had always understood, and the American Embassy here have fostered the view, that King Saud has accepted the Eisenhower Doctrine, though we can find no definite Saudi statement to that effect. The farthest that Saud appears to have committed himself is in the statement reported in . . . despatch . . . of February 19 that 'the Eisenhower Doctrine as explained to him was a good thing and he thought that his Arab friends would see its merits if the same explanations were made to them.' The Saudis got U.S. financial aid for Damman harbor but Saudi Arabia would no doubt say this is not connected with the Eisenhower Doctrine but with the Dhahran airbase renewal." (British Foreign Office, letter from J.B. Denson to W. Morris, October 14, 1957, FO 371/127155, PRO).

31. "Who Lined Up the Arabs?" *The Economist,* October 5, 1957, pp. 50–51; FBIS, October 2, 1957, p. A1.

32. Ibid.

33. "Who Lined Up the Arabs," *The Economist,* October 5, 1957, pp. 50–51.

34. British Embassy-Amman, September 30, 1957, FO 371/128230, PRO; British Embassy-Beirut, October 1, 1957, FO 371/128230, PRO.

35. Seale, p. 305–306; *Christian Science Monitor,* September 12, 1957.

36. FBIS, September 30, 1957, p. B1–2.

37. Ibid.

38. British Embassy-Beirut, September 24, 1957, FO 371/128229, PRO.

39. *Middle East Journal,* vol. IX (Winter 1958), p. 83–84; FBIS, October 14, 1957, p. C1.

40. Telegram From the Embassy in Egypt to the Department of State, December 11, 1957, *FRUS,* pp. 744–746.

41. "Syria's Egyptian Visitors," *The Economist,* October 19, 1957, p. 230–231.

42. Rabinovich, however, suggests the possibility that the two main factions within the Ba'th Party, led by Hawrani and Michel 'Aflaq respectively, also intended to use Nasser's intervention and eventual union with Egypt to help one "neutralize the other." The author obtained this information from indirect references made in the protocols of the March–April 1963 unity talks between Egypt, Iraq, and Syria, published by Nasser's friend and confidante, Muhammad Hasanain Heikal, in *Ma alladhi jara fi surya?* (What Happened in Syria?) (Cairo, 1962). Rabinovich, p. 15.

43. Torrey, p. 373. Moshe Perlmann suggested at the time that there was a "behind-the-scenes struggle . . . between full Sovietists and those who are glad to use Soviet aid but are wary of becoming subservient to Moscow. . . . " "The Syrian Affair," *Middle Eastern Affairs,* vol. 8 (1957), p. 407.

44. Torrey, pp. 373–374.

45. Hawrani revealed his intentions by calling the Communist Party in Syria "insignificant" at a parliamentary session on September 12 (one day after Bizri's and Sarraj's meeting with Nasser in Cairo). This led to a postponement of a Syrian parliamentary delegation trip to Moscow until the spring of 1958, when, as speaker, Hawrani would lead the delegation (thus preventing any more surprise packages with the Soviets like the one negotiated by Khalid al-'Azm in July–August 1957). *Christian Science Monitor,* September 17, 1957.

46. Elias Murqus, a former Syrian communist, gives an interesting criticism of the Communist Party's activities at this time. He feels its

over-aggressiveness vis-à-vis the Ba'th seriously damaged its chances to gain power. *Ta'rikh al-ahzab al-shuyu'iyya fi al-watan al-'arabi* (History of the Communist Parties in the Arab Homeland) (Beirut, 1964), pp. 91–92.

47. British Embassy-Beirut, October 18, 1957, FO 371/128231, PRO.

48. FBIS, October 14, 1957, p. C3.

49. FBIS, October 17, 1957, p. A2.

50. See, for instance, Jordanian Prime Minister Samir Rifa'i's remarks to British officials, British Embassy-Amman, October 19, 1957, FO 371/128232, PRO.

51. British Embassy-Amman, October 21, 1957, FO 371/128242, PRO.

52. Telegram From the Embassy in Lebanon to the Department of State, October 16, 1957, *FRUS*, p. 508–509.

53. Ibid.

54. FBIS, October 21, 1957, p. A2.

55. *Middle East Journal*, vol. IX (Winter 1958), p. 84.

56. Ibid.

57. As a bone to Sa'ud, or possibly to put the onus of action on him, the Syrian council of ministers, as reported in the October 27 *al-Hadara*, decided to invite Saudi military forces to come to Syria to "consolidate the position of the liberated Arab states." The belated nature of the invitation was blamed on the confusion surrounding the mediation offer.

11

The International Crisis

While the regional diplomatic game intensified from mid-September through October, the United States began to shift its confrontation with the Soviet Union from the Middle East to the United Nations. Sa'ud's diplomacy, the subsequent "retreat" by Syria's Arab neighbors, and the Kremlin's deterrence against Turkish intervention forced Dulles to try to claim victory in the American-Syrian crisis in an alternative forum. Dulles believed the United States had to regain the diplomatic initiative.[1] He still felt very strongly about arresting the "deterioration" in the Middle East, but was not very clear on exactly what to do, especially when the "flabbiness" of Syria's neighbors was exposed.[2] The secretary of state then decided to launch his counterattack with his opening address to the United Nations General Assembly on September 19, 1957.[3]

The decision to go on the counteroffensive in the UN, however, may have precluded the opportunity to reduce tensions in the region and resolve the crisis before the superpowers became dangerously involved. In September, after the uproar over the Henderson trip had faded, there was a series of "gestures" emanating from Syria that indicated it wanted to improve its relations with the United States (we know from the Istanbul meetings that the Arab states already preferred a diplomatic solution to the crisis). This essentially just reflected the relatively mild Syrian response to the uncovering of the coup attempt in August prior to the announcement of the Henderson mission. We have already seen Bizri's and Sarraj's mollifying remarks at various press conferences in mid-September. At the same time, Salah al-Din Tarazi commented that relations between the United States and Syria had improved, and the chairman of the foreign affairs committee, Ihsan al-Jabri, stated that while Syria had intended to bring its complaint against American interference to the UN, it "now may not do so."[4] Khalid al-'Azm remarked that the threat of aggression against Syria had receded,[5] and referred to the Soviet-Syrian agreement in the following manner:

> We have obtained arms for the defense of our country. We have also obtained economic aid for promoting the prosperity of our people. Thereby we are banishing the ghost of communism which is a system unsuitable for our country. I affirm that these plans of ours will not lead us to communism. Rather, it is poverty and economic domination which would do that. When Russia agreed to grant us economic aid it thereby combatted communism in our country.[6]

There were also several indications that the Syrians were willing to come to some sort of an accommodation with the Turks and improve relations.[7] Upon assuming his post in Ankara on October 3, the new Syrian chargés d'affaires stated that Syria's "only desire is to see the existence of good relations between the two countries. . . . " and that " . . . the only country from which Syria expects an attack is Israel. We have no anxieties about any other country."[8] In addition, Syria was not exactly preparing itself for battle. Several eyewitnesses at the time reported that there was little or no evidence of a crisis atmosphere in the country. There were only the standard one or two military checkpoints between Damascus and the Jordanian border and there were reportedly no checkpoints between Damascus and the Lebanese border.[9] There was also a noticeable lack of military activity in Damascus, contrary to what one would expect if the regime truly felt it was in imminent danger.[10] Confirming these observations, the Soviet naval squadron that had been anchored off Latakia, ostensibly as a show of force to counter the American Sixth Fleet, sailed for home on October 2.[11]

It was also, of course, in mid to late September that Sa'ud launched his diplomatic effort to mediate a resolution to the crisis, one that was embraced at first by Syria and most of the other Arab states. The American chargés d'affaires in Damascus, Robert Strong, suggested to the State Department that it should leave "the handling of the problem to King Saud and other moderate Arab states. Continuation of . . . military threats simply gives the Soviets and Syrian extremists another golden propaganda opportunity."[12] He also commented that "the best we can hope for from Syria for a long time would be genuine neutrality. No one in Syria can bring Syria back into the western camp under any foreseeable circumstances. We can contribute to adoption of truer neutrality by Syria and to insulation of other Arab states, but we cannot do it by ourselves."[13]

Left to itself, the American-Syrian crisis just might have harmlessly petered out at this time, even though Nasser may have still tried to regain the initiative from Sa'ud, but this would have been totally a regional affair, and if the tensions had dissipated along the Syrian-Turkish border, Nasser's pretext for landing troops at Latakia would have been removed (and Sa'ud's efforts possibly crowned with success, thus making him the effective counterpoise to Nasser the Eisenhower administration had hoped for). The Syrian leadership was satisfied that the crisis atmosphere had helped it solidify domestic support for the regime and allowed it to weather the storm created by the Soviet economic aid agreement. The opposition had expressed its full-fledged support for 'Asali, and even the outlawed SSNP, exiled in Lebanon, called on its members in Syria to come to the regime's defense.[14] Syria was prepared to settle the crisis.

The superpowers, however, were not yet ready to put their guns in their holsters. In response to Strong's suggestions, Assistant Secretary of State William Rountree wrote the following: " . . . we must meet threats by the Soviet Union with firmness whatever the reaction of the Syrian government or press may be."[15] In Washington and Moscow, the only thing that mattered was the perception of claiming victory over the other. Dulles switched venues to the UN in an attempt to do this, and in the process had unwittingly reignited at the international level what was a diminishing crisis. The Kremlin, in turn, could not take Dulles' onslaught in the UN lying down, and it subsequently added more fuel to the fire with equally bellicose remarks in early October. This diplomatic confrontation correspondingly spilled over into the regional arena and resulted in a heightening of tension between the superpowers' respective client-states, Syria and Turkey, which, in turn, could have led to a direct superpower confrontation.

During his General Assembly speech, while deriding the Soviet Union for its historic ambitions to dominate the Middle East and its aggressive intentions vis-à-vis Syria and Turkey, Dulles brought to life an obscure resolution passed by the UN General Assembly in 1949 entitled the "Essentials for Peace."[16] Dulles pointed out that this resolution called upon every nation "to refrain from any threat or acts, direct and indirect, aimed at impairing the freedom, independence or integrity of any state," adding that the only nations who voted against the resolution were the five Soviet bloc states, while the United States had "consistently supported" it from the beginning. Dulles then accused the "Soviet Communists" of violating the Essentials for Peace Resolution vis-à-vis "certain Near East nations" and stated that "when there is such a situation as now exists in the Middle East, this General Assembly ought at least to consider it and to discuss it." In essence then, Dulles' promotion of the resolution conceded that the critics of the Eisenhower Doctrine were correct when they pointed out that it did not adequately address the nebulous problem of indirect aggression/subversion. The introduction of the Essentials for Peace Resolution was a belated and capricious attempt to correct this flaw.

Dulles' harsh words aimed at the Soviet Union and the sharpness of his tone took the General Assembly by surprise and made a "considerable impression" upon many of them.[17] His speech indicated to UN members that the administration's position had reverted to its more strident position reflected in the September 7 statement and away from the more conciliatory remarks made by Dulles at his September 10 press conference. In Syria, Quwatli was reportedly "enraged" by the speech and saw it as representative of American policy, i.e., "something must be done about Syria—if no one else is going to do anything, the United States will be prepared to go it alone."[18] Sabri al-'Asali stated that the speech "marks the climax of the campaign of lies, threats and accusations against Syria."[19] *Al-Ra'i al-'Am* on September 22 asserted that Dulles' concern over the possibility of Syria attacking Turkey "was the excuse used to justify Turkish [troop] concentrations on the border" and that "Turkish fear of Syria is the greatest deception ever attempted." Reaction from Egypt was no less critical. *Al-Jumhuriyya* stated also on the 22nd that "the real danger threatening peace in the Middle East wears a Turkish military uniform and has Dulles' head on its shoulders." On the same day, *al-Ahram* accused Dulles of exploiting the UN to advance the interests of the United States and asked why he was all of a sudden anxious to work through this world body when in January he "ignored the United Nations when his government issued its miserable Eisenhower plan."

Not wanting the United States to gain the upper hand, Soviet Foreign Minister Gromyko lashed back on September 20 that the West was transforming the Middle East into a "hotbed of international conflict" and called upon the UN to defend its independence.[20] The next day, Gromyko repeated his charges against the West and submitted two requests to the General Assembly to debate the issue. At about the same time, the Soviets launched another propaganda campaign in the Middle East, purporting to have discovered continued American plotting in Syria to overthrow the regime.[21] The Kremlin wanted to make sure that Syria, not Turkey, was perceived to be the victim of aggression.[22]

The Turks were bolstered by Dulles' speech. Prime Minister Menderes issued a statement on September 24 in which he accused Syria of being "on the way to becoming a bridgehead for destructive ends and aggressive ambitions" and as a result Turkey must be "very vigilant" in maintaining its national security concern.[23] He went on to state that "the existence of Syria as an independent state and her security are not being threatened in any way," but the statement did not preclude action against the Syrian *regime* and essentially only made assurances that Syria would continue to be an independent state in some form. In his General Assembly speech on September 27, Turkey's chief delegate, Seyfullah Esin, attacked the "campaign of propaganda and false rumors" directed at Turkey made by "a powerful country with which we have long common frontiers to the north."[24] The Turkish government, in principle however, felt that it was time to "pipe down" on Syria and "were all for keeping silent and getting on with the preparation of whatever practical measures might be required for dealing with the Syrian situation."[25]

The Turks also believed Sa'ud was losing faith in Quwatli (this was said *before* the Egyptian landing) and that despite his known attachment to the cause of Arab solidarity, he would cast an approving blind eye toward any action by the neighboring Arab states to bring down the Syrian regime[26] (a view with which Dulles concurred, and by the time of the Egyptian move, was probably correct, but by then it was too late). It is clear that the Turks were still very anxious about the situation to their south, but as long as they received the support of the United States to check the Soviet Union, they would maintain their military pressure. Dulles even expressed concern to Senator Mansfield in a conversation on October 6 over what action Turkey might take.[27] After letting the genie out of the bottle with his tacit approval of whatever the Turks decided to do regarding Syria, the secretary of state was beginning to feel a bit nervous about what they *might* do, the possibility of a superpower confrontation, and the negative repercussions this would have for the American position in the Arab world.

In October, however, the effects of the regional diplomatic chess game in the Middle East began to alter the framework of the UN debate over Syria. On October 2, the Saudi Arabian delegate to the UN, Ahmad Shuqayri, denounced Dulles' suggestion that the UN should discuss the Syrian situation and stated that the UN had no right to interfere with Soviet arms shipments to Syria.[28] The next day, the Egyptian delegate, Mahmud Fawzi, declared in the General Assembly that Egypt would not tolerate any form of aggression against Syria. The American delegate to the UN, Henry Cabot Lodge, described Fawzi's speech as "awful"[29] and Shuqayri's as "not good."[30] In an exasperated tone, Dulles stated that "it is hard for us to say it's dangerous when they [the Arabs] say the opposite."[31] It was hard indeed — in fact, Eisenhower felt it necessary to address the incongruities in a press conference on October 3, in which he stated that "the original alarm of countries like Lebanon, Jordan, and Iraq, and to some extent Saudi Arabia, seems to have been quieted by what they have learned" and that the affair "should be handled locally and internally."[32] The Saudis obviously did not want the UN to "handle" the Syrian situation because their king was in the midst of his diplomatic efforts to resolve the crisis peacefully. The Egyptians, in a game of one-upmanship and with an eye toward upcoming plans (i.e., the landing at Latakia), followed the Saudi delegate in the UN with a robust speech depicting Egypt as the protector of Syria (which, of course, would be manifestly displayed on October 13). The Eisenhower administration, however, was immediately unaware of the effects of the diplomatic struggle occurring at the regional level on American policy and found itself in the awkward position of trying to rationalize to a confused public why it was still claiming that Syria was a threat while at the same time its erstwhile allies in the region were all proclaiming their solidarity *with* Syria against outside aggression.

On October 5, Dulles met with Gromyko in New York and made it very clear to him that American resolve on the Syrian matter was unflinching. He stated that "we didn't move to get our friends the British and French out [of Suez] merely to see them replaced by the Soviet Union. If we took such strong action then, you can calculate as to how strongly we would feel about keeping the Soviet Union out."[33] Although the intent was to put the Kremlin on guard, the effect of Dulles' warning might have had the opposite effect. All it did was confirm, in Moscow's eyes, continued attempts by Washington to keep the Soviets totally out of the Middle East. This, in turn, only made it that much more important for the Soviets to stand their ground in Syria and maintain their entry point into the heartland of the area so that they would be indispensable to the diplomatic process in the region. This is exactly what the Soviets had been attempting to accomplish with the various notes they had sent to the governments in the West during the course of 1957 — all of which were summarily rejected. Now they engaged themselves in the area by directly supporting an Arab state and gained increased access to a regime which was forced to turn to them for protection against American-sponsored encroachment. Therefore, it is not surprising that when *New York Times* correspondent William Reston interviewed Khrushchev on October 7, the Soviet leader lashed out at the United States and Turkey, again raising international tension.[34]

Khrushchev told Reston that "if the rifles fired the rockets could start flying." He accused the United States of sending Henderson to the Middle East in order to plan an attack on Syria by its Arab neighbors, and when this failed, the Eisenhower administration then turned to Turkey to do the job. Commenting on the interview, an official at the United States embassy in Moscow stated that "it would appear that [the] Soviets have some specific information [on U.S. plans], possibly intercepts of Arab communications, which they consider genuine." Indeed, the Kremlin claimed that it had evidence of Turkish military intentions in the form of documents which Soviet agents had allegedly taken out of an American diplomatic pouch that was on a ferry crossing the Bosporus.[35] This accusation was never substantiated by the Soviets, but Dulles did admit that "no doubt the Soviets have gotten hold of war plans which we all have. There is a difference between having them and putting them into operation. The proof of attacking is not in [the] plans — it is in the political decision."[36] There was plenty of hearsay evidence to put the Kremlin on guard, and after digesting the recent history of American-sponsored action in Guatemala, Iran, and Jordan, the Henderson mission was understandably seen as provocative. As one correspondent aptly stated, "Moscow was as naturally alarmed by Mr. Loy Henderson's tour . . . as Washington would be were a special Soviet envoy to sign up the Mexicans."

The Soviet press obediently started publishing numerous reports of shooting incidents on the Turkish-Syrian border, the continued massing of Turkish troops, and violations of Syrian airspace by Turkish aircraft. On October 8, the day after the Khrushchev interview, the Syrian government, emboldened by the Soviet leader's supportive statements, formally complained about Turkish activities on its borders to the secretary-general of the United Nations and lodged a protest with the Turkish government. Moscow kept the pot boiling on October 11 when it sent letters over the heads of various governments in the West to the British Labor party and the socialist parties of France, Belgium, Norway, Italy, the Netherlands, and Denmark, urging all of them to exercise their influence to restrain their respective governments from sanctioning aggressive action in the Middle East.

Dulles responded to Khrushchev's interview on October 10, stating that "despite distances, he [Khrushchev] should be under no illusion that the United States, Turkey's friend and ally, takes lightly its obligations under the North Atlantic Treaty or is not determined to carry out the national policy expressed in the joint congressional resolution on the Middle East." At a press conference on October 16, he said "if there is an attack on Turkey by the Soviet Union, it would not mean a purely defensive operation by the United States, with the Soviet Union a privileged sanctuary from which to attack Turkey."[37] Global prestige was at stake and neither side wanted to back down.

Syrian Inscription in the United Nations

The Syrian delegation at the United Nations, led by Foreign Minister Bitar, requested on October 16 formal inscription of their "complaint about threats to the security of Syria and to international peace" for debate in the General Assembly. The Syrians called attention to the concentration of Turkish troops on the border and asked that an impartial commission be set up by the assembly to investigate the situation on the Syrian-Turkish border. Gromyko followed with a "request for the inclusion of an additional item" in which he wholly supported the Syrians and stated that "the fact should be taken into account that the United States, while prodding Turkey to commit aggression against Syria, is urging that this operation should be carried out with lightning speed and that the United Nations should be confronted with a fait accompli so that it may have no time to take steps to prevent aggression. Evidently, the United States intends in this case to apply in Syria the methods already used by it to suppress the independence of Guatemala."[38] He added that his government "declares that the Soviet Union is prepared to take part with its forces in suppressing aggression and punishing the violators of peace."

There was some debate within the Eisenhower administration over whether to accept inscription of the Syrian complaint in the General Assembly or propose to refer it directly to the Security Council. Those in favor of the latter maintained that the Security Council was the appropriate forum for discussing "urgent" situations. They felt that if the Syrians were really afraid of an attack they would have brought their complaint directly to the Security Council since it could act in a matter of hours if necessary, as opposed to the more cumbersome assembly process.[39] United Nations Secretary-General Dag Hammarskjold also believed that the Syrian complaint was better suited for the Security Council, but admitted that a Security Council debate would dramatize the incident to an unwarranted level; therefore, he suggested that the complaint be allowed to be inscribed in the General Assembly and then hopefully have it sent to a special political committee.[40] Dulles preferred a Security Council debate, for he was wary of setting a precedent of agreeing to investigations by the assembly before prior reference to the Security Council (i.e., he wanted an opportunity to veto any investigating commission).[41] The British were especially concerned about establishing this sort of precedent because they felt it could be effectively used against them in the Arabian Peninsula, but they decided to let the United States take the initiative in this instance and support whatever approach the administration adopted.[42]

A compromise solution was reached between Dulles and Lodge, the latter felt that by not voting for inscription in the assembly the United States would be perceived as trying to avoid debate on the issue.[43] In addition, if action in the Security Council resulted in a veto of an investigation, the West would be accused of having maneuvered the process to this end. As one British official pointed out, "there would be a certain contradiction between arguing on the one hand that the Syrian move is a propaganda stunt organized by the Russians and on the other hand that the Security Council which is concerned with threats to the peace . . . should be brought into play."[44] This last point (with some convincing from Lodge and Wadsworth) became especially important, for Dulles wanted to publicly exploit the contradictions on the Syrian-Soviet side of going through the General Assembly rather than the Security Council.

Handling the matter in the General Assembly seemed more consistent with American charges that the whole thing had been overblown by the Soviets and Syrians in order to gain ground in the Middle East. Dulles also wanted to turn the tables on the Soviets at the UN and "point up the threat to independence of Syria arising from indirect Soviet aggression and to security of ME [Middle East] arising from [the] pile-up of Soviet arms in Syria. We also believe that [the] outright Soviet threat against Turkey, and reported Bulgarian military movements on the Turkish border . . . will lend themselves to exploitation."[45] Dulles mentioned to Ambassador

Wadsworth, a member of the American United Nations delegation, that he expected to "have fun with the Russians before we are through."[46] Dulles and Lodge agreed to accept inscription of the Syrian complaint while introducing a resolution whereby the assembly, after its discussion of the issue, would refer the item to the Security Council, which would in turn "determine the scope of [the] investigation."[47] The American delegation officially supported inscription on October 18, emphasizing the need to address the problem of indirect aggression and "possible violation" of the Essentials for Peace resolution, and called for plenary discussion of the matter in the assembly "on an urgent basis."

Before Dulles could implement his grand strategy in the United Nations, however, Sa'ud made his formal offer on October 20 to mediate the Syrian-Turkish problem. This action sent UN strategists back to the drawing board and, serendipitously, helped the United States escape an unintended diplomatic dilemma.

Dulles correctly suspected the Turks would not approve of an investigatory commission visiting the Turkish-Syrian border zone. Indeed, Turkish Foreign Minister Esenbel claimed it would hamper his government's ability to act against Syria.[48] What Dulles did not realize was that it would also have adverse effects on the American position there as well. Not until October 19 did Dulles have his "military people" examine the repercussions of such an investigation. They found that the areas to be investigated were of "the most highly sensitive character" and stated that it "would be disastrous to have anything exposed."[49] Dulles suddenly was confronted with more than just the question of how to satisfy the Turks on the investigation issue, now he had to find a way, as he commented to Lodge, for the United States "to get out of it."[50]

Dulles then must have viewed Sa'ud's mediation offer as a godsend—it provided the way "out of it." There is no reason to suggest that the timing of Sa'ud's announcement was more than just a coincidental blessing for the Eisenhower administration; the Saudis had been acting on their own all along and were essentially at odds with the administration's policy toward the American-Syrian crisis. Dulles jumped at the opportunity and officially proclaimed the wholehearted support of the United States for Sa'ud's plan (after irreparably damaging Sa'ud's mediation effort by keeping tension high, thus allowing Nasser a pretext to land troops at Latakia). Simultaneously, the American delegation at the UN called for a delay of the debate on the Syrian complaint until Sa'ud had a chance to pursue his plan. This meant, of course, a delay in a decision on the investigatory commission. With British and American encouragement, the Arab states, with the exception of Egypt, agreed not to hear the Syrian complaint in order to give Sa'ud time to succeed with his mediation.

Even if the United States could not take advantage of Sa'ud's propitious intervention, Dulles had alternate plans to kill a UN investigation of the Turkish-Syrian border. One was to support the Turkish call for a postponement of the debate until after the Turkish national elections on October 27. Another was to insist that if a commission was sent to Turkey then one must be sent to the Turkish-Soviet and the Turkish-Bulgarian borders. In both areas the Turks and the Americans complained of threatening moves by foreign troops — the Soviets would naturally reject this option and the investigation would become a dead issue. But neither option was employed. As Dulles told Lodge, "the Saudi thing is wonderful because an Arab state wants to mediate between an Arab state and a non-Arab one and the Arab state won't do it."[51] On October 22, the General Assembly officially suspended its debate on the Syrian-Turkish dispute pending the outcome of Sa'ud's mediation.

The Syrian, Soviet, and Egyptian delegations at the UN were caught totally off-guard by Sa'ud's gambit (thinking he should have abandoned his efforts) and reacted in the General Assembly on October 22 in a very confused and petulant fashion. They objected to any delay in the proceedings, and lashed out with vicious attacks against American policy, the Eisenhower Doctrine, NATO, Western imperialism, and Turkish aggression. Assistant Secretary of State William Rountree described the scene as a "three-ring circus."[52]

At this time, the Kremlin decided to turn up the heat again in order to give the impression that the Turkish threat still existed, which, in turn, might induce the Arab states and other nations in the Third World to press for an immediate assembly debate of the issue rather than wait for the outcome of Sa'ud's mediation. Soviet press and radio began labelling Sa'ud's offer as an American device to remove the Syrian complaint from discussion at the United Nations. The Kremlin also intensified its accusations that Turkey and the United States planned to invade Syria, emphasizing an alleged Israeli role in such plans. Cairo and Damascus radio exhorted the UN to send an investigatory commission to the Syrian-Turkish border and, while not directly accusing Sa'ud of being an accomplice of the West, criticized the Eisenhower administration for maneuvering to remove the Syrian debate from the UN.

In addition, in an unusual move, the Kremlin announced on October 23, amid much publicity, that one of its senior deputy ministers of defense, Marshal Konstantin Rokossovski, had been reassigned as commander of the Trans-Caucasus military district bordering Turkey and Iran.[53] The Soviet ministry of defense announced on the 24th combined military and naval exercises by the Trans-Caucasus armies and the Black Sea fleet.[54] As Mackintosh observes, the transfers of military district commanders in the Soviet Union, as well as the dates of military or naval exercises, are never publicized in the Soviet press.[55] The Kremlin also reportedly pressured the Syrian government to show some consistency with the Soviet line and maintain the tense atmosphere.[56] Bizri seemed to comply and on October 23 accused the Sixth Fleet of sending aircraft deep into Syrian territory. Three days later, he made some rather bellicose statements aimed at the United States, bravely asserting that "if they want to fight, they are welcome . . . we will compel it to retreat."[57] On October 24, Quwatli reportedly asked Sa'ud to withdraw his mediation offer so the UN could resume its discussion.[58] And on the 28th, the Soviet-Syrian economic accord, despite continued opposition in the chamber, was finally signed by Syrian and Soviet representatives in Damascus (and ratified by the Syrian parliament on November 6).[59]

Dulles suspected that Sa'ud's efforts would in the end fail and thus planned to table a resolution in the UN which would reflect the course of recent events. He did not want to prematurely introduce a resolution and "assume the onus of rejecting Saud's offer of mediation," but he also wanted to be prepared just in case the Arabs turned away from Sa'ud and allowed the Syrians to reintroduce their complaint in the General Assembly.[60] The best outcome as far as Dulles was concerned was for the debate to simply "peter out," something with which both the British and Hammarksjold agreed.[61]

As the Soviet-Syrian position in the UN became more hollow with each passing day of Saudi mediation and general Arab support of his efforts, there were discussions within the Eisenhower administration on whether or not to take further advantage of the Soviet vulnerability in the UN. Cooler heads prevailed, however, mainly because of the fear of a Soviet reprisal elsewhere in the world to even up the score. The decision was made to let the crisis take its natural course and fade away. With this in mind, the administration urged the Turks to play down the Syrian threat for the time being and allow tensions to ease.[62] At an extended press conference on October 29, Dulles barely touched upon the subject of the Middle East and only mentioned the word "Syria" on one occasion, and that in general terms.[63] Even the Arab League position turned lukewarm on the subject. In its statement released on October 31 in Cairo, the Arab League Council denounced in pro forma fashion any aggression against Syria and reiterated its solidarity with the Syrian regime, but concluded with a rather passive and innocuous request "to communicate this resolution to the U.N. Secretary-General and the President of the General Assembly in order that they may in turn communicate it to the member states."[64] There was no demand for debate in the UN and there was no mention of a commission of investigation—the Arabs obviously did not want to see the issue heat up again. Now if only the Soviets would cooperate.

This they did. Khrushchev must have realized the untenable Soviet-Syrian position at the United Nations in the wake of Sa'ud's mediation offer. His objective of deterring the Turks (and the United States) from actively intervening in Syria had been successful, with the concomitant rise in prestige and popularity in the Arab world and increased influence in Syria. It was time to end the crisis before the Soviets lost at the UN much of what they had won in the Middle East. With this in mind, Khrushchev unexpectedly and dramatically appeared at a reception at the Turkish embassy in Moscow on the evening of October 29. The signing of the Soviet-Syrian economic accord the day before may have made the Soviet leader feel more secure about reducing the tension in the crisis — the maintenance of the fever pitch intensity had served its purpose.[65]   Indeed, the Soviet Union had escalated the tension level in early October in order to counter the administration's maneuvers in the United Nations. But the Kremlin's stiff reply to the Turkish threat in early September in large measure prevented the engagement of open hostilities in the region. Contrary to most studies on the American-Syrian crisis, which purport that the United States and Turkey never seriously considered armed intervention in Syria, Dulles essentially had given the Turks the green light to move into Syria. The bellicosity of the Soviet Union in early September was necessary in order to deter any forward policy the Turks might have been contemplating. Whether or not the Kremlin's initial rejoinder was above and beyond what was necessary is a moot point — who can accurately calculate an exact reciprocal response when dealing with such potentially volatile and catastrophic circumstances. Moscow thought, probably correctly, that it was best to err on the side of overreaction, if purely diplomatic ruffling is considered such. We must remember that the Soviets were well aware of and feared, probably more so than the West, the possible calamitous results of appeasement. Their sensitivity to appeasement was as or more pronounced than that which was felt in the White House, especially considering the close geographic proximity of Syria to the Soviet border. Now it was time for the Kremlin to take stock of and secure its newly won position in the Middle East. Asked if his presence at the reception indicated a lessening of tensions, Khrushchev replied, "yes, this is a gesture, a gesture toward peace" and held up one finger saying "if you look at this as a compass needle, you can say it has gone a little way towards peace."[66]

Syrian recriminations against the Turks would continue for a few weeks, along with some threatening noises from Moscow, primarily because the Turks were being "somewhat unnecessarily reticent" about removing their troops from the Syrian border.[67] The Turks began to withdraw their troops on November 19 and announced on November 29 that "an important part of its defense forces" would be reassigned from the border region.[68] Deflated by Sa'ud's mediation and Khrushchev's timely visit to the Turkish Embassy, the UN General Assembly debate on the Syrian complaint was officially put to rest on November 1, with the rival resolutions being mercifully withdrawn and without the issue ever having gone to an official vote.

Bitar had a cordial meeting with Rountree in New York on November 7, in which he clearly expressed Syria's desire for friendlier relations with the United States.[69] Syria did not want a commission of investigation "under any circumstances" and approached Hammarskjǫld asking him to make informal contacts with the Turks in an attempt to resolve the situation in a quiet manner.[70] The crisis had indeed ended, with Khrushchev taking the initiative to remove it from the superpower agenda, which is where it had been prolonged and intensified in the first place.

American-Egyptian Modus Vivendi?

The American-Syrian crisis showed how similar objectives can sometimes make strange bedfellows. Both Egypt and the United States were very interested in keeping Syria from becoming communist and from falling too deeply in the Soviet orbit. To wit, a confidante of Nasser informed American officials on December 11, 1957, that the Egyptian president "had investigated recent information we [United States] had given him relative to the communist connections of Bizri and is now convinced Bizri [is] a communist and that something must be done about it. . . . He [Nasser] asks of us only that we keep hands off Syria for a maximum period of three months and particularly that we do nothing which could have unintentional effect of making heroes out of Bizri, Bakdash and Khalid Al Azm."[71] The informer suggested that there were "several ways of attacking the Syrian problem" but the "only country with capability [to] succeed, and which can do so with minimal repercussions is Egypt. Of [the] countries primarily concerned with [the] Syrian situation, US and Egypt have greatest interest in ensuring that country [has] a stable, anti-communist government."[72] On December 10, Ambassador Hare had a conversation with a member of the inner circle of the Revolutionary Command Council, Ali Sabri, in which the latter stated that Egypt had more reason to worry than the United States about the prospect of Arab nationalism taking too much of a left-hand turn, since Egypt "had to live in the area and could not escape the consequences."[73] The State Department reacted by stating that "we wish [to] avoid impeding any Egyptian efforts to bring about change and in particular appreciate considerations re[garding] Bizri, Bakdash and Azm . . . "[74]

The three months Nasser had asked for was one more than he needed. The long talked about union between Egypt and Syria was finally consummated on February 1, 1958. The regional solution to the Syrian problem that Eisenhower and Dulles so desperately wanted had occurred, although from an unexpected source. The Eisenhower administration calculated that if it could not keep the Soviets out of Syria, it might as well trust the job to someone who could. The United States had tried just about everything short of invasion to keep Syria from becoming a Soviet base in the Middle East.

Dulles turned to a policy of containment "plus" – at least keep the "virus" from spreading out from Syria. Nasser successfully kept the Soviets at arms-length, maybe his stature and power in the Arab world was enough to also keep Syria at arm's length as well.

The American-Egyptian rapprochement did not occur overnight. There had been signs during the crisis that their coinciding interest vis-à-vis Syria might produce some sort of working relationship. In early October the State Department publicly expressed its desire for closer relations with Egypt. Egyptian press and radio commented that this was generally favorable and welcomed American friendship. *Al-Sha'b* of October 12 stated that Egypt "is anxious to have good relations with the United States and other states." The next day, *al-Jumhuriya* printed that "we antagonize those who antagonize us and pacify those who pacify us."

This budding cooperation was clearly evident early on at the UN debate over the Syrian complaint. The Egyptian representative to the UN, Mahmud Fawzi, apparently told Hammarskjold that the Egyptians were doing the best they could to keep the Syrians from proceeding with their complaint in the General Assembly, including trying to dissuade them from insisting on an investigatory commission.[75] They felt the debate would not be confined to the relatively narrow Syrian-Turkish item, but would expand to cover broader issues in the Middle East that could place Nasser in some rather uncomfortable diplomatic positions. Fawzi also told the secretary-general that he was "bitter" over how the Soviets were forcing the hand of the Syrians in the UN.[76] This tended to confirm suspicions that the Syrians (or at least some of them) were less than enthusiastic about approaching the UN on the matter. This might explain some of Bitar's more conciliatory remarks to the Turks on his stopover in Istanbul on his way to New York for the UN debate, as well as his expressed eagerness to meet with American officials (which he did on November 7). There were also reports that the Syrian military, which was under pressure from the Soviet general staff, prevailed upon the government to follow the Soviet strategy in the UN.[77] The remarks on American policy disseminated by Syrian officials, ranging from outright hostility to subtle calls for better relations, revealed the divisions within the Syrian hierarchy over the extent of Soviet influence. Indeed, Soviet guidance of Syrian actions at the UN seemed to have awakened the American and Egyptian delegations to the possibility of limited cooperation. From the Eisenhower administration's point of view, this possibility became more desirable after Sa'ud's mediation had failed and Nasser had regained his paramount position in the Middle East. Evidence of this is found in a summary record of conversations American officials had with Fawzi. One went as follows: "We told Fawzi in our opinion his statement . . . was restrained and we appreciated [the] tone he had struck in it. We said we believed objectives which had outlined to us for handling this item [Syrian complaint] . . . were shared by U.S. Fawzi said Egypt and U.S. share desire to see in Middle East peaceful, constructive, independent states, free from outside interference of *any kind*. . . . Fawzi said he appreciated our initiative and our approach which, as far as he was concerned, represented a clean slate from which to start."[78] (emphasis mine).

The administration began to realize what the Egyptians already knew, i.e., the latter were the only ones capable of preventing an increase of Soviet influence in Syria.[79] Fawzi's actions at the UN and other indications from Cairo convinced Dulles that Nasser was sincere in his desire to "save" Syria. Having exhausted all other reasonable avenues, Dulles had to acquiesce to Nasser's plan.

Recognizing the new political balance in the Middle East, *al-Ahram* of November 6 stated that the Soviet Union "may be on its way to the conquest of space but America can certainly conquer people's hearts." As Mackintosh observed, one of the ironies of this particular moment in Middle East history is that "at the height of this apparent triumph of Soviet diplomacy . . . the neutralist Arab governments turned to the United States with a plea to improve relations."

For Nasser, however, he had just traded in one headache for another. Most Syrians saw union with Egypt as a necessary step to avoid more internal turmoil and external interference. But the problems of the United Arab Republic are the subject of a different story.

Notes

1. Telegram From the Department of State to the Embassy in Turkey, September 16, 1957, *FRUS,* pp. 704–705.

2. British UN Delegation-New York, September 17, 1957, FO 371/128228, PRO.

3. For text of speech, see Department of State For the Press, no. 529, John Foster Dulles Papers, Box 119, Seeley G. Mudd Library, Princeton.

4. British Embassy-Beirut, September 17, 1957, FO 371/128228, PRO.

5. Ibid.

6. FBIS, September 10, 1957, p. C17.

7. For example, see British Embassy-Ankara, September 29, 1957, FO 371/128242, PRO; British Embassy-Ankara, September 27, 1957, FO 371/128242, PRO.

8. British Embassy-Ankara, October 4, 1957, FO 371/128231, PRO.

9. British Embassy-Amman, September, 2, 1957, FO 371/128226, PRO; and British Embassy-Baghdad, September 17, 1957, FO 371/128228, PRO.

10. Ibid.

11. J. M. Mackintosh, *Strategy and Tactics of Soviet Foreign Policy,* p. 227.

12. Letter From the Charge in Syria (Strong) to the Assistant Secretary of State for Near Eastern, South Asian, and African Affairs (Rountree), October 16, 1957, *FRUS,* pp. 718–719.

13. Ibid.

14. British Embassy-Beirut, October 23, 1957, FO 371/128232, PRO.

15. Letter From the Assistant Secretary of State for Near Eastern, South Asian, and African Affairs (Rountree) to the Charge in Syria (Strong), October 29, 1957, *FRUS,* pp. 735–737.

16. General Assembly Resolution No. 290, passed December 1, 1949.

17. British UN Delegation-New York, September 20, 1957, FO 371/127743, PRO.

18. Reported to the British by Dr. Ernest Altounyan, a British subject of Armenian descent, who had a personal meeting on September 22 with Quwatli, who was a longtime friend of his. On the meeting see: British Foreign Office, September 26, 1957, FO 371/128230, PRO; British Embassy-Beirut, September 24, 1957, FO 371/128229, PRO; British Foreign Office, no date, FO 371/128230, PRO (profile of Altounyan).

19. FBIS, September 23, 1957, p. A1.

20. *Middle East Journal,* vol. XIII (Autumn 1957), p. 413.

21. For example, see TASS bulletin on this subject published in the September 27, 1957, *Le Caire,* and interview with Gromyko in *al-Jumhuriyya,* September 30, 1957.

22. Also concerning the Soviets was a meeting in London in late September of the anti-subversion committee of the Baghdad Pact. On September 27, the Baghdad Pact powers agreed to expand their program against communist subversion in the Middle East (obviously with Syria as the focus of attention). *Middle East Journal,* vol. XIII (Autumn, 1957), p. 413. The Soviet press denounced the meeting and its results as further evidence of continued plotting against the Syrian regime.

23. British Embassy-Ankara, September 25, 1957, FO 371/128242, PRO. A Turkish official said that the only reason Menderes made this statement was because of Dulles' speech at the United Nations, which forestalled a possible Soviet "onslaught" in the UN, and because the prime minister did not want to give the impression that the United States spoke for Turkey. (British Embassy-Ankara, October 9, 1957, FO 371/128231, PRO).

24. British UN Delegation-New York, September 27, 1957, FO 371/128229, PRO.

25. British Embassy-Ankara, October 9, 1957, FO 371/128231, PRO.

26. Ibid.

27. Memorandum of Conversation Between Dulles, Mansfield and Macomber re Middle East and Turkey, October 6, 1957, John Foster Dulles Papers, General Correspondence and Memoranda Series, Box 1, DDEL.

28. *Middle East Journal,* vol. IX (Winter 1958), p. 83.

29. Dulles Telephone Call to Lodge, October 3, 1957, 6:06 p.m., John Foster Dulles Papers, Telephone Calls Series, Box 7, DDEL.

30. Telephone Call to Dulles From Lodge, October 2, 1957, 12:46 p.m., John Foster Dulles Papers, Telephone Calls Series, Box 7, DDEL.

31. Ibid.

32. *NYT,* October 4, 1957.

33. Memorandum of Conversation Between Dulles and Gromyko, October 5, 1957, Ann Whitman File, Dulles-Herter Series, Box 7, DDEL.

34. Interview published in *New York Times,* October 10, 1957.

35. *The Economist,* October 26, 1957, p. 291. British opposition leader Bevan, who met with Khrushchev, stated that the Soviet leader told him that he had "irrefragable" evidence that Henderson had been sent to the Middle East to organize a coup d'etat in Syria, with the cutting of the oil pipelines as the pretext for Arab and Turkish intervention. Bevan said that Khrushchev added that if this should happen "we will show the Turks how they can bleed." (British Foreign Office to Washington, October 15, 1957, FO 371/128241, PRO). The above scenario was being considered by American and British officials. (British Embassy-Beirut, August 31, 1957, FO 371/127743). Tass made an official statement on the disclosure on October 18. On September 10, *Kraznaya Zvezda* published a detailed report of a five-stage plan to attack Syria, to be carried out by Turkey, Iraq and Israel; however, Laqueur claims the validity of this assertion was highly questionable since it was based on a report by an "obscure Indian newspaper." (Walter Z. Laqueur, *The Soviet Union and the Middle East* (London: Routledge & Kegan Paul, 1959), pp. 257–258). For purposes of disinformation, Moscow often cited articles in Indian newspapers.

36. Telephone Call from Lodge to Dulles, October 23, 1957, 12:32 p.m., John Foster Dulles Papers, Telephone Calls Series, Box 7, DDEL. The Soviet army paper *Red Star* (September 1957) published what it termed as an Order of Battle of the Turkish army along the Syrian frontier, describing the whereabouts and movements of divisions and armored brigades near the border. (Mackintosh, p. 228).

37. Department of State For the Press, no. 579, John Foster Dulles Papers, Box 122, Seeley G. Mudd Library, Princeton.

38. It is interesting that Gromyko brought up the Guatemalan incident at this time. In his October 16 press conference, Dulles stated that "it seemed that the Arab states preferred to deal with this matter on a regional basis, and the charter of the United Nations provides that in the event of a dispute the nations shall, first of all, deal with it by means of their own choosing, including among other things a regional approach." This aspect of the UN Charter became an issue during the Guatemalan crisis. To at least give the impression that the United States supported a peaceful resolution to the crisis and was following the prescriptions of the UN, Dulles supported and

attended the 10th Inter-American Conference (with the other OAS states) in Caracas, Venezuela, held from March 1 to 28, 1954 (held while the U.S. was planning to overthrow Guatemalan President Jacobo Arbenz Guzman, which would occur only a few months later). Known as the Declaration of Caracas, Dulles introduced a draft resolution entitled, "Declaration of Solidarity for the Preservation of the Political Integrity of the American States against International Communism." The OAS states, except for Guatemala, tacitly approved Dulles' resolution, although many expressed apprehension that it could be used to sanction American intervention in the internal affairs of the Latin American nations. In other words, the Soviets had a precedent for treating as suspect administration claims that the American-Syrian crisis should be resolved under regional and/or UN auspices. See Richard H. Immerman, *The CIA in Guatemala: The Foreign Policy of Intervention* (Austin: University of Texas Press, 1982); and, Stephen G. Rabe, *Eisenhower and Latin America: The Foreign Policy of Anticommunism* (Chapel Hill: The University of North Carolina Press, 1988).

39. Article 24 of the UN Charter gives the Security Council "primary responsibility for the maintenance of international peace and security."

40. British UN Delegation-New York, October 16, 1957, FO 371/128242, PRO.

41. Telephone Call from Dulles to Wadsworth, October 18, 1957, 10:46, John Foster Dulles Papers, Telephone Calls Series, Box 7, DDEL.

42. British UN Delegation-New York, October 16, 1957, FO 371/128242, PRO.

43. Telephone from Dulles to Lodge, October 16, 1957, John Foster Dulles Papers, Telephone Calls Series, Box 7, DDEL.

44. British UN Delegation-New York, October 19, 1957, FO 371/128242, PRO.

45. Telegram from the Department of State to the Embassy in Turkey, October 18, 1957, *FRUS,* pp. 723–724.

46. Telephone Call from Dulles to Wadsworth, October 18, 1957, 11:40, John Foster Dulles Papers, Telephone Calls Series, Box 7, DDEL.

47. Ibid.; and call from Dulles to Lodge, October 16, 1957, 6:48 p.m., John Foster Dulles Papers, Telephone Calls Series, Box 7, DDEL.

48. British Embassy-Ankara, October 18, 1957, FO 371/128242, PRO.

49. Telephone call from Dulles to Lodge, October 20, 1957, 12:49 p.m., John Foster Dulles Papers, Telephone Calls Series, Box 7, DDEL.

50. Ibid.

51. Telephone call from Dulles to Lodge, October 23, 1957, 2:37, John Foster Dulles Papers, Telephone Calls Series, Box 7, DDEL.

52. Telephone call from Dulles to Rountree, October 22, 1957, 4:30 p.m., John Foster Dulles Papers, Telephone Calls Series, Box 7, DDEL.

53. Mackintosh, p. 228.

54. Ibid., p. 229.

55. Ibid., p. 230.

56. British Embassy-Ankara, October 24, 1957, FO 371/128243, PRO.

57. FBIS, October 28, 1957, pp. C9–10.

58. *Middle East Journal*, Vol. IX (Winter 1958), p. 84.

59. British Embassy-Beirut, November 7, 1957, FO 371/128232, PRO.

60. Memorandum of a Conversation, Department of State, Washington, October 25, 1957, 10:30 a.m., *FRUS*, pp. 730–731. The proposed resolution called on the UN Secretary-General to "undertake informal discussions with representatives of Syria and Turkey," as provided for under Article 33 of the Charter (which states that the parties of a dispute shall first seek a solution through peaceful means of their own choice). (text of draft resolution in British UN Delegation-New York, October 23, 1957, FO 371/128243, PRO). In other words, Dulles was seeking to reduce the level of discussion to that of a diplomatic "misdemeanor" in order to create an atmosphere in which the crisis could end without any further superpower confrontation.

61. British UN Delegation-New York, October 28, 1957, FO 371/128244, PRO.

62. British UN Delegation-New York, October 23, 1957, FO 371/128243, PRO.

63. For text of press conference, see Department of State For the Press, no. 601, John Foster Dulles Papers, Box 119, Seeley G. Mudd Library, Princeton.

64. Text of communique in *al-Ahram*, November 1, 1957.

65. In addition, Khrushchev might also have had his eye on the domestic situation in the Soviet Union. On October 26, the Central Committee of the Soviet Communist Party expelled former defense minister and military hero Marshal Zhukov from the party's Presidium and Central Committee, accusing him of creating a "cult of personality" and "adventurism" in foreign policy. (Dictated by PDB to News Division for Immediate Release, November 2, 1957, John Foster Dulles Papers, Telephone Calls Series, Box 7, DDEL). Zhukov was formally dismissed for "violating Leninist principles concerning the administration of the armed forces." Strobe Talbott (ed.), *Khrushchev Remembers: The Last Testament* (Boston: Little, Brown and Company, 1974), p. 15. Khrushchev avoided discussing the topic in his memoirs, only referring to the incident as "a rather interesting episode in the history of our Party." (Ibid.).

By visiting the Turkish embassy, Khrushchev might have had in mind ridding himself of a possible foreign policy nightmare in order to concentrate on solidifying his position at home in the wake of the expulsion of the popular Zhukov and a potential counter-attack within the Soviet hierarchy. Calling Zhukov an adventurist in foreign policy and three days later making a peaceful gesture at the Turkish reception seemed to be an attempt by

Khrushchev to lay some of the blame for the Syrian-Turkish crisis at the former defense minister's feet—which was, in actuality, an open admission that the Kremlin may have played too heavy a hand vis-à-vis Syria in the latter stages of the crisis.

66. British Foreign Office to UN Delegation-New York, October 30, 1957, FO 371/128244, PRO.

67. British Foreign Office, November 15, 1957, FO 371/128244, PRO.

68. *Middle East Journal,* vol. IX (Winter 1958), p. 85. The announcement on November 29 was made after Premier Bulganin sent another accusatory and threatening note to Menderes on the 25th and after Foreign Minister Bitar stated on the 26th that Syria would ask the General Assembly to again take up its complaint against Turkey if the Turkish troop presence along the border was not sufficiently reduced.

69. For record of meeting, see Memorandum of a Conversation, New York, November 7, 1957, *FRUS,* pp. 740–744.

70. British UN Delegation-New York, November 15, 1957, FO 371/128244, PRO.

71. Telegram From the Embassy in Egypt to the Department of State, December 11, 1957, *FRUS,* pp. 744–746.

72. Ibid.

73. Ibid.

74. Telegram From the Department of State to the Embassy in Egypt, December 12, 1957, *FRUS,* pp. 746–747.

75. British UN Delegation-New York, October 16, 1957, FO 371/128242, PRO.

76. British UN Delegation-New York, October 18, 1957, FO 371/128242, PRO; Henry Cabot Lodge told Dulles that "Bitar is here and is lonely and overwhelmed by Soviet overtures and would like to talk with someone from the West." (Telephone call from Lodge to Dulles, October 2, 1957, 5:40 p.m., John Foster Dulles Papers, Telephone Calls Series, Box 7, DDEL).

77. British UN Delegation-New York, October 18, 1957, FO 371/128242, PRO.

78. Telegram From the Mission at the United Nations to the Department of State, October 24, 1957, *FRUS,* pp. 728–729.

79. It is interesting to note that Khalid Baqdash fled Syria three days before the Syrian parliament voted to join the United Arab Republic. (Mohamed Hassanein Heikal, *The Cairo Documents* (New York: Doubleday, 1973), p. 124.

12

Conclusion

By mid-August 1957, the Syrian government felt secure enough in its position to manipulate the parliamentary process, push through the chamber obvious political devices (the tax exemption to the Czech firm), and agree to a far-reaching economic accord with the Soviet Union. The regime could not be defeated through the election process, and as long as there remained a consistent external threat it would maintain popular support. The leftist regime had built up its power position through a series of convulsions that pitted it against the disorganized right-wing opposition groups. It played upon popular Arab nationalist, anti-imperialist, and anti-Zionist themes that forced the right-wing elements to ultimately look to the outside for assistance, which, in turn, only confirmed suspicions that they were merely instruments of imperialism.

The Eisenhower Doctrine awakened the Syrian regime to the possibility of American interference and to the nature of the international cold war game as it applied to the Middle East. In a sense, the Syrian regime had been battle-hardened by the repeated attempts by the opposition to regain power. The regime also effectively weathered Sa'ud's pro-American posture and King Hussein's reorientation of Jordan toward the West; indeed, Syria was able to turn the table on the Eisenhower administration by effectively playing upon Arab nationalist themes that forced the Jordanian, Iraqi, and Saudi regimes to distance themselves from American policy.

The American attempt to overthrow the Syrian regime was expected and the leftist groups could exploit it to their own advantage. One could say that the Syrian leadership played the international diplomatic game at the domestic level better than the United States played the domestic diplomatic game at the international level. It was the Syrians who successfully forced the showdowns with the right-wing opposition, to the latter's detriment. The Eisenhower administration miscalculated the strength and agility of the Syrian government and overestimated the influence and flexibility of the Iraqi and Saudi governments. Sa'ud, Jawdat, and Nasser had their own agendas regarding the disposition of Syria, and decided to pursue their objectives in the more accessible environment of the inter-Arab rather than the international arena. Befuddled as it was, the Eisenhower administration sent mixed signals to allies and enemies alike regarding its response to the American-Syrian crisis. It was unable to organize a regional response and ultimately reverted to an application of the Munich mentality to the Soviet position in the Middle East; in the process, it exponentially raised the level of tension in the area. Blocked at the domestic level by the disclosure of the coup attempt in Syria, at the regional level by the actions of, inter alia, Sa'ud, Nasser, and Jawdat, and at the international level by the threats emanating from the Kremlin, the Eisenhower administration opted to pursue "victory" in the United Nations, where the whole affair, guided at that point by the regional dynamics in the Middle East, unceremoniously faded into memory.

Nasser's sangfroid during the crisis and his country's ultimate union with Syria signaled Egypt's final victory over Iraq in the regional struggle for supremacy in the Arab world — a triumph that rested on his ability to "win" Syria over to his side. The pro-West regime in Iraq, despite its desperate attempt to offset the UAR by unifying with Jordan, was isolated in the region and under increasing pressure from Egypt and Syria; as a result, it fell in July 1958, and with it went any hopes of establishing a pro-West conglomerate in the Middle East.

The denouement of Sa'ud's mediation efforts during the American-Syrian crisis signaled the end to his brief tenure in the spotlight of Arab politics. Beyond Sa'ud's putative limitations as an effective leader, this episode revealed the constraints upon Saudi Arabia any time it attempted to assert itself politically in the inter-Arab arena. Sa'ud realized that he could not totally alienate the United States, which was, and still is, Saudi Arabia's ultimate guarantor of security. This limited Sa'ud's ability to strike out in bold fashion on behalf of Syria in the way that Nasser was free to do. He viewed American overtures as a stepladder to obtain his ambitions; however, to do so meant he had to simultaneously distance himself from American policy. But the limitations upon Sa'ud's ability to enhance his stature in the region became apparent, and Nasser was willing and able to exploit them. The specter of a Syrian-Egyptian union frightened Sa'ud to the point where he sloppily tried to arrange for Nasser's assassination. The uncovering of the plot by pro-Nasser elements soon led to Sa'ud's effectual abdication in March 1958 in favor of his brother, Crown Prince Faisal.[1]

The crisis also resulted in a significant increase in Soviet influence in the Middle East at the expense of the United States; indeed, before the Kremlin itself began to realize the liability of becoming too involved in inter-Arab politics, by the end of 1958 it could legitimately count as its allies in the region the three most powerful nations in the Arab heartland: Syria, Iraq, and Egypt. This, of course, was exactly what the Eisenhower administration tried to prevent. Washington and Moscow mistakenly believed they could control the 1957 crisis to their own advantage, only to discover that it was actions taken in the regional and domestic arenas in the Middle East that dictated the course of events during the crisis itself. With an air of desperation, the United States and Great Britain felt compelled to militarily intervene in Lebanon and Jordan in July 1958 following the Iraqi revolution in order to preserve two of the lone remaining pro-West outposts in the region. Considering its active support of King Hussein in April 1957, the wooing of King Sa'ud throughout the year, the action taken against the Syrian regime, and its intervention in Lebanon, the Eisenhower administration only sharpened the distinction between the "progressive, democratic" regimes supported by the Soviets and the reactionary regimes that were identified with the United States.[2] In other words, the attempt by the Eisenhower administration to increase its influence in the Middle East could not be "expected to support, make up for, or rescue a poorly conceived and misdirected foreign policy" that did not take into account the domestic and regional motivations of and actions taken by the various players in the Middle East arena.[3]

The Eisenhower administration's efforts to lure and ultimately force Syria to look toward Washington rather than Moscow failed. In fact, Syria probably would not have tacitly aligned itself with the Soviet Union if not for the pressure exerted upon it by the United States, Great Britain, Turkey, Iraq, and Israel. Syria was forced into the position of having to choose between East and West, as were other Middle East countries. It was not allowed to develop its political system without the debilitating effects of outside intervention, and it had to think in terms of its national survival rather than its national development. The American-British alternative was to return to power a military dictator like Adib al-Shishakli, who had already been brought down by popular will — not exactly a policy consistent with the espousals of democratic values and self-determination so often heard from the White House at the time. It was more cost-effective to support the status quo (i.e., the older class of conservatives and reactionaries) in the face of political change, and to support a dictatorial leader (and his police/intelligence forces) who could clamp down on unrest and provide stability rather than implement a policy truly designed to promote the social and economic well-being of a particular society; this latter path would take too long and would not meet the immediate strategic objective of reducing Soviet influence. These individuals and groups, according to Washington, were less unpredictable than the younger class of nationalists who had for the most part been bred in anti-Westernism. Stability in the Middle East was one of the strategic premises upon which the administration based its foreign policy, and it was intended to keep the Soviets from fishing in troubled waters; however, American policies at best (i.e., when the maintenance of the status quo or status quo ante was successful) placed a country into a kind of developmental holding pattern — "buying" relative stability — and at worst, increased political tension at the domestic, regional, and international levels. This exacerbated and, indeed, sometimes caused instability that contributed to the political and economic retardation of its society.

But the Eisenhower administration could not finesse its way through the rocky political landscape that comprised the Middle East. It could not hope to keep the Soviets out and maintain cordial relations with the radical Arab states at the same time it supported Israel, tried to construct a pro-West defense system in the region, propped-up reactionary regimes, and intervened in the internal affairs of sovereign states. By assessing its strategic needs in the Middle East in terms of the Soviet threat the administration failed to seriously consider on their own terms other problems existing in the region, such as political and economic development, inter-Arab disputes, and the Arab-Israeli conflict. Unfortunately, one of the most propitious opportunities for an Arab-Isaeli peace was lost because of the administration's preoccupation with regional defense systems and the prevention of any appreciable increase in Soviet influence in the area. This tunnel vision analysis also frequently resulted in misinterpretations of the motivations and actions of various actors in the Middle East political arena, all to the detriment of a cogent American policy—especially that which existed during a crisis situation.

In light of this study, the scorecard for the Eisenhower administration's policies in the Middle East is certainly less than impressive. The interventionist side of the Eisenhower administration becomes apparent, and the benign president whose success has been measured in post-Vietnam scholarship on his ability to keep the United States out of war, has also in this study shown an ability to create conditions conducive to war by interfering in the affairs of third world nations. A Hungary was off-limits, but a Syria was not.

By focusing solely on the American-Soviet dynamic, the revisionist scholarship on the Eisenhower administration fell victim to the same cold war mentality that plagued America's relations with the Third World. This tended to obscure the rather non-democratic means employed by the administration toward these countries in order to obtain its global objectives. This study is but one example. It would seem more appropriate then that when Eisenhower, Dulles, and their strategic conceptions are attributed with greater acumen and cunning, we should also acknowledge their capacity for deception, militarism (through non-conventional military means), and cold-blooded interventionism. This would certainly offer a more complete and accurate picture of the overall effects of the Eisenhower administration's foreign policy and its motivations.

The cold war between the United States and the Soviet Union is over, but American administrations from this point on will find that serious and potentially explosive problems still exist in the Middle East. The root causes to these problems have long been largely independent of the East-West conflict. Hopefully, these issues will not be discreetly shelved in favor of more tractable problems. Now that the Soviet strategic/military threat in the region has been removed, policymakers should address these issues on their own terms, something which should have been done more often during the Eisenhower years.

Notes

1. According to Heikal, Sa'ud paid nearly 2 million British pounds to, of all people, 'Abd al-Hamid Sarraj to carry out the execution (reportedly by putting a bomb on Nasser's plane). Sarraj then went straight to Nasser with the news and publicly revealed the plot on March 5. (Mohamed Hassanein Heikal, *The Cairo Documents,* pp. 127–128; also, see George Lenczowski, *The Middle East in World Affairs,* 4th ed. (Ithaca: Cornell University Press, 1980), p. 593–594).

2. For a discussion on how the Eisenhower Doctrine was perceived as an instrument of the reactionaries, see George Lichtheim, "The U.S. Backs the Arab Monarchs: The Eisenhower Doctrine and the Anti-Nasser Bloc," *Commentary* vol. 23 (June 1957), pp. 516–522.

3. Alexander L. George and Richard Smoke, *Deterrence in American Foreign Policy: Theory and Practice,* (New York: Columbia University Press, 1974), p. 355.

Bibliography

Archives

John Foster Dulles Collection, Seeley G. Mudd Library, Princeton University, Princeton, New Jersey.
Dwight D. Eisenhower Library, Abilene, Kansas.
Library of Congress, Washington, DC.
Ministere des Affaires Etrangeres, Paris, France.
National Archives, Washington, DC.
National Archives and Record Administration, Suitland, Maryland.
Public Record Office (Kew Gardens), London, England.

Public Documents

Documents on American Foreign Relations, 1954. New York: Harper & Row, 1955.
The President's Proposal on the Middle East. Hearing Before the Committee on Foreign Relations and the Committee on Armed Services, US Senate, 85th congress, 1st Session, on S.J. Res. 19 and H.J. Res. 117. Joint Resolution to Authorize the President to Undertake Economic and Military Cooperation with Nations in the General Area of the Middle East in Order to Assist in the Strengthening and Defense of their Independence. Washington: Government Printing Office, 1957.
Report of the Committee on Foreign Relations and the Committee of Armed Services on S.J. Res. 19 to Promote Peace and Stability in the Middle East, 85th Congress, 1st Session. Washington: Government Printing Office, 1957.
Senate Historical Office. *The Executive Sessions of the Senate Foreign Relations Committee* (Historical Series), vol. 9:1957.
State Department *Bulletin.*
U.S. Department of State. *American Foreign Policy 1950–1955, Basic Documents.* Washington: Government Printing Office, 1957.
_____. Historical Office. *American Foreign Policy, Current Documents.* Washington: Government Printing Office.
_____. Historical Office. *Foreign Relations of the United States, 1952–54, vol. IX.* Washington: Government Printing Office, 1984.

_____. Historical Office. *Foreign Relations of the United States, 1955–57, vol. XIII.* Washington: Government Printing Office, 1988.

U.S. President. *Public Papers of the Presidents of the United States.* Dwight D. Eisenhower, 1953–1958. Washington: Office of the Federal Register, National Archives and Record Services.

United States Treaties and Other International Agreements. Washington: Government Printing Office, 1953–1957.

Watson, Robert J. *History of the Joint Chiefs of Staff: The JCS and National Policy, 1953–54, vol. V.* Washington: Government Printing Office, 1986.

Newspapers

al-Ahram (Cairo)
al-Akhbar (Baghdad)
al-Akhbar al-yawm (Cairo)
Alif ba' (Damascus)
al-Ayyam (Damascus)
al-Ba'th (Damascus)
Baltimore Sun
al-Bina (Damascus)
Le Caire (Cairo)
Daily Mail (London)
Daily Star (Beirut)
Daily Telegraph (London)
al-Difai (Jerusalem)
Barada (Damascus)
Christian Science Monitor
The Economist
Egyptian Gazette (Cairo)
Falastin (Jerusalem)
al-Hadara (Damascus)
al-Hawadith (Baghdad)
al-Hayat (Beirut)
al-Hurriyyah (Baghdad)
al-Insha (Damascus)
al-Jarida (Beirut)
Jerusalem Post
al-Jihad (Amman)
Le Jour (Beirut)
al-Jumhur al-Arabi (Aleppo)
al-Jumhuriyya (Cairo)
Manchester Guardian
al-Misri (Cairo)

Le Monde (Paris)
al-Mussawar (Cairo)
al-Nahar (Beirut)
al-Nasr (Damascus)
New Statesman
New York Herald Tribune
New York Times
Observer Foreign News Service (London)
L'Orient (Beirut)
al-Qabas (Damascus)
al-Rai al-Am (Damascus)
Rose al-Yusuf (Cairo)
al-Sarkha (Damascus)
al-Shaab (Cairo)
al-Sham (Damascus)
Le Soir (Beirut)
al-Tali'a (Damascus)
The Times (London)
Washington Post
al-Zaman (Baghdad)

Books

Adams, Michael. *Suez and After: Year of Crisis.* Boston: Beacon Press, 1958.

Adams, Sherman. *Firsthand Report: The Story of the Eisenhower Administration.* New York: Harper & Brothers, 1961.

Alexander, Charles C. *Holding the Line: The Eisenhower Era 1952–1961.* Bloomington: Indiana University Press, 1975.

Ambrose, Stephen E. *Eisenhower: The President.* New York: Simon & Schuster, 1984.

_____. *Ike's Spies: Eisenhower and the Espionage Establishment,* Garden City, NY: Doubleday, 1981.

Asfour, Edmund Y. *Syria: Development and Monetary Policy.* Cambridge, MA: Center for Middle Eastern Studies, Harvard University Press, 1959.

Barnet, Richard J. *Intervention and Revolution: The United States in the Third World.* New York: World Publishing, 1968.

Batatu, Hanna. *The Old Social Classes and the Revolutionary Movements of Iraq.* Princeton: Princeton University Press, 1978.

Bell, Coral. *The Debatable Alliance: An Essay in Anglo-American Relations.* New York: Oxford University Press, 1964.

Berliner, Joseph S. *Soviet Economic Aid: The New Aid and Trade Policy in Underdeveloped Countries.* New York: Praeger, 1958.

Birdwood, Lord. *Nuri as-Said: A Study in Arab Leadership.* London: Cassell, 1959.

Bitar, Salah al-Din and 'Aflaq, Michel. *al-Ba'th wa al-hizb al-shuyu'i.* Damascus, 1944.

Bloch, Jonathan and Fitzgerald, Patrick. *British Intelligence and Covert Action: Africa, Middle East and Europe Since 1945.* London: Brandon Junction, 1983.

Blum, William. *The CIA: A Forgotten History: US Global Interventions Since World War 2.* London: Zed Books, 1986.

Campbell, John C. *Defense of the Middle East: Problems of American Policy.* New York: Harper & Brothers, 1960.

Caroz, Yaacov. *The Arab Secret Service.* Glasgow: Corgi Books, 1978.

Cook, Blanche Wiesen. *The Declassified Eisenhower: A Divided Legacy.* Garden City, NY: Doubleday, 1981.

Cooper, Chester L. *The Lion's Last Roar: Suez, 1956.* New York: Harper & Row, 1978.

Copeland, Miles. *The Game of Nations: The Amorality of Power Politics.* London: Weidenfeld and Nicolson, 1969.

Crabb, Cecil V., Jr. *The Doctrines of American Foreign Policy.* Baton Rouge: Louisiana State University Press, 1982.

Cutler, Robert. *No Time for Rest.* Boston: Little, Brown and Company, 1966.

Dallin, David J. *Soviet Foreign Policy After Stalin.* New York: J.B. Lippincott Company, 1961.

al-Dawuq, Bashir. *Nidal Hizb al-Ba'th al-Arabi al-Ishtiraki 'abr Mu'tamarat al-Qawmiya, 1947–1963.* Beirut: Dar al-Tali'a, 1971.

Devlin, John F. *The Ba'th Party: A History from Its Origins to 1966.* Stanford: Hoover Institution Press, 1976.

Dietl, Gulshan. *The Dulles Era: America Enters West Asia.* New Delhi: Lancer International, 1986.

Divine, Robert A. *Eisenhower and the Cold War.* New York: Oxford University Press, 1981.

_____. *Since 1945: Politics and Diplomacy in Recent American History.* New York: John Wiley & Sons, 1979.

Dulles, Allen. *The Craft of Intelligence.* New York: Harper & Row, 1963.

Eden, Anthony. *Full Circle.* Boston: Houghton Mifflin, 1960.

Eisenhower, Dwight D. *Mandate for Change 1953–1956.* Garden City, NY: Doubleday, 1963.

_____. *Waging Peace 1956–1961.* Garden City, NY: Doubleday, 1965.

Ellis, Harry B. *Challenge in the Middle East: Communist Influence and American Policy.* New York: The Ronald Press Company, 1960.

Evans, Rowland and Novak, Robert. *Lyndon B. Johnson: The Exercise of Power.* New York: Signet Books, 1966.

Eveland, Wilbur Crane. *Ropes of Sand: America's Failure in the Middle East.* New York: W.W. Norton, 1980.

Finer, Herman. *Dulles Over Suez: The Theory and Practice of His Diplomacy.* Chicago: Quadrangle Books, 1964.

Gaddis, John Lewis. *Strategies of Containment: A Critical Appraisal of Postwar American National Security Policy.* New York: Oxford University Press, 1982.

Gallman, Waldemar J. *Iraq Under General Nuri: My Recollections of Nuri al-said, 1954–1958.* Baltimore: The Johns Hopkins Press, 1964.

Gelber, Lionel. *America in Britain's Place: The Leadership of the West and Anglo-American Unity.* New York: Frederick A. Praeger, 1961.

George, Alexander L. and Smoke, Richard. *Deterrence in American Foreign Policy: Theory and Practice.* New York: Columbia University Press, 1974.

Goold-Adams, Richard. *John Foster Dulles: A Reappraisal.* New York: Appleton-Century-Crofts, 1962.

Greenstein, Fred I. *The Hidden-Hand Presidency: Eisenhower as Leader.* New York: Basic Books, 1982.

Halpern, Manfred. "Middle Eastern Armies and the New Middle Class," in John J. Johnson, *The Role of the Military in Underdeveloped Countries.* Princeton: Princeton University Press, 1962.

al-Hawrani, Akram. *Ra'yi fi al-Wahda al-Arabiya.* Damascus: al-Matba'a al-Jumhuriya, 1962.

Hayter, Sir William. *The Kremlin and the Embassy.* New York: The MacMillan Company, 1966.

Heikal, Mohamed Hassanein. *The Cairo Documents.* Garden City, NY: Doubleday, 1973.

_____. *Ma alladhi jara fi Suriyya?.* Cairo: Dar al-Qawmiya, 1962.

Hoopes, Townsend. *The Devil and John Foster Dulles.* Boston: Little, Brown & Company, 1973.

Hughes, John Emmet. *The Ordeal of Power: A Political Memoir of the Eisenhower Years.* New York: Atheneum, 1963.

Huntington, Samuel P. *The Common Defense: Strategic Programs in National Politics.* New York: Columbia University Press, 1961.

Hussein, King. *Uneasy Lies the Head: The Autobiography of His Majesty King Hussein I of the Hashemite Kingdom of Jordan.* New York: Bernard Geis Associates, 1962.

Immerman, Richard H. *The CIA in Guatemala: The Foreign Policy of Intervention.* Austin: University of Texas Press, 1982.

Ionides, Michael. *Divide and Lose: The Arab Revolt of 1955–1958.* London: Geoffrey Bles, 1960.

James, Robert Rhodes. *Anthony Eden.* London: Weidenfeld and Nicolson, 1986.

al-Jundi, Sami. *al-Ba'th.* Beirut: Dar al-Nahar, 1969.

Kaufman, Burton I. *Trade and Aid: Eisenhower's Foreign Economic Policy 1953-1961.* Baltimore: The Johns Hopkins University Press, 1982.

Kerr, Malcolm H. *The Arab Cold War: Gamal 'Abd al-Nasir and His Rivals, 1958-1970.* New York: Oxford University Press, 1971.

Khoury, Philip S. *Syria and the French Mandate: The Politics of Arab Nationalism, 1920-1945.* Princeton: Princeton University Press, 1987.

Kinnard, Douglas. *President Eisenhower and Strategy Management: A Study in Defense Politics.* Lexington: The University Press of Kentucky, 1977.

Kirk, George E. *Contemporary Arab Politics: A Concise History.* New York: Frederick A. Praeger, 1961.

Laqueur, Walter Z. *Communism and Nationalism in the Middle East.* New York: Praeger, 1956.

_____. *The Soviet Union and the Middle East.* London: Routledge & Regan Paul, 1959.

Lederer, Ivo J. and Vucinich, Wayne S. (eds.). *The Soviet Union and the Middle East: The Post-World War II Era.* Stanford: Hoover Institution Press, 1974.

Lenczowski, George. *The Middle East in World Affairs.* Ithaca: Cornell University Press, 1980.

_____. *Soviet Advances in the Middle East.* Washington: American Enterprise Institute, 1971.

Longrigg, Stephen Hemsley. *Syria and Lebanon Under French Mandate.* New York: Oxford University Press, 1958.

Louis, Wm. Roger. *The British Empire in the Middle East 1945-1951: Arab Nationalism, the United States, and Postwar Imperialism.* Oxford: Clarendon Press, 1984.

Love, Kennett. *Suez: The Twice-Fought War.* New York: McGraw-Hill, 1969.

Mackintosh, J.M. *Strategy and Tactics of Soviet Foreign Policy.* New York: Oxford University Press, 1963.

MacMillan, Harold. *Riding the Storm 1956-1959.* New York: Harper & Row, 1971.

Magnus, Ralph H. (ed.). *Documents on the Middle East.* Washington: American Enterprise Institute, 1969.

Marlowe, John. *Arab Nationalism and British Imperialism: A Study in Power Politics.* New York: Frederick A. Praeger, 1961.

Monroe, Elizabeth. *Britain's Moment in the Middle East 1914-1956.* London: Chatto & Windus, 1963.

Murqus, Ilyas. *Tarikh al-Azhab al-Shuyu'iyya fi al-Watan al-Arabi.* Beirut: al-Jam'a al-Lubnaniya, 1974.

Neff, Donald. *Warriors at Suez.* Brattleboro, VT: Amana Books, 1988.

Neustadt, Richard E. *Alliance Politics.* New York: Columbia University Press, 1970.

Nutting, Anthony. *I Saw For Myself: The Aftermath of Suez.* Garden City, NY: Doubleday, 1958.

_____. *Nasser.* London: Constable, 1972.

_____. *No End of a Lesson: The Story of Suez.* New York: Clarkson N. Potter, 1967.

Nye, Joseph S., Jr. (ed.). *The Making of America's Soviet Policy.* New Haven: Yale University Press, 1984.

Patai, Raphael. *The Kingdom of Jordan.* Westport, CT: Greenwood Press, 1958.

Paterson, Thomas G. (ed.). *The Origins of the Cold War.* Lexington, MA: D.C. Heath, 1974.

Prados, John. *President's Secret Wars: CIA and Pentagon Covert Operations Since World War II.* New York: William Morrow and Company, 1986.

Ra'anan, Uri. *The USSR Arms the Third World: Case Studies in Soviet Foreign Policy.* Cambridge, MA: The M.I.T. Press, 1969.

Rabe, Stephen G. *Eisenhower and Latin America: The Foreign Policy of Anticommunism.* Chapel Hill: The University of North Carolina Press, 1988.

Rabinovich, Itamar. *Syria Under the Ba'th 1963–66: The Army Party Symbiosis.* Tel Aviv: The Shiloah Center for Middle Eastern and African Studies, 1972.

Richardson, Elmo. *The Presidency of Dwight D. Eisenhower.* Lawrence: The Regents Press of Kansas, 1979.

Robertson, Terrence. *Crisis: The Inside Story of the Suez Conspiracy.* New York: Atheneum, 1965.

Rondot, Pierre. *The Changing Patterns of the Middle East.* New York: Frederick A. Praeger, 1962.

Royal Insitute of International Affairs. *British Interests in the Mediterranean and Middle East.* New York: Oxford University Press, 1958.

Safran, Nadav. *Israel, The Embattled Ally.* Cambridge, MA: Harvard University Press, 1981.

Seale, Patrick. *The Struggle for Syria: A Study of Post-War Arab Politics.* New Haven: Yale University Press, 1986.

Shair, Khaled A. *Planning for a Middle Eastern Economy: Model for Syria.* London: Chapman and Hall, 1965.

Shwadran, Benjamin. *Jordan: A State of Tension.* New York: Council for Middle Eastern Affairs Press, 1959.

Smith, Charles D. *Palestine and the Arab-Israeli Conflict.* New York: St. Martin's Press, 1988.

Smolansky, Oles M. *The Soviet Union and the Arab East Under Khrushchev.* Lewisburg, PA: Bucknell University Press, 1974.

Spiegel, Steven L. *The Other Arab-Israeli Conflict: Making America's Middle East Policy, from Truman to Reagan.* Chicago: The University of Chicago Press, 1985.

Stivers, William. *America's Confrontation with Revolutionary Change in the Middle East, 1948–83.* London: The MacMillan Press, 1986.

Sulzberger, C.L. *What's Wrong with U.S. Foreign Policy.* New York: Harcourt, Brace and Company, 1959.

Talbott, Strobe (ed.). *Khrushchev Remembers: The Last Testament.* Boston: Little, Brown and Company, 1974.

Tomeh, George J. (ed.). *United Nations Resolutions on Palestine and the Arab-Israeli Conflict, Volume I: 1947–1974.* Washington: Institute for Palestine Studies, 1975.

Torrey, Gordon H. *Syrian Politics and the Military 1945–1958.* Columbus, OH: Ohio State University Press, 1964.

Trevelyan, Humphrey. *The Middle East in Revolution.* London: MacMillan, 1970.

Umran, Muhammad. *Tajribati fi al-Thawra.* Beirut: 1970.

Van Dam, Nikolaos. *The Struggle for Power in Syria: Sectarianism, Regionalism and Tribalism in Politics, 1961–1978.* New York: St. Martin's Press, 1979.

Vatikiotis, P.J. *The History of Egypt: From Muhammad Ali to Mubarak.* Baltimore: The Johns Hopkins University Press, 1985.

Vatter, Harold G. *The U.S. Economy in the 1950s: An Economic History.* Chicago: University of Chicago Press, 1985.

Yamak, Labib Zuwiyya. *The Syrian Social Nationalist Party: An Ideological Analysis.* Cambridge, MA: Center For Middle Eastern Studies, Harvard University Press, 1966.

Yodfat, Aryeh. *Arab Politics in the Soviet Mirror.* New York: Halsted Press, 1973.

Articles

Abu-Jaber, Faiz S. "The Egyptian Revolution and Middle East Defense." *Middle East Forum,* XLV, 4, 1969.

_____. "Eisenhower, Israel and the Jordan Valley Authority Scheme." *Middle East Forum,* XLV, 2, 1969.

Attlee, Clement R. "Britain and America: Common Aims, Different Opinions." *Foreign Affairs,* XXXII, 1954.

Bakdash, Khalid. "Document: For the Successful Struggle for Peace . . . . ," *Middle East Journal,* VI, 1, 1953.

Bertier, F. "L'Egypte et le Pacte de Bagdad." *Politique Etrangere,* XXII, 1957.

Bitar, Salaheddin. "The Rise and Decline of the Baath." *Middle East International,* 3, 1971.

_____. "The Baath Party." *Middle East International*, 4, 1971.

Bowen, N. St.J. F. and Hughes, E.J. "Guatemala, 1954: Intervention and Jurisdiction." *International Relations*, 4, 1972.

Brands, H.W. "The Age of Vulnerability: Eisenhower and the National Insecurity State." *The American Historical Review*, 94, 4, 1989.

B.S.-E. "The Middle East since Suez." *The World Today*, 13, 12, 1957.

Bustani, Emile. "The Arab World and Britain." *International Affairs*, XXXV, 1959.

Colombe, Marcel. "Interpretations Orientales de la Doctrine Eisenhower." *Orient*, 1, 1957.

Davenport, John. "Arms and the Welfare State." *The Yale Review*, XLVII, 3, 1958.

Dulles, John Foster. "A Policy of Boldness." *Life*, 32, 1952.

_____. "Policy for Security and Peace." *Foreign Affairs*, XXXII, 1954.

_____. "Challenge and Response in United States Policy." *Foreign Affairs*, XXXVI, 1957.

"Evolving Doctrine." *New Republic*, January 21, 1957.

Gilead, Baruch. "Turkish-Egyptian Relations 1952–1957." *Middle Eastern Affairs*, X, 1959.

Henderson, Loy. "Statement Summarizing the Objectives of United States Policy in the Near and Middle East." *Middle East Journal*, I, 1, 1947.

Holsti, Ole R. "Cognitive Dynamics and Images of the Enemy." *Journal of International Affairs*, 21, 1967.

"How CIA 'Foul-ups' Happen." (interview with Wilbur Crane Eveland). *The Middle East*, October 1980.

Howard, Harry N. "The Regional Pacts and the Eisenhower Doctrine." *Annals of the American Academy of Political and Social Science*, 401, 1972.

Immerman, Richard H. "Eisenhower and Dulles: Who Made the Decisions?" *Political Psychology*, I, 1979.

Issawi, Charles. "United States Policy and the Arabs." *Current History*, 34, 1958.

Johnson, Paul. "The Struggle for the Middle East; Part I: American Takes Over." *New Statesman*, July 6, 1957.

Kaplan, Stephen S. "United States Aid and Regime Maintenance in Jordan, 1957–1973." *Public Policy*, 23, 2, 1975.

Kaufman, Burton I. "The United States Response to the Soviet Economic Offensive of the 1950s." *Diplomatic History*, 2, 1978.

Kaylani, Nabil M. "The Rise of the Syrian Ba'th, 1940–1958: Political Success, Party Failure." *International Journal of Middle East Studies*, 3, 1972.

Kedourie, Elie. "Panarabism and British Policy." *Political Quarterly*, XXVIII, 1957.

Kerr, Malcolm. "American Attitudes to 'Nasserism.'" *Middle East Forum*, XXXVI, 4, 1959.

Khadduri, Majid. "The Problem of Regional Security in the Middle East: An Appraisal." *Middle East Journal*, X, 1, 1957.

Khalidi, Walid. "Nasser and the Arab World." *Middle East Forum*, XXXVI, 4, 1959.

Kirk, George. "The Syrian Crisis of 1957 – Fact and Fiction." *International Affairs*, XXXVI, 1, 1960.

Lichtheim, George. "The U.S. Backs the Arab Monarchs." *Commentary*, 23, 1957.

Little, Douglas. "Cold War and Covert Action: The United States and Syria, 1945–1958." *Middle East Journal*, 44, 1, 1990.

London, Isaac. "Evolution of the U.S.S.R.'s Policy in the Middle East 1950–1956." *Middle Eastern Affairs*, VII, 1956.

McGhee, George C. "Turkey Joins the West." *Foreign Affairs*, XXII, 1954.

McKitterick, T.E.M. "The Problem of Egypt." *Political Quarterly*, XXVIII, 1957.

Minganti, Paolo. "Considerazioni sull'unione fra Siria ed Egitto." *Oriente Moderno*, XXXVIII, 1958.

Nelson, Anna Kasten. "The 'Top of Policy Hill': President Eisenhower and the National Security Council." *Diplomatic History*, 7, 1983.

Nolte, Richard H. "Arab Nationalism and the Cold War." *The Yale Review*, XLIX, 1, 1959.

"Notez Varie." *Oriente Moderno*, XXXVII, 1957.

"Notez Varie." *Oriente Moderno*, XXXVI, 1956.

Perlmann, M. "The Syrian Affair." *Middle Eastern Affairs*, VIII, 1957.

Philby, H.A.R. "Nasser and the West." *Middle East Forum*, XXXVI, 4, 1959.

al-Qazzaz, Ayad. "Political Order, Stability and Officers: A Comparative Study of Iraq, Syria and Egypt from Independence till June 1967." *Middle East Forum*, XLV, 4, 1969.

Reichard, Gary W. "Divisions and Dissent: Democrats and Foreign Policy, 1952–1956." *Political Science Quarterly*, 93, 1978.

Rondot, Pierre. "Les Etats Unis devant L'Orient d'aujourd'hui." *Orient*, 1, 1957.

_____. "Tendances particularistes et tendances unitaires en Syria." *Orient*, 2, 1958.

Sterling, Claire. "Syria: Communism, Nasserism, and a Man Named Serraj." *The Reporter*, 16, 13, 1957.

Stevens, Georgiana G. "Arab Neutralism and Bandung." *Middle East Journal*, XI, 2, 1957.

Tobin, James. "Defense, Dollars, and Doctrines." *The Yale Review*, XLVII, 3, 1958.

Winder, R. Bayly. "Syrian Deputies and Cabinet Ministers, 1919–1959." *Middle East Journal*, XVII, 1, 1963.

Wright, Esmond. "Defence and the Bagdad Pact." *Western Political Quarterly,* XXVII, 1957.

W.Z.L. "Syria on the Move: The Ascendancy of the Left Wing." *The World Today,* 13, 1, 1957.

Yizhar, Michael. "The Cold War Struggle over the Middle East: The Syrian Crisis, 1957." *International Problems,* XVI, 3–4, 1977.

_____. "Israel and the Eisenhower Doctrine." *Wiener Library Bulletin,* 28, 33/34, 1975.

Dissertations

al-Akhrass, Mouhamad Safouh. *Revolutionary Change and Modernization in the Arab World: A Case from Syria* (University of California, Berkeley), 1969.

Kingseed, Cole Christian. *Eisenhower and Suez: A Reappraisal of Presidential Activism and Crisis Management* (Ohio State University), 1983.

Lindley, Wilber Terry. *The Tag End of Diplomacy: American Policy in the Near East, 1949–1953* (Texas Christian University), 1985.

Polster, Deborah. *The Need for Oil Shapes the American Diplomatic Response to the Invasion of Suez* (Case Western Reserve University), 1985.

Sadowski, Yahya M. *Political Power and Economic Organization in Syria: The Course of State Intervention, 1946–1958* (University of California, Los Angeles), 1984.

Salami, George Raymond. *The Eisenhower Doctrine: A Study in Alliance Politics* (Catholic University of America), 1974.

Tyson, Carolyn Ann. *Making Foreign Policy: The Eisenhower Doctrine* (George Washington University), 1984.

About the Book and Author

The "Syrian crisis" of 1957, sparked by a covert attempt by the Eisenhower administration to overthrow what it perceived to be an emerging Soviet client state in the Middle East, represented the denouement of a badly misguided U.S. foreign policy, according to David Lesch. The repercussions of this incident, which almost precipitated a superpower confrontation, made glaringly obvious the pitfalls of a Middle East policy so obsessed with the "Soviet threat" that it precluded a reasoned analysis of the complex dynamics of the region.

Focusing on regional politics and utilizing newly available primary documentation, *Syria and the United States* offers a multidimensional analysis of Syrian-American relations during the Eisenhower years and presents a new interpretation of the "Syrian crisis" and the evolution of U.S. foreign policy that led to it. In addition, Lesch offers important new insight into the roles played by Iraq, Syria, Egypt, and the United Nations as well as a thorough examination of the Syrian political scene. The implications of the past for the present, Dr. Lesch emphasizes, should not go unremarked in light of current events – and Syria's pivotal role in them – in the Middle East.

David Lesch is assistant professor of Middle East history at Trinity University in San Antonio.

Index